THE GAMBLER

By the same author

TURNING WHEELS
WATCH FOR THE DAWN
THE HILL OF DOVES
CONGO SONG
AFRICAN PORTRAITS
THE CURVE AND THE TUSK
THE AFRICAN GIANT
MAMBA
THE MASK
GAZELLA
THE SOLDIER'S PEACHES
THE FIERCEST HEART
THE SILVER TRUMPET
WEST WITH THE SUN
THE LOOKING GLASS
RAGS OF GLORY
THE HONEY BIRD
THE THOUSAND AND ONE NIGHTS
OF JEAN MACAQUE
THE WRITING ON THE WALL
HOW YOUNG THEY DIED
THE ABDUCTORS
THREE WHITE SWANS
THE COMPANY WITH THE
HEART OF GOLD

Autobiography

A VICTORIAN SON

STUART CLOETE

THE GAMBLER

AN AUTOBIOGRAPHY

VOLUME II

1920 – 1939

COLLINS
ST JAMES'S PLACE, LONDON
1973

William Collins Sons & Co Ltd
London · Glasgow · Sydney · Auckland
Toronto · Johannesburg

First published 1973

ISBN 0 00 216262 8
Set in Monotype Garamond
Made and Printed in Great Britain by
William Collins Sons & Co Ltd Glasgow

CONTENTS

TO TINY WHOM I HAD THE GOOD FORTUNE
TO MEET IN THIS PERIOD AND TO EILEEN
WHOSE FRIENDSHIP I HAVE REGAINED AFTER
THIRTY YEARS OF SILENCE

FOREWORD

This is the story of the rehabilitation of a soldier home from the wars. It was the most eventful period of my life. It covers my convalescence, my emigration to Africa, the break-up of my marriage and home, my beginning to write at the age of forty, my meeting with Tiny who later became my wife, my arrival in the United States, and ends with the success of *Turning Wheels*, a Book Society Choice in both England and America.

It is the story of a gamble that came off and the start of a new career in a new country with a new companion.

For the first time in my life I was to find myself with some money, a position in society, my name in *Who's Who* – all of which I found astonishing. I was to meet a lot of well-known people, to travel, to make a thousand acquaintances and a few friends.

Part One

FRANCE

CHAPTER I

EDEN

It was 1920. I had been put on half-pay for five years. This period was punctuated by six-monthly medical boards. My life as a soldier was over, though it had not yet been made final. But I knew I should never march again. I was still in a state of shock, and now that I was back in France at Condette I could let go, which I did, reverting to the simplest things in life, to woman – my love was everything – and the land. To dig, to sow, to plant and watch things grow, became a passion. It was a Garden of Eden existence. I avoided strangers. I cried easily. I read no newspapers. I escaped into the primitive reality of my Eve and my garden. I was a lover of everything that lived. The birds, the butterflies, the flowers. I looked at everything with the greatest care: the wings of a bee, the pistils and stamens of a flower, my wife's body, my own hands. How fragile everything was! How curious was the interlocking pattern of life: of man, animal, plant and insect. How wonderful to have survived to share in all this! The world seemed to have been made for my enjoyment of its beauties. White-flowered hawthorn hedges, ditches gold with marsh marigolds, birdsong, the flash of butterfly wings, the darting flight of giant turquoise dragon-flies. There could have been no better therapy. Instinctively I must have known it.

Today I should probably have been sent to a mental hospital, which might have been the end of me. Woman, Eileen, was the answer. The beautiful girl of my dreams come true. And she was beautiful: five foot eight with a lovely figure, long dark brown hair, grey-blue Irish eyes fringed with long lashes. People turned round to look at her. Several men had wanted to marry her – so she too was a kind of triumph, a success scored against great odds. Another piece of luck, like coming through the war alive.

It is difficult to estimate the state of my mind at that time. I had no experience of life as I had gone into the army straight from school at the age of seventeen. I had been first wounded when I was nineteen and again when I was twenty-one. I had had my twenty-first birthday in the line at Ayette on the Somme and only Eileen had written to me. My mother had forgotten but she was very bad at birthdays, even those of her sons. I thought of the festivities and presents most boys got when they came of age in peace-time. But of course I had really come of age long before my birthday, with my first dead body, my first battle, the first man I had killed. So at the same time I was still a boy, just a kid, and also a twice-wounded veteran. This was a difficult paradox to live with. In many ways I had enjoyed the war. The comradeship of the army, the feeling of being part of something and being engaged in an historic occasion. I was terrified much of the time but learnt to overcome my fear. I was bored, I was exhausted with long marches and fighting, but I was excited by action. The sound of the guns as we marched towards them, even the smell of the dead, was a kind of aphrodisiac. Then there were the wonderful rest periods while we were being fattened up again for more action. There were the horses; out of the line I got plenty of riding. There was the beautiful peace of the countryside: the cultivated fields, the orchards, the cottages with their cows and poultry.

Sometimes I would sit by the fire with Eileen and think of it. The terror, and wonder that a man could live through it all. I thought of the trenches. The Germans' and ours stretching from the Channel to the Alps. Great ditches full of armed men both wired in: separated by a stretch of no-man's-land; uncultivated, grass-covered, untouched except by occasional patrols, where game – hares, rabbits and partridges – bred undisturbed by the shells that passed over them in both directions. A haven for the great rats that lived on the dead.

This was a world of young men, utterly womanless. Behind the lines, though still within range of the big guns, there were people – peasants – farming their land, *estaminets* catering to the troops, a few souvenir shops, women of the looser kind whose avarice overcame their fear, old men and cripples, many of them wounded. Behind this there was another zone. The rest of France, in fact, where there were respectable women and children, and again old men and wounded soldiers. This pattern must have been duplicated behind the German lines, a curious rearrangement of human beings according to sex and age.

I was lucky enough to find in those first months at home an

advertisement in a magazine for the Pelman system of memory training. I sent for the course, which consisted of a series of little grey books, and it helped me a lot.

There were tests. I had to memorize and describe everything in a room. Everything on my wife's dressing-table. I had to observe everyone I could see sitting in a bus and later describe their clothes and appearance. There were tricks for remembering things, words, names, based, I should say, on the Freudian system of word association. All this was useful when I began to write. Another thing I studied was psychology, in an effort to understand myself and others. To some extent a novelist must be a psychologist, so it too came in useful later. A girl has asthma because she hates her home and does not realize it. A boy is forced into homosexuality by a doting mother.

The cottage my people let us have was old, built of wattle and daub on a framework of oak and beech. It had once been used by Louis and Stephanie, our gardener and his wife. It had probably been built before the Revolution. The stables and cow-byre had been converted into rooms. The sitting-room had an enormous open fireplace ten foot in diameter in which in earlier times all the cooking had been done in iron pots over an open fire. I built ingle-nook seats in the corners where we could sit and watch the flames.

The common of close-cropped grass began twenty yards from the front door. Beyond the common where the village cows and horses grazed was the lake, and beyond the lake the great forest of Hardelot, once a hunting ground of kings. No sheep, goats or geese were allowed on the common as they grazed too close. Most of the peasants had a cow or two and a horse that they used to cart their produce to the weekly market in Boulogne.

We made a little garden in front of our cottage with hollyhocks, climbing roses and a wide border of double arabis. We grew splendid delphiniums, Michaelmas daisies, monkshood, wallflowers and foxgloves. It looked like a Christmas-card cottage with its old red-tiled roof, white-washed walls, and black doors and shutters.

We used to walk over the common to the lake – *Lac des Miroires* it was called because everything was reflected in its black water.

The old man who used to make peat bricks by baling the mud

out of the lake bottom and putting it into forms that he set out to dry on a bed of reeds was dead. So was the other old man who used to call the cattle and horses out of the peasants' stables and drive them on to the common to graze. He used to blow a cow's horn and everyone opened their stable doors to let out their stock.

But apart from these quite normal deaths and the blanks left by the war dead there seemed to be little change in the tempo of country life. There was still the sweet sickly smell of meadow-sweet in the ditches, still the sound of the corn-crake in the meadows, and the croaking of frogs. The women still took their white enamel buckets, that looked like slop pails, and three-legged stools to milk their cows in the open – cows that stood placidly chewing their cud. The chalky white roads were still the same with chickens scratching in front of every cottage. There were still chained watchdogs and hovering kestrels. Still pigs killed in the village street. What was happening in the world was happening elsewhere in an urban background. The ripples of progress had not yet reached us. Everything was going to be all right. Perhaps the dead had not died in vain.

Eileen and I were very happy in our cottage, with its low-beamed ceilings and white-washed walls. It was cool in summer, and with a big fire in the open hearth it was very cosy in the winter.

We used lamps and candles, and I thought back to those of my childhood in Paris. Lamplight was among my first memories. No one today realizes the soft light they give or wonderful shadows they throw.

My nursery had a central illuminated pool that faded slowly out into the corners of the room which remained quite dark and might conceal anything: wild men, animals, monsters.

Then there was the ceremony of lighting up. First the glass was taken off, then came the sharp sound of a striking match and the smell of its sulphur head. The wick took where the match touched it, and flames spread slowly in a circle till they met. The glass was now put on, the wick adjusted. If the flame was too high the glass was blackened by smoke and it was turned down. The shade was put on like a dress over a girl's head. Accompanying all this was a homely smell of kerosene.

When night had fallen, all over the Paris flat these miniature suns burned softly, silently. They gave off some heat as well as light. In the nursery there was an oil stove with a red glass covered in wire like a Sparklet's bottle. The table-like top was of blue enamel and hollow. This caught the heat and distributed it. The light through the red glass was very beautiful. I always thought of it when I saw the little red lamps burning in Roman Catholic churches. The stove gave out a much stronger smell than the lamps which I enjoyed.

There were a lot of odours in those days. Roses, Parma violets or the lilies of the valley that my mother wore in her dress when she was going out. Eau de Javel when laundry was being done. Of savon noire when a floor was scrubbed, of wax and turpentine being melted on the stove for floor and furniture polish. Outside in the streets there was the smell of horse manure, of urinals, of heavily perfumed women, of unwashed crowds, of sweat, of baking bread, of meat in butcher shops, of cheese, milk and butter from the *Laiteries*. There were no automobile fumes. No smog.

And there was noise: the hammer of iron horseshoes on the *pavé*, the cracking of whips, the shouts of carters. The cries of hawkers selling their goods: fish, flowers, toys. There were barrel organs, street singers and musicians. Mountebanks, tumblers and street jugglers.

It was a highly differentiated world of sound and sight and scent. Of well-dressed people and people in rags. Of clean people and dirty people, of good women and bad. There were *apaches* in corduroy trousers, caps and scarves. There was infinite variety, contrasts of all kinds. The whole world was a stage-set with everyone in costume, each playing a part. For a middle-class child Paris was a wonderful place; for a poor child it must have been terrible.

Though we did not realize it at the time – we, that is Eileen and I and all the people around us – were living in a world which no longer existed. It was a world which had either gone or was going, though all we noticed was that there were suddenly more cars on the road. It was rather like an old photographic print. The picture was still there but it was turning yellow, the images were getting blurred and faint. Today, fifty years later, the picture has completely gone. The print is blank.

It is difficult to remember that the world of the twenties did not really differ much from the world of the eighteen-sixties, the American Civil War period or even that of my great-grandfather's time. He, for instance, would have been able to adapt himself without much difficulty. There were new inventions but they were not too complex to understand. There were very few new materials. Till the turn of the century every educated man knew more or less everything there was to be known. World history, geography, politics, natural science. There were few experts in the sense of experts today: of course there were doctors, geologists and engineers, but their knowledge was not so specialized as to be inexplicable to ordinary educated people. Education was not yet general. In every country the masses were illiterate or semi-literate.

All this crept up on us as we lived in our little post-honeymoon bubble. Machines, gadgets, synthetic fibres increased. The craftsmen died off. Their work disappeared. Farriers and saddlers went with horses, carpenters gave way to mass-produced goods, domestic servants went to work in factories. Food was being grown in vast quantities, much less came from family farms. Every year there were new inventions. Technocracy was born, and the world moved slowly towards the state it is now in – overpopulated, polluted, lawless and computerized. But it took another world war, a lot of lesser wars and fifty years of time for it to reach the point where the future of the human race may be in jeopardy.

Eileen took to living in France very easily. She was a country girl except for her war experience in London, and she knew Condette and Hardelot from the sick leave we had spent there. Her schoolgirl '*Plume de ma Tante*' French soon improved enough for her to be able to shop and chat with tradesmen, though she made some curious mistakes, such as the one in which she told the maid to take the wet sailor off the bed and put him in the sun. This was after a hot water bottle had leaked, and *matelot* for *matelas* was an easy mistake to make, but we all laughed about it.

Eileen and I were both happy in having a home of our own at last instead of flats and furnished rooms. The cottage had great charm. It was built on the ground without a step, so on opening the front door one was right in the garden. The floors were cement, but that did not bother us as my mother had given us some old rugs and carpets.

My parents, who lived next door, the cottages were joined together, gave us furniture, blankets, linen and silver. We cooked with a double Beatrice stove which had an oven. When we married Eileen could only make tea and toast and boil an egg, but she learnt to cook from the *Daily Mail* cookery book which, with each recipe, gave reasons for failure. We generally read these first and managed fairly well. Felix Potin delivered groceries once a week, at the same time taking orders for the following week. They came in a van drawn by two horses. Meat came twice a week from Pont de Briques. Fish was brought, or not brought, by fishwives from Equien or Le Portel. They came on bare feet carrying the fish in a basket on their backs.

On one occasion my big Rhode Island cock, disapproving of the fishwife's presence in the yard, followed her and, flying up, gave her such a strong, two-legged kick in the bottom that she fell on her face screaming 'Murder! Assassin!' and scattering her fish – red mullet and soles – on the ground in front of her. I apologized and bought more fish than I needed to compensate her for this indignity.

I have had two other cocks that would go for people – one game cock that attacked all dogs and strangers impartially, and the other a Light Sussex who had the greatest objection to my feeling under his sitting wives when I looked for eggs. A cock with a great sense of decency.

The way of life here had hardly changed for a century. The tramline had only been completed in 1912. When I first came to Condette as a boy the last part of the journey was made by a horse-drawn diligence.

I bought rabbits, a mixed lot of hens and a grey-and-white goat that I called Lavender. She was in full milk and had a male kid at foot. We drank the milk and made butter from the cream. The butter was white. There is no goaty taste to the milk if the goat is kept clean. I killed the kid and, contrary to the biblical injunction, seethed it in its mother's milk. It was excellent. Later she had twins, and I took a very nice snapshot of Eileen wearing a sun bonnet and carrying a kid under either arm.

I bought a French spade. These spades are straight from the bottom of the blade to the crosspiece of the handle. They were kept sharp and clean, standing in the chimney corner when not in use. The foot is not used in digging. The spade is driven into the ground by a kind of forward throw.

The soil was sand that had been turned black by what could easily have been a thousand years of culture by the peasants whose huts had once clustered round the castle whose foundations were Roman. There were several Roman camps in the vicinity, and prehistoric remains. Neolithic and Paleolithic implements could be found in certain areas. As a boy I had made a collection of them. Hand axes, spearheads, hammers, even a tiny flint saw probably used for reaping crops. There is a certain fascination in living in an area that has been inhabited for so long.

The soil was rich with life, never having known a chemical fertilizer or a poison spray. Only animal manure and human refuse had ever been applied to it and it was one of the finest kitchen-garden areas in France. Most of the blackcurrants exported to England came from round here.

I was soon growing all the vegetables I needed, including potatoes, and for a while I became a vegetarian except for poultry, fish and eggs. Curiously enough, during this two-year period I had no tooth trouble, no cavities or fillings.

The poultry, both chickens and ducks, were on free range on the common and were excellent eating. We set our own eggs. There were no day-olds then and we raised both chicks and ducklings. Hens' eggs took twenty-one days to hatch – ducks' twenty-eight. As ducks – except Muscovies – do not sit on their eggs, they were hatched under hens. The eggs, usually twelve in number, were put under a broody hen in a straw-filled box. Once a day she was lifted off the nest to have food and water and to defecate. She was held by the wings about three feet from the ground and dropped so that she flapped them as she fell. If this was not done she was likely to sit for too long without moving. I was very fond of duck eggs and our roast duck, killed when it was six months old, was something one cannot get today. Hens were variable as mothers, some were excellent and could raise eight or ten out of twelve chicks, others could only manage two or three. The good mothers we kept year after year no matter how little they laid. Our hens were crossbred with Rhode Island cocks if I could get them. Later we got all Rhode Islands except for the old mother hens which we kept on and on for sitting purposes. They were usually cross-bred Buff Orpingtons, Faverolles or Plymouth Rocks. I had one lovely pure-bred Buff

Orpington hen that followed me about and liked to sit in my lap. I also had a tame duckling that followed me and always went with me when I was digging or working in the garden.

There were leeches in the ditches, and I lost one duckling through a leech fastening itself in its throat. I lost others to rats but still managed to raise enough poultry to keep us going.

The ducks were Rouen. They are like enormous mallards, the drakes with lovely green heads and necks.

With no refrigeration we only got things in their season – strawberries, green peas, apples, pears – and therefore looked forward to them. The varieties grown were much less commercial or suited to mass production than the kinds we get today. There were no factory farms or battery hens, calves and pigs. Nothing was fed on fishmeal or pellets. Most farms were still mixed. Mono-culture almost unknown. The pattern of husbandry had been relatively unchanged for a thousand years.

I bought army surplus corrugated iron and timber and, with the aid of a man called Lamarche – one of the finest and fastest workmen I have ever seen – built some quite hideous but practical stabling.

I got a half-Jersey, half-Flemish heifer that I called Buttercup. She was red like her mother with a mealie ring round her nose. I raised her on goat's milk and she followed us about like a dog. Because no vet was available, I lost her calving and was much distressed.

Eileen suddenly became ill and I got Dr Bachelet from Pont de Briques. He saw her in bed and he asked me for a face towel which he put over her chest and then, bending over, applied his ear to her breast. At that time French doctors did not use stethoscopes. He prescribed a purge, as all French doctors do for any illness whatsoever, and friction with spirit – eau de cologne – to be rubbed on her back and front every four hours. I nursed her myself and would hardly even let my mother near her. In a week she was well.

Having come into a small legacy, I bought a field that adjoined my parents' property. The owners were not keen on selling it but were prepared, after some persuasion, to let me buy the lower half, which was very boggy, at what seemed to them a good price, and indeed it was for so poor a piece of land. In their pleasure at off-loading this almost valueless section, they signed a deed, giving me an option on the top half, which was valuable as building land apart from its grazing, which was of excellent quality, at the same price. They were much upset when, a year later, I exercised my option.

I remember a very fine funeral given to an old man called César. He was a veteran of the 1870 war and very fat with red-rimmed, watery eyes. He said he had only washed twice in his life, once when he was born – and for that he took no responsibility – and again when he married, because this was the conventional thing to do, a politeness as it were. He would never wash again, he said, but no doubt they would wash him when he died. He considered his health and long life entirely due to his fortunate abomination of water.

We got excellent mussels from the village of Equien where they grew on the rocks in profusion. This was a fishing village and the smacks, being without engines, were entirely dependent on the wind. In bad weather they were sometimes wrecked as the women stood on the cliff-tops watching and praying for their men. There was not a family which had not lost men to the sea. When the boats were beyond service they were dragged on to the grass highlands and turned into houses by inverting them so that their keels became the roof. Doors and windows were cut into them and a very picturesque effect was achieved. Inside, the beds were bunks set above each other in large cupboards whose doors, I was told, were closed when the last person got in.

With the rest of the money I had been left I now bought a bigger house on mortgage. It had good stables and I got Nadine, a pedigree in calf Jersey heifer. The calf, a heifer, was born without trouble and I called her Nera. I also got a good Alsatian bitch whose name I forget. We had a very good maid, Louise, who was like one of the family. She could neither read nor write, but liked to work. She cooked, milked, made butter, did the laundry, and worked with me in the garden in her spare time.

An ex-soldier, Sergeant Twiddy of the 18th Hussars, now turned up and I took him on. He was just what I needed as I was negotiating the purchase of a mare from a horse dealer who ran a stable at Hardelot Plage in the summer months, catering to visitors and tourists. Stella was a nice bay mare eight years old with black points and a white star on her forehead. She was very quiet and suited Eileen, whom I had taught to ride on an army horse when we had been here on leave in 1919. I was soon able to pick up a very nice sixteen-hand bay Irish mare, ride and drive, that I called Sheilah; and a high-wheeled English dogcart. We had some lovely rides in the forest, the dunes and the beach, and as I enjoyed driving a good horse, we often visited friends ten miles away – twenty miles the round trip was not too much if we gave the mare a feed and a rest. With horse transport our social circle had to be kept within a ten-mile limit. In this horse-drawn period people were much more punctual, for horses once harnessed could not be kept waiting. They got restive or, if the weather was bad, could catch cold standing still.

Driving along the country roads was most enjoyable, with yellow-hammers in the hedge-tops saying, 'A little bit of bread and no cheese,' and the glimpse of an occasional rabbit or pheasant. The roads were metalled with white limestone and had grass verges where old women and children picked weeds for their rabbits.

Cars were still relatively few and far between, and the peasants' carts – the traditional hooded, two-wheeled vehicles – hogged the road, clip-clopping along, both horse and driver half asleep. Unless they heard a car hoot they refused to move. The French system of driving a car differed from the English and American style in that they drove with the horn sounding almost continuously, and, on the principle of a police car or fire engine, they expected to find the road clear in front of them which, since they drove at high speeds, usually proved to be the case.

I found it was no use shouting at these carts to give me room. Sheilah was very fast and rather hot. She did not like being kept back, so, finding that all the carts responded to was a klaxon horn, I fitted a big one to the dashboard of my dogcart. The first time I sounded it Sheilah tried to bolt, but she soon got used to it. Now the carts got out of my way, and were very angry when they found it was only a horse and trap that had made all that noise.

The house we moved to I called, with great originality, Belle Vue. At least a name everyone could remember and pronounce. Except for the stabling, hay barn and carriage house it had nothing to recommend it. The rooms were large, cold and faced north. I built a lean-to bedroom, sitting-room, sun porch and bathroom and lavatory on the south side, and we hardly used the rest of the house. The kitchen was on the south so it really was rather like a sunny flat giving right on to the garden. The flat wooden roof of the extension was covered with overlapping lead sheets, something that could cost a fortune today but was then quite reasonable. The house was painted blue and white by a very nice painter who taught me how to paint as I worked with him. In the kitchen yard against the wall of the barn which formed one side of it there was a very fine hyspalia Bon Chrétien pear tree twenty feet high which bore heavy crops.

We had some amusing and exciting experiences while living here. One day a commercial traveller visited us, a short, fat, red-haired man with a Homburg hat.

'Did Monsieur require lace? Lingerie?'

He opened his suitcase, pulled out a pair of ladies' drawers – lace-edged – and held them against his fat little stomach. He then held them up and demonstrated that the legs were divided.

'*Très pratique*,' he said.

Yes indeed, I thought, but we did not buy them. By this time Eileen was blushing scarlet. We did, however, buy some very nice *point de Venise* medallions – one was quite large and depicted two cupids holding a shield. We used this on the frill we had round the top of our four-poster bed.

Then we had a mad dog scare. It crossed our garden with the whole male population of the village after it, armed with pitch-forks and ancient pin-fire hammer shotguns. They killed it in the next field. I hoped it was really mad. It may have been as it was frothing at the mouth.

Twice a horse got bogged on the common and again the villagers turned out, this time with spades and ropes. They lifted one of our doors off its hinges, we were the nearest house. The hinges were male and female, the female on the door fitting on to the male portion on the frame, and lifted off easily. The rescuers set the door in front of the horse, dug under its barrel, passed a rope through the mud and then, with four or five men pulling from either side, raised the animal so that it could get its forelegs up and set its hooves on the door. Once it had this foothold it could pull itself free of the liquid peat that had engulfed it. If not found it would soon have disappeared completely.

There was the incident of my hat. I had a brown felt hat made by Christie in London which I wore all the time and refused to part with no matter how often Eileen said I should get rid of it. I, like many other men, only like clothes when they are broken in, which often means ready to discard. Anyway, one day my beloved hat disappeared. No one knew where it was. A conspiracy of silence. Then later when I was manuring the garden I found it buried in a mixture of horse and cow dung. I picked it up, soaked it and washed it with soap and hot water. It lasted so well that I took it to Africa with me. They made things to last in those days.

The mare, Stella, that I had bought for Eileen had one defect as I found out the first time I rode her over to Gobert, the blacksmith, to be shod. Even with a twitch on her nose he could not manage her and she had to be put in the stocks. A twitch is a whipcord loop fastened to a short stick which is put over a horse's nose or ear. Twisted tight, it generally restrains them. Stocks are a kind of heavy parallel bars in which the horse is fastened by straps. A French farrier shoes horses alone without the helper as is usual in England. He holds the horse's hindleg by means of a looped strap passed over the hock and under the pastern.

Twiddy kept the horses and saddlery in beautiful condition. All the steel – bits, stirrup irons – were burnished in real cavalry fashion. He never discussed his affairs, but I gathered he was a time-expired man who had returned to the service in 1914. He had served with the 18th in the Boer War. He had a small pension and had decided to stay in France at the end of the war, probably because of a woman, though I never really heard his story. On Sundays he put white cotton head ropes on the headstalls and a plaited straw rope along the edge of the stalls. Then in the passage he scattered ordinary sand and a line of special orange-coloured sand against the plaited straw rope. This Sunday stables business was quite a ceremony.

When we went out the trap harness shone, its brass work gold. The dark green dogcart, its high wheels picked out with red, glistened like glass in the sun. I was very pleased by the turnout and loved bowling along at a fast flying trot with the mare feeling the bit and enjoying herself too.

By now I had developed a small milk, poultry and flower business with the summer visitors. I had built up my small dairy herd to three tuberculin-tested pedigree Jerseys, and with two hundred head of poultry I was doing quite well. But horse transport was not enough to make my deliveries. I was very sorry to see my horses go, knowing they would pass from hand to hand downhill on their way to the knacker's yard and the horse butcher. I should like to have been in a position to shoot them myself and bury them where they fell in their own paddock. To replace them my mother gave me a T model Ford van which I learnt to drive.

That the French are a very logical race was proved by their driving test which was performed almost entirely in reverse, their reasoning being that no one would attempt to drive backwards till they were pretty good at going forwards.

It was quite a good little business supplying the English and American visitors at Hardelot Plage with milk, cream, eggs, poultry and flowers. There was no price control and I charged double the usual price for everything. When people ordered two dozen eggs a day I would refuse to supply them. I would say: 'I only sell breakfast eggs that I guarantee to be less than twenty-four hours old. They are much too good for cooking. Get your cooking eggs elsewhere.' My poultry was the same. Carefully hand-plucked, powdered with boracic, their heads wrapped in white paper, with their feet washed and their toenails cleaned. With each bird went a label stating breed, age, weight, time killed and suggested eating date. People in Europe did not use much ice then and there was no other means of refrigeration.

I had standing orders for flowers, usually a big mixed bunch twice a week. But the milk was the important thing as all milk in France had to be boiled, and the English and American babies refused boiled milk. That was where I came in. I approached the distracted and often very pretty young mothers and said I could supply them with tuberculin-tested Jersey milk twice a day, but it would cost – 'Oh, I don't care what it costs,' they answered.

I had some trouble with my poultry at first till I found that French cooks required a discount of ten per cent – dix pour cent, as they called it – on everything they bought for the house. Before I solved the problem my clients were complaining that my poultry was inedible. Afterwards they said how good it was. I never told them why.

It was at one of these villas that I met the chef who had cooked at Lennel for Lady Clementine Waring where I had convalesced after being wounded in 1916.

When I could not supply enough poultry of my own I took the truck to market towns fifty miles away and brought birds home to fatten. It paid well, and if the season had lasted six months instead of a maximum of four it would have been a gold mine, though all of it was not particularly pleasant. I used to get covered with red mite plucking the chickens, and I never cared for the drawing and cleaning anything, nor did I like killing things.

I planted a very nice orchard of standard fruit trees. That must have been in about 1922, and when I saw them in '39 they were bearing well. I made a good garden – lawns, herbaceous borders, and a little wood of about half an acre planted chiefly with elms, poplars and lilacs.

When my first cow, Nadine, was dried off to calve, we had to buy milk for a month. After a few days of this Eileen complained of a sore mouth. The doctor came and said it was *Fièvre aphteuse* – foot and mouth disease. Treatment? None. It would pass. In Europe they do not take Foot and Mouth very seriously. Cattle get it and get over it, whereas in England whole herds are destroyed if there is an outbreak. Another time, just as we were going to Paris for a few days' holiday, Eileen got ringworm on her chest, just where it would show if she wore evening dress, which naturally she wanted to do. This she caught from Nera who had it. I was treating her with tincture of iodine painted on with a brush. Ringworm is a fungus and easily cured this way. So I painted both Eileen and the cow. They were both soon well and we went to Paris a few days late which really did not matter.

My cows were very tame. I had raised Nera and Pearl by hand, removing them from their mother at birth. They followed me like dogs and sometimes in the winter when there was no one on the golf course we would take them walking with us over the fairway. On one occasion as I was milking one cow in the fields, another was licking my neck and the third lay down and tried to put her head in my lap.

A neighbour a couple of miles away had a Jersey herd and ran a bull with his cows. I got permission to have my cows served by him and would walk over there with my cow following me without a rope or halter. I turned her into the pasture and a month later would go to the gate, call her, and she would come galloping up to me, sliding to a halt a couple of feet away. Then we would go home as we had come. I never then or later had the slightest trouble milking a newly calved heifer, as even when they were quite small calves I had handled their udders and pulled at their teats. I have been more attached to cows than horses, but that may be because I have raised them, whereas I have never bred a foal. The so-called stupidity of horses can be in part at least accounted for by the way they are brought up, trained and stabled. Arab mares living in the tents of the tribe were certainly, from what one reads, quite different.

In this part of the world, the Pas de Calais, there is a breed of draught horse, the Boulonnais, that I consider unequalled anywhere. They are descended from the Flemish draught horses with a strong infusion of Arab blood. This makes a wonderful animal, at the same time strong and full of fire. Their breastplates and collars were always made double strength because, when they cannot move a load by leaning into it as Clydesdales, Shires and Percherons do, they go back in their traces and jump into the harness with such force that if it were not reinforced they would burst right through it. In colour they were chiefly grey, but I have seen blacks and bays. I once had one bogged down on my farm. It was very wet but she came through with her load although she was in over her knees and hocks in mud. She was handled by a very good young carter who stood beside her talking to her as she struggled. A whip can never be used on these horses except to wave it over them or to crack it to excite them.

As well as farming I now went into an incubator business with my brother-in-law, Frank Horsman, who had obtained the agency for an English model. This was a correspondence business. We imported the machines, advertised them in the agricultural papers, and took stands on agricultural shows where we demonstrated them. I turned out to be a first-class salesman, my best effort being to sell a hundred-egg model to a couple who had no chickens.

While at Lille, during a poultry show, I went to a night club and saw one of the most beautiful girls I have ever seen – a Jewess of seventeen or eighteen – splendidly dressed, and who was said to be the mistress of one of the big industrialists. I have seldom seen such grace and beauty and, seeing her, I visualized all the lovely women of the Old Testament. She was the Song of Songs, dressed by Worth. I have no doubt she died in a German concentration camp twenty years later. But it was impossible to think of such things then, any more than I dreamed that the apples of my orchard, which I never tasted myself, would be eaten by German occupation troops.

The incubator business went very well until the exchange rate went against me, that is to say, became more stable, and I was left with the farm again as my only source of income apart from my pension which was now also worth much less.

CHAPTER 2

THE LONG GOODBYE

At last I got a good German shepherd bitch. It had been my ambition to possess one since I had seen my first pair, then known as *chien loup*, in the Ratadrome as a child in Paris. I bred some good dogs from her, and one of them, Bodo, that I sold when he was nine months old, caught and held a burglar within a month of his purchase. His new owner drove over to tell us about it and was delighted with his bargain. I joined a dog-training club called the Societé du Chien de Défence du Boulonnais. We had a trainer and grounds with small huts in which a man dressed in canvas and leather and a fencing mask would hide while we sent our dogs in to find him. They were trained to seek and to bark when they found. *Cherche et Aboye* was the order. Then came the *Attaque*, and the dog leapt at the man. With a fully trained dog it was possible to call him off in mid-air, so that he changed his course, passing by the man's shoulder. They were taught to go back and seek objects dropped by their masters, to guard objects, to face blank pistol shots, to jump up to two metres (they did not actually jump but could clamber up a wall of this height), to make long and high jumps over hurdles similar to those used in horse shows. Most of the dogs were Alsatians, as the English call them, but which the French call Berger Allemand, Groenendales, a similarly shaped black sheep-dog from Belgium, Beauceron, a cattle dog from central France, and a Briard or two.

It was at this time that a rather terrible thing happened. A little long brown dog that had been lost turned up and we took him in. He was the most splendid and loving little dog I have ever had, but because I was afraid of his serving my pedigree bitch I eventually shot him. I have never forgiven myself for this. I do not think I understood love then. It embarrassed me. Love, as I have since found, when I have offered it, is very hard to give away. People, women, are like I was with Kiki. It is too much for them. They do not want everything. Flattery, presents, caresses – these are in universal demand – but love, with the responsibility it entails to the beloved, is seldom wanted.

Kiki, as I called him, was the first of the many dogs I have shot for various reasons. They were unsatisfactory, or old, or sick. One thing I have never done is to allow anyone else to destroy my dogs. I have shot dogs that I knew for my friends. I do not think they should be handed over to strangers. My method is very simple. I give the dog a good meal – something he likes – and stand beside him with my left hand on his back while I shoot him with a pistol in the head. He knows nothing. His last sensation is one of pleasure – a meal before him, his master's hand upon his shoulder.

I also had to destroy – shoot – another very nice animal. A young tom cat called Blee. He was a half Persian that had been given to us by some English people who had had a villa for a year and were returning to England. He was beautifully marked with tiger stripes and very large. He was the best walking cat I have ever had and would go three or four miles, walking at heel, like a dog, with his tail straight up and purring much of the time. He was most devoted but took to messing on the very middle of the bed. I tried hitting him to cure him but without any effect, so finally I shot him. I did not try rubbing his nose in it, which will generally cure them of such habits, as I did not know about it or thought it was an old wife's tale. Nor did I know enough about cats then to realize that this act was a sign of affection, though somewhat misplaced, an extraordinary effect that love and happiness may produce as a reflex in some cats. It may also have been to establish territory or to call attention to himself or get more love. The cats we have now, even if we have only been away for the day, immediately run to meet the car when they hear it and then settle down to dig holes, perform and fill them in, all in the most solemn manner.

There is something terrible about killing one's pets. It is the ultimate betrayal of their confidence. One can only say that they felt nothing and had had a happy life till it ended. As they die the light of life and love fades from their eyes. Suddenly, if shot; slowly like the light of a lamp being turned down if done by a vet. Held in my arms I have had dogs and cats die like this, painlessly after the injection, but one can watch their spirit departing. Life leaving them. Love leaving them.

Invariably I have wept. Men are too afraid of tears these days. General Sir Harry Smith, in his memoirs, mentions several occasions when he cried at the death of a comrade, a horse or a dog. Nelson wept, so did Cromwell. In the nineteenth century men lived more fully. Loving, fighting, dying with a style unknown today. They played nothing cool, their emotions had not been denatured by TV and films. When we see violence and death today it lacks reality because we have seen it all before on the screen. We tend to say, 'It's just like the pictures,' but it isn't, because in pictures all the protagonists come alive again to play another role.

We had various other interesting experiences. As I stood in my garden one day two mounted *gendarmes* arrived, clattering into the yard on their shining chargers, all spurs, chains, jackboots, white breeches and tricorne hats. These men are a kind of mounted state police who deal with all serious crime in their area. Their uniform is Napoleonic and very impressive. Local order is kept by the *garde champêtre*, a man who wears no uniform except an official *képi*, carries no arms except a stout walking-stick, nor does he need any, for the country districts are very peaceful. The *gendarmes* live in small cavalry barracks scattered over the country and work in pairs. I have seen them riding with a prisoner walking beside them with a long chain running from his handcuffed wrists to the saddle of his captor.

I was somewhat astonished to see these magnificent men dismount in my yard, tie their horses to the railings and come towards me with their notebooks in their hands.

I said: 'How do you do?'

They greeted me.

I said: 'And what can I do for you gentlemen?'

They said: 'We have come to investigate a crime.'

'A crime?'

'Yes. It is said that you are growing illegal tobacco. You have no permit.'

I began to laugh. 'Yes,' I said. 'I am growing tobacco.'

'It is a serious crime,' they said. 'We must investigate the crop.'

'Come, gentlemen,' I said. I led them round the house and there, by the bedroom window, were the criminal plants, six of them, white, sweet-scented Nicotiana.

'Look,' I said. 'Flowers. Tobacco, but a flowering variety.'

They apologized very handsomely. 'We were misinformed,' they said.

'No, you weren't,' I said. 'It's tobacco all right, but not a crop of sufficient importance to warrant sending two splendid mounted policemen some twenty miles to see it.' I gave them coffee with rum in it. I gave the horses water and a feed of oats, and they clattered away.

The only other time I had them on the place was when I had tried to help a Swedish sailor. I had put him up and fed him for a couple of days. I forget the hard-luck story he told me, but it was a good one and he looked pretty beaten up. He talked English and was very religious. He said God would bless me for my charity and quoted a lot from the Bible. A few days later when he was rested he left with my new bicycle. The police came again and told me how foolish I had been. They said neither sailors nor anyone else should ever be helped, this seemed very hard to me then, but I think it was probably good advice.

We made one or two trips to England, which was after all only thirty miles or so away across the Channel, to see friends and relations, and on one of them we crossed on the same boat as a detachment of Denekin's Cossacks, fine-looking men who sat on the deck eating bully beef and biscuits and drinking what I supposed was vodka out of bottles. They had their saddles and bridles with them, and some of them amused themselves singing to the music of a concertina, while others demonstrated their skill and sureness of hand and eye by throwing up large daggers and catching them point first in their teeth. Fortunately it was very calm.

Cossacks have always interested me. They are among the romantic troops, like Bengal Lancers, Gurkhas and Bersaglieri – something special. I thought of them mounted on their shaggy ponies, armed with long lances, hanging like wolves on the flanks of the *grande armée*. Of how they galloped out of the mist and snow and spitted any miserable French straggler who had become separated from his companions. And now I was actually seeing them. What was left of the thousands of those picked troops who had remained loyal to the Czar. These were the men who had ridden down the crowds in Russia, flogging them into submission with their knouts. Wild horsemen, very little changed in their habits in the last three hundred years.

A fortnight later I went to see them at Olympia. In this short time they had trained English horses so that they could do all their tricks from their backs. Some of them were breathtaking. Picking up a handkerchief with their teeth at full gallop was one of the most spectacular. The slightest mistake in timing would have wiped the skin off their faces. They demonstrated their lance charges. Showed how, at a gallop, they could sweep up a wounded comrade. They galloped standing in the saddle, they ran beside their horses and leapt on to them, they dropped off them to the ground, all at high speed. They sang, they danced, they threw daggers and caught them in their teeth as we had seen them do on the Channel steamer. Among them was one of the most magnificent men I have ever seen. He was six foot six and wonderfully developed, with an enormous chest and a waist like a girl's. The Cossack uniform was very attractive with its long blue coat, soft high boots and astrakhan cap, the coat being ornamented with cartridges arranged diagonally across each breast, with a heavy dagger belt round the waist.

I have seen other fine men, and three stand out in my memory. Two American Negro sergeants, each at least six foot four and built in perfect proportion, and a Jewish soldier, also American, at a night club in New York where, getting on to the stage during the floor show, he deliberately danced one of the girls into his arms and took her off. I have never seen such an example of natural courting by means of the dance. He danced in front of her and to her. No one thought of interrupting them. This was a phenomenon.

Shortly after this my friend George Buchanan, Laird of Gask, with whom I had served in the Household Battalion, said he was going to visit the war graves and would we like to come with him as I spoke French. I said we would be delighted and off we went in a hired car.

How strange our battlefields looked! Most of them in cultivation again, with the pill-boxes that had proved too hard to destroy serving as storerooms for tools and seed potatoes. The shelled villages had been rebuilt with orange-red tiled roofs. Along the roads there were heaps of war debris that had been ploughed up – wire, unexploded shells and bombs, pieces of equipment, and even human bones. There had been quite a number of accidents where both the farmer and his team had been blown up by the plough striking live shells or bombs, but this did not deter anyone. Nothing can separate a French peasant from his land. I remember a competition with a substantial prize offered by the *Vie à la Campagne* for the family that could prove they had cultivated the same fields for the longest time. The winning family had worked the same land for more than a thousand years from father to son. Since the time of Charlemagne.

These men were truly men of the soil, their soil, and it was certainly a part of them, for everything they ate was grown upon it and all they voided was returned to it and served to grow a new crop.

The peasants or cultivators, as they called themselves, of the war area, resembled my neighbours at home. The houses were the same. A living-room-kitchen flanked by two bedrooms with a lean-to at the back. Behind the house was the kitchen garden where most of the work was done by the women and children while the men went off each day on bicycles to factories five or even ten miles away. The garden produce, poultry and rabbits were taken to market once a week by the women in their covered carts. In front of the house, between it and the road, was a yard with a manure heap (*fumier*) in the centre. On either side were outbuildings. The whole establishment a hollow square with one side open to the road. When the garden was fertilized the manure was taken through the living-room in a wheelbarrow.

Round all the cottages and farms, in the roads and nearby fields, poultry scratched and foraged for insects, ranging several hundred yards from their homes, often making nests in the hedgerows and returning after three weeks' absence, followed by the chicks they had hatched in secret. Each peasant had twenty hens or so in his *poulaier*, each had a handsome cock that crowed with pride in the dawn. Cock answering cock in a chorus of challenge. When the hens laid an egg they cackled. Only because of the noise they made was it possible to find their 'stolen' nests hidden in a bed of nettles or in the undergrowth of a hedge. Most of the hens used the nest boxes in the fowl house, but there were always some of independent spirits that wished to keep and hatch their eggs instead of having them picked up each day. These were among the sounds we heard, the crow and cackle from the poultry that speckled the countryside, the lowing of cattle and the barking of dogs.

How all this would have delighted Sir Albert Howard or Lady Eve Balfour, as examples of the wheel of life.

The Somme was the area we first visited and sought the graves of our friends. George was photographing those we could find for their families. This was where we saw the Graves Commission at their macabre work. They still looked for bodies and collected the bones the peasants had dug up – I am inclined to think that many a grave contains remains that do not correspond to the name on the white cross that surmounts it. But does this matter? The bones are those of a comrade, or even an enemy, but in death there is peace. There is rest, British and German bones no longer fight. The Graves Commission dug in patches where the wheat grew greenest and tallest, first testing with a long steel rod. The difference in the crop where it was growing over a dead man was easy to spot.

We stayed at YMCA hostels and at hotels and visited the military cemeteries and monuments erected to commemorate the action of various divisions. The cemetery below the battered walls of Ypres was the most beautiful, with wonderfully kept grass paths, flowers, shrubs and trees. These were kept up by a staff of English gardeners. Gardening seems to be a peculiarly English talent. Wherever an Englishman goes he tends to make a garden. I brought back a rooted slip of moss rose wrapped in wet newspaper and planted it. It grew very nicely and bore flowers the following year.

It was now time for my final medical board. I had been on half-pay for five years and they had to decide if I was to be permanently pensioned or not. As I was quite lame in the left leg, they wrote me off as twenty-five per cent disabled and gave me a life pension. Fortunately I could still ride, my buttock wounds being clear of the saddle. The board sat at Calais. On the way we visited the lighthouse at Cap Gris Nez. This was where Napoleon's army had camped as he prepared his attack on England. Calais was interesting with its long history of war with the English. We wandered over the walled battlements and through the cobbled streets. We went to the museum where they had some very fine paintings, and I bought Eileen a pretty white organdie hat that was trimmed with blue kid, the colour of her eyes. It was a lovely hat, and in a way its purchase marked the end of a phase. I was out of the army for good.

I sometimes wondered at the problems I should have had to face if I had not been retired and stayed on with the Regiment. When

I joined the Coldstream as a regular officer in 1918 the Colonel said I would need a minimum of £300 a year private means. Had I got it? 'Oh, yes,' I said, though I had nothing but my pay and a couple of hundred pounds saved while I was in France with the BEF. Most officers spent all their money in case they were killed, whereas I saved mine in case I was not killed.

The plan I had in mind had been to go and see the Colonel again when the war was over and say that though I had money when I came to the Regiment I had none now, as my parents had lost all their fortune in Russia owing to the revolution. I then hoped the Colonel would get me attached to the WAFF – the West African Frontier Force – or the King's African Rifles in East Africa, where I could live on my pay and save money, enough to come back and do a tour in with the Regiment in England. The uniform alone would cost £600 which would have to be found somehow. A bearskin cap cost £40. More than a bear.

Later when I had got permission to marry, the Colonel asked if Eileen had money. 'Oh, yes,' I said again, her parents were very well off. Another invention I should have had to talk my way out of.

Had I gone on foreign service, seconded to some colonial force, I would have left Eileen with her parents, something I should have hated to do. All these financial problems were however solved by my retirement on pension.

In many ways I was glad it was over, as I was not by nature a peace-time, parade-ground soldier. I remember one senior officer in the mess after the war saying: 'Thank God all that is over and we can get back to real soldiering.' Real soldiering, indeed: marching up and down and doing castle guards.

I was out of date anyway, even then. What I should have liked was to have been a cavalry officer in the nineteenth century, fighting mounted with lance and sabre.

I suppose it is a terrible admission today but, frightened as I often was, I still remained a fighting man and liked soldiering. I believe this is the nature of man, he is a savage animal; life in a good regiment canalizes and disciplines these atavistic instincts. A regiment is, or was, a kind of family and gave men a place in a particular social hierarchy. This was one reason that men enlisted for long periods. In the army they were safe: fed, clothed and taken care of. If wounded they were hospitalized, pensioned if no longer able to serve. If they died they were buried free of charge.

Anyway, all this was over now. I was a civilian and on my own.

Eileen and I now decided to ask my uncle, Montrose Cloete, of 52 Berkeley Square, to spend a few days with us. We hardly knew him, but he said he would be delighted to come. We met his boat in Boulogne and had a very pleasant week together, during which I broached the subject of my name.

I said, 'I want to take my real name. I am not a Graham. What do you think about it?'

He said, 'I think you should have your real name.'

I said, 'How do I do it?'

'By deed poll,' he said, 'I'll see to it.' And he did. The notice duly appeared in *The Times* and *Telegraph* on June 12, 1925. The name Cloete was simply added on to my other names of Edward, Fairley, Stuart, Graham, thus giving me four Christian names. I sent a clipping to the Regimental Adjutant, and when the next army list appeared, I was in it under 'C' instead of 'G' in the retired section.

The name would have been a great help to me in the war, as most of the senior officers had served in South Africa, and a great number knew my family there, which had entertained the army in quite a big way. It was one of the oldest families in the Cape, our original ancestors having come from Holland with Van Riebeeck in 1652 to establish a settlement for the Dutch East India Company. My great-great-grandfather had been Chief Justice of the Colony and First High Commissioner of Natal. Numerous members of the family were in the British army and navy, and many of the girls had married soldiers or sailors who had been stationed in South Africa.

But that was all water over the dam. At least now I would no longer be sailing under false colours.

While he was with us, Montrose took us to Paris for three days where we had a very gay time. It was still home to me. We saw Josephine Baker at the *Folies Bergères* – a most beautiful woman – and bought records of her songs. From a musical point of view she is probably no songstress, but her voice has a strange quality that appealed to me, to something in my blood, a wildness, a femaleness. We went to the Concert Mayole and saw Maurice Chevalier and Yvonne Printemps. She was another singer whose voice, as natural as a bird's, attracted me.

The prostitutes at the *Folies Bergères* were unchanged and the atmosphere of Paris remained the same. It was what it has always been – my home town. The place to which, perhaps before I die, I shall return. I have a theory about old men going back to where they lived as children. It is not sentiment. It is dietetics. The time comes, I think, when the palate yearns for the first food it ever knew. For the food on which it was weaned. In my case it consisted very largely of sole and other fish – good for my brains, my mother said. And sheep's brains for the same purpose, I suppose. My favourite meal, which I was allowed to choose for my birthday, the way a condemned criminal chooses his last breakfast, was French fried potatoes and fried eggs. It still remains one of my favourites. For breakfast as a child I had porridge – there were no Quaker Oats then – which often had pieces of oat husk mixed with it that I spat out, served with milk and brown sugar or golden syrup which I trickled on with a spoon in splendid voluptuous circles. I was taught geography on my porridge plate. I made peninsulas, islands, isthmuses and lakes. This served the purpose of instruction as well as tricking me into eating the map I had made. I have never been a good doer and caused my mother a lot of trouble by being finicky with my food.

There were some splendid male dancers at the *Folies Bergères*. I have always been interested in dancing and saw more of it later with the Joos Ballet at Dartington and with Katherine Dunham in New York. This must be a wonderful profession, combining grace and beauty with the maximum controlled exertion and the interpretation of music. I have always been attracted to such isolated and spectacular things as exhibition dancing, skating and ski-ing, having a natural leaning towards showing off, an over-compensation, I suppose, for an inferiority complex. Actually I am a poor dancer and do not skate at all except in my head.

The *Folies Bergères* shows which are supposed to be put on for tourists only are always a fine spectacle, wonderfully staged and produced. The show runs for a year and towards the end the costumes – what there is of them – tend to become shabby. But since most of it is human skin this does not matter much. There are always some of the same features – beautiful female statues that come to life. Ladies with nothing on floating in the air like wingless angels, and a slowly turning silver wheel on which more lovely unclad ladies hang or recline. The French take their sex lightly – as a pleasure – and the cuckolding of a husband is a standard joke. They are very fond of a libertine being introduced as a school master into a young ladies' seminary, or a dried-up virginal lady suddenly finding herself in a brothel. None of this strikes me as particularly vicious and seems less harmful than many of the violent films we see today, where men kill each other and even strike women. This is considered quite in order whereas should a man do more than kiss a woman the film would be banned, though this has now changed in Europe and America. Yet in life very few men ever hit a woman and all caress them.

We drank coffee at the Café de la Paix, we had dinner at the Café de la Régence where Napoleon used to eat sometimes, and we saw the table on which he played chess. We crossed the bridges of the Seine and looked at the open-air bookstalls on the *quais*. We did what every tourist does. We ate, we drank, we stared, we went to shows, we danced in the night clubs and lunched in the open air in the *bois* at Armenville where they had those delightfully naughty menus, some of which I saw later framed in the men's room at the Stork Club in New York, and then went back home.

Among the summer visitors I met at Hardelot was Colonel Karri Davies who was with Jameson on his raid into the Transvaal in 1896. He drove a Pierce Arrow – a car which impressed me very much by its size and the fact that it had a pump which automatically kept up the pressure of the tyres. One day while we were having coffee in Boulogne he traced out the course of the raiders on the marble table top by dipping his finger into the coffee. He was one of the leaders and lay for some time in the Pretoria gaol under sentence of death. I little thought then that one day I should drive past it every time I went to town, or ever write about the history of South Africa.

My Uncle Montrose Servas Cloete was a character. He had married his cousin, Mary van der Byl, who was therefore both my cousin and my aunt. She was a great beauty, with her portrait in the Academy (this picture is now hanging at Alphen Hotel in Constantia), and an heiress. Her father, who had lived most of his life in England, was an MP. Their house, 52 Berkeley Square, on the corner of Charles Street, was a wedding present. It had belonged to the old Duke of Cambridge, once the Commander-in-Chief of the British army, and chiefly famous for his remark: 'No change of any kind for any purpose whatsoever.' My uncle's house was, I think, the only one in Berkeley Square without a telephone. He said people only rang up when they wanted something. He did not want anything. If they wanted anything they could send him a postcard or call.

When he left us I settled down thinking what I should now do. I could not be recalled into the service and could go ahead with new plans. The man who had the Jersey bull died and his herd was dispersed, so I bought, through the French Jersey Society, a young pedigree bull of my own – Costaux des Prés Haut. I also bought, through the French German Shepherd Society, a beautiful bitch pup, black and tan – *noire et feu*, as they call it, Uraine de Beauchamps. Everything was going nicely. Electric light reached our village and we installed it. We bought some antique furniture and my mother gave us her mother's dressing-table, a large one made of solid bird's-eye walnut, the kind of wood that is now only seen as a veneer. We had picked up old brass candlesticks, steel firedogs, pre-revolutionary fire backs made of cast iron decorated with coats of arms. We had found brass and copper kettles and saucepans at sales and secondhand shops and had quite a lot of old pewter. Europe was full of what is now described as genuine antiques but which then were in common use. We were, in fact, very comfortably settled.

Life was still very simple. Peasants still cultivated their land by hand with spades, hoes and rakes. Our hay was still mown with a scythe. The village carpenter – Vasseur – made everything from a wheelbarrow or a cart to a coffin. The blacksmith – Gobert – at the traditional crossroads shod horses, put iron tyres on wheels, mended ploughs and did any other kind of iron work that was needed. He made the blades for Vasseur's planes. He had dozens of various shapes and sizes. Vasseur made the wooden parts himself. These men were real craftsmen. Their skills are now lost forever.

There can have been little change in the rhythm of peasant life for a hundred years or more. The *château* still dominated the village as it had done for centuries. Part of it was in ruins, part had been reconditioned and modernized. The 'Rose of Picardy' was written there by Guy d'Hardelot when his family had owned the property. It had been bought by the company that was developing the area, and the tee of the first hole of the golf course was built on the top of one of the wide round towers. Under the building there were dungeons and prisons with rings and chains still welded into the walls, and an *oubliette* – a kind of well into which unsuspecting prisoners could fall as they groped their way about in the dark. The moat had been filled in long ago. In the courtyard there were some very fine trees – a very big ilex and a walnut among others – and a lawn where once knights and soldiers must have exercised their skill at arms. The walls were covered with ivy centuries old, the main stems thicker than my arm, in which thousands of house sparrows nested. It is curious that the common sparrow is now rare. It was dependent on horses, eating the undigested oats in their droppings, and the horse was dependent on the gentleman, *chevalier*, *cabalero*, *Ritter*. This always seemed to me a rather amusing situation that the sparrow, the horse and the gentleman – now an archaic term – should have disappeared together. Their relationship was symbiotic.

We had so many nightingales in our garden that sometimes they kept us awake. The charm of the nightingale is that it sings at night. If it sang in the daytime it could not compete with the wren, blackbird or thrush. But on a moonlight night it was wonderful. There were plenty of birds and butterflies in those days because there were no pesticides or poison sprays. Our buddleias were at times a mass of peacock and red admirals. I miss birds and butterflies and the insect hum of summer. Even wild flowers along the roadside have disappeared.

We went on picnics, just the two of us. We went to the sea and bathed. It was so empty that we could go in naked which always makes bathing so much more enjoyable. In the spring we picked wild daffodils and branches of wild cherry in the forest. In the autumn we went blackberrying, there were always lots of blackberries as the peasants thought them poisonous. We went to Boulogne to shop once a week. Lunch at the *Meurice*. Chocolate with whipped cream cakes and pastries at Caveng's shop. Robin's Gun Shop, where I had bought my .22 rifle ammunition, was still there. He also sold daggers and knuckle-dusters, which were then quite legal. Parsons, the English chemist, still filled in prescriptions. It was here as a boy I had bought liquorice root to chew. Merridew's Library and Bookshop still supplied our literary needs. Eileen bought her clothes from Madame Martin's shop in the Rue Victor Hugo. Very smart and not too dear. The whole tempo of life had even now, in spite of the war, a nineteenth-century flavour. The fisher people wore their costumes, and big carts drawn by big horses went rattling over the *pavé*. The market still took place once a week, with the peasant women sitting by their stalls with their home-grown vegetables, chickens and ducks tied by their legs at their feet. Rabbits in baskets. Dogs still pulled carts harnessed under them or, more rarely, to shafts. The baker at Condette had two beautiful cross-bred Danes, one yellow and one a grey that was almost mauve, harnessed to a little cart. One day they ran away pursuing a rabbit which had somehow escaped into the street. The loaves were scattered everywhere.

In the winter there were wild duck and geese, curlews and plover. Once against a dark grey sky above brown winter-killed reeds we saw three wild swans flying low, a sight I never forgot. Fifty years later I wrote a short story about it called 'Three White Swans'.

There were other events I still remember. An accident with Douai, a fox terrier bitch the army had left with my father. She was accustomed to going through a hole in the fence. She tried to go through the usual way when she was heavily in pup and tore open the skin of her belly, which I was able to stitch up. Another day my father returned from Boulogne and said he had had all his teeth out without gas. There was no Novocaine in those days.

I said: 'Without gas?'

He said: 'Without anything.'

I said: 'Why?'

He said: 'To see if I could stand it.' This was an interesting sidelight on his character.

There was still a kind of awed hush over the country. Over all Europe in fact. It was a manless world. Manless, that is, of prime men in their twenties and thirties and early forties. There were old men and boys coming to manhood, and us – the *ancien combattants*, as the French called us – the damaged goods. Tested by the fire but inevitably distorted by it. There had never been such a generation before. Never one so lonely.

Never had women been faced with such a shortage of men.

Anyone at all presentable could have married almost any girl he fancied. Good looks and money were to be had for the asking. I remember my father before the war when I was a boy talking about marriage and saying: 'Don't marry for money; just go where money is.' If you did that you were bound to meet rich girls. I did not follow his advice either time and do not regret it, for I have seldom known a man married to a rich woman to be happy.

But this was the end of our idyll: of love in the forest and sand dunes, of nightingales, wild swans and daffodils, of the strange and happy relationship I had established with my wife, my animals and the living earth. For to me, this long-cultivated soil really lived; it was rich in the palm of the hand, fecund. Blessed by the ancient phallic gods of fertility, old with rites and blood, with footsteps obliterated by still more footsteps over millennia. It had brought me health and sanity, and the strength to leave it, for here rather than in the first years had my marriage been consummated. That it had already in a way failed, in one aspect, was neither here nor there. Something profound as far as I was concerned had taken place. A trinity of man, woman and the earth; and of the living things upon the earth of which we were a part. This period was to form the backbone of my life, but it had come to an end.

I now realized I could go no further here, that I was dependent on Twiddy and Louise, and I determined to go to South Africa. My father got in touch with Francis Dormer, an old friend who had not completely forgotten him. Dormer had many interests in South Africa, the magazine called *South Africa* was one of them. The Transvaal Estates & Development Company was another. We went to London, I had an interview with him and he promised me a farming job.

Eileen was quite willing to go even though she knew it would cut her off from her parents and friends in England. So we sold our cows and poultry and packed up what we called our best things and the personal luggage which was actually going with us. Most difficult of all was to part with the library I had been collecting since boyhood. The *Harmsworth Natural History of the World* in three volumes, my bird books, my collection of Nelson's sevenpenny hardback novels, my Everyman's then costing a shilling, my other natural history books. Old leather-bound books I had bought for a few francs for their bindings. All were abandoned.

Eileen bought some new clothes from Madame Martin. One was a navy coat frock which fastened with a nickel-plated zipper in front. It had pockets on the breast, also fastened with the same decorative zippers. They were quite new then. When used for men's flies they were called talon fasteners, and there were a lot of jokes about them. Until 1926 men's flies had buttons and ladies' dresses fastened with hooks and eyes. The zipper has certainly facilitated dressing and undressing as has the disappearance of the corset, then universally worn. These were signs of the times, but we never noticed them.

South Africa was in my blood. I had been brought up on stories of hunting lion and elephant, of Kaffir wars. The story I used in *Turning Wheels* about a buffalo licking the flesh off the legs of a treed hunter he could not reach with his horns had been told me by my father. So with this background I felt myself a South African though I had never been there.

We sold our property and realized a few hundred pounds once the mortgages had been paid up. We had packed ammunition boxes, trunks and canvas bags with linen, china, some pictures, silver, brass and the odd ornaments that go to make a home. There was also a bag of saddlery. Twenty-six pieces in all. Everything was clearly numbered and sent to Cape Town by Thomas Cook, who had also arranged the dog's quarantine at Hackbridge. I parted from her on the Boulogne Docks. The next thing was to say goodbye to my parents and Eileen's people who were now living near us as France was much cheaper than England at that time. This was the long goodbye. My people were old, my father over seventy, and six thousand miles a long way away. It was all very well conducted in a stiff-upper-lipped manner. We did not really expect to see them again. Eileen was very brave. But war had made people used to partings that were so often final.

Part Two

LAND OF MY FATHERS

AFRICA

CHAPTER 3

BIRDS OF PASSAGE

SUPERFICIALLY London had not changed much since I had been stationed there with the 2nd Battalion. There was still a lot of horse-drawn transport, even a few private carriages and pairs. But the shortage of young men was noticeable, and there were men decorated with DCMs and MMs selling matches and boot-laces in the streets. We sometimes saw a brass band entirely composed of crippled men. England was still bleeding slowly. The widows were not so conspicuous as they were in crêpe-draped France. But they were there all right. Widows of all kinds – apathetic, heart-broken, or man hungry. Sometimes all three at once. And there were the new rich. Profiteers – fat, sleek as seals with their befurred and jewelled women. The age of vulgarity had got into its stride. The class structure was cracked from top to bottom. Things still looked much the same, but there were no quality replacements and social vacuums, like any others, are soon filled.

But none of this meant very much to me. Most of my friends were dead and I had already projected myself into the future. I was just passing the time, a bird of passage, till our new life began.

I still remember thinking about money, security, having no proper skills, no education, no real earning capacity. These fears have always obsessed me and I still suffer a kind of psychological hangover from those days. I knew by now that my marriage was not perfect but still hoped that Eileen would change. English women were said to be late maturing. People had been getting at her. They said she was spoiling me. She must make me do this or stop me doing that. She must make me over according to the popular conception of what a young man should be. Make me dress better, go out more, be more sociable. However, I make over badly. I remember once at a party when I was quite small going to my hostess and saying: 'Thank you, and can I go home now?' She said: 'Aren't you happy here? What are you going to do when you get home?' 'Go to bed,' I said.

I still like going to bed early – as soon as it is dark almost, even in winter – with a good book, a jug of milk or chocolate, and a bowl of fruit. What could be nicer? I have no difficulty in sleeping for eight or ten hours. I have never understood why it is so virtuous to be able to do with only five hours' sleep. No animal except man is so stupid as to stay awake when its work, which is getting enough to eat, is done.

But it was this breach in our happiness, this outside influence on our affairs, that had helped me to decide I must get out. This was apart from the fact that I had gone as far as I could in France. And luckily I did too, for only a few years later France was overrun by the Germans.

In London we saw the Military Tournament with the Royal Horse Artillery, gun teams criss-crossing each other at a gallop, and a musical ride by the Greys. Montrose took us to the Tattoo at Aldershot, a flood-lit sight that ended with the massed bands of the Highland Brigade playing 'The Flowers of the Forest' which brought tears to my eyes. I always find bagpipes very moving. They are an emotional instrument, appealing to the guts rather than the intellect.

We saw some shows and dined at the Spread Eagle at Thame, whose host and owner, Fothergill, wore knee breeches, and whose table arrangements were impeccable with real silver, cut-glass and linen napery.

My Uncle Montrose took us to Ranelagh several times. It was a beautiful place with a lovely clubhouse, golf course, polo ground and tennis courts. All very luxurious and the epitome of what a country club should be. The food was first class and the waiters in scarlet coats most decorative. Montrose was a foundation member and had won a number of golf trophies which he later gave me. The club no longer exists.

My uncle was a remarkable man, a character of the kind which is now extinct. As a young man he had worked on his brother Broderick's ranch, Sabinas, in Mexico, and told many stories about his adventures, which unfortunately I forgot, never dreaming I should ever need story plots. The ranch, eventually expropriated, was very large – three or four hundred square miles in extent. At one time two hundred pedigree Hereford bulls were imported from England and they lost the lot with disease.

Montrose gave me a Colt pistol with which one of the cowboys had shot a man. An early model now in the hands of Hugh Bairnsfather Cloete of Alphen. He gave me the enormous Mexican silver bit and silver stirrup irons which he used on Sundays and fiestas when he rode a black parade horse called Prince. When he talked of Prince he choked and tears came into his eyes. He was a very emotional man. Short but very powerful, he had been described as a pocket Hercules. He had grey eyes like my father. His nose had been spoilt by being thrown from a horse and landing with his face on a broken bottle.

He took us to his wine merchant – Justerini & Brooks in Pall Mall – where we sampled sherry and port. He was a judge of port and could generally tell not only the vintage but the importer. Once we went to their cellars which were under Charing Cross Station. They were enormous and filled with barrels and thousands of bottles of maturing wine. There we drank more wine. No smoking, of course, and a Bath bun to clear the palate before we began. We had sardines on toast with the wine. It was all very impressive eating and drinking in those dimly lit cellars deep underground.

One day when we were lunching at Ranelagh the waiter upset a glass of port and my uncle, instead of being angry, said: 'If you have to pay for that, put an extra one on my bill.' This taught me a lesson in manners.

We met a lot of interesting people at 52, among them at lunch one day was Lady Wolseley, the widow of the late Commander-in-Chief of the British Army. She was going to South Africa later in the year and asked if she could visit us. I said: 'Of course,' although I did not know where we would be except that it was likely to be somewhere in the Transvaal, and thought no more of it.

This month or so was an interlude and without reality to me. I had already projected myself into the unknown future. I have always done this. Once my mind was made up to go I had already left spiritually. These periods are, as it were, bridges over a void where I had no valid existence. A period of waiting in the wings for the scenery to be changed. I watched what was going on but was almost completely detached from it.

We did everything one could do in London and then came more goodbyes to my Uncle Montrose and Aunt Mary. We embarked on the old *Garth Castle*, a ten-thousand-ton intermediate ship, at Tilbury and soon saw the last of England. This was a big thing. Emigration to a country six thousand miles away. It was the first time either of us had made a long voyage.

On board we met Matabele Thompson, an old-timer from Rhodesia, who had known Freddie Selous' father well. We became friends with a very good-looking man a little older than I, Tobin Maunsell, who had been a Dublin Fusilier, then gone on the stage and was now a mine captain on the Reef. He was a wonderful dancer. He could tap-dance and do a lot of fancy steps. He taught me some kitchen kaffir, as it was called, the *lingua franca* of the mine natives, and gave me lessons in double-entry book-keeping. We had a very rough passage, particularly in the Bay of Biscay, and it took us twenty-six days to reach the Cape.

We had one amusing coincidence: the black satin evening dress with beaded red and white flowers that Eileen had bought from Mme Martin in Boulogne was exactly duplicated by another passenger.

Intermediate ships carried a more varied lot of passengers than the mailships. They were also slower and cheaper, so we had District Commissioners, soldiers returning from leave, civil servants, farmers and their wives. An interesting collection.

We saw several whales blowing and schools of flying fish flicking from wave crest to wave crest. It was strange to see in reality things we had only read about. We stopped for a few hours at Las Palmas and went ashore by launch. In the cathedral we saw in a bottle an object which was said to be the heart of a pope, and watched casks of wine being skidded downhill on ox-drawn sleighs. The mules did not have bits in their mouths but were controlled by iron nose-bands to which the reins were fastened. I succeeded in buying one. We bought sandwiches, which we had in the open air, and then returned to the ship which sailed before dark.

I was very excited at seeing Table Mountain, the landfall of so many of my ancestors. The great flat-topped peak in whose shadow they had lived and died for three hundred years. I had, curiously, a feeling of coming home as we docked.

Here was a new life beginning. I was cut off from the old by the Atlantic Ocean. I was an emigrant, in a sense a settler. We had even come in under the auspices of the 1820 Settlers' Association, but I was at the same time returning to the land where my father, my brothers and all my ancestors had been born, where I had many relations and connections though I knew none of them.

My boats were burned as effectually as if I had set fire to them, for I had not the money to return nor had I any place to go. So, like Rhodes' young men, I was going north, towards the interior which was being developed about the time I was born. I had not missed Mr Rhodes by so long. Only a generation. Had I lived in his time I would have liked to serve him, for he was a giant.

What do I remember of the landing? Very little. The bulk of Table Mountain, the hansom cabs in Adderley Street, named Lily White and Blue Bell, the hotel we stayed at – the Grand, I think. My cousin, P. A. M. Cloete, a lawyer, whom we visited at Constantia, lunching there with his two very pretty daughters. One of them, Doris, married Fred Searle, who became a judge, and the other, Claudine, married Dale Lace, whose mother, José, had been my mother's greatest friend and intimate. She told me a lot about King Edward VII when I met her a few years later at the races in Johannesburg. She had been one of his friends and was a woman of striking good looks.

She said: 'So you are Edie's son. You have a spot in your eye. You will be lucky.' She was right. I have been. In the big things – to be alive, to be happily married, to have achieved some measure of success and security. This is luck indeed.

P. A. M. Cloete's house, Four Winds, where we lunched, was subsequently sold to Hugh Tevis who pulled it down and replaced it with an immense bastard Tudor villa and a terraced garden on which he spent hundreds of thousands of pounds. The property was later sold again, the asking price being said to be a million sterling. The furnishings were put up for auction – a sale which took the best part of a week – and we liked nothing except the waste-paper baskets which were old leather fire-buckets. There were also some regimental drums made into tables that were nice. The rest of the furniture was massive, expensive, with no line whatsoever. The house seemed an unhappy one and the garden, beautiful as it was, without gaiety.

It must be very hard to be rich and happy. The ideal amount of money to have would be enough not to have to think about it. If every whim can be satisfied at once, if a blanket of dollars can be hung between oneself and every difficulty, if each sound of reality be perpetually muted by the whispering banknotes, the mind becomes warped on the questions of love and friendship – for on these subjects the rich man can have little assurance and happiness must be very difficult to achieve, though its pursuit is the rich man's only occupation. That, and the making of more money, but riches are like beauty. To both the law of diminishing returns seems to apply in a greater or lesser degree. Though most girls desire beauty above all things, it almost always fails to bring them happiness. Things come to them too easily. They are met everywhere with smiles as royalty are met with flags. There are too many men ready to help them. The possibilities in their lives are too diverse. Only a few are strong enough in character to stand the gift of real beauty. Men are afraid to marry them, thinking they are bound to be spoilt or expensive to keep. Beauty is a form of riches and the law of diminishing returns operates with both.

I remember what Eileen wore at that luncheon with P.A.M. It was the navy wool frock that fastened with zippers. They were the only decoration on the frock and were the first to be seen in South Africa. I had chosen it for her. It was very expensive but I was always extravagant with women's clothes. My own always bored me and I felt that if one of us was well dressed it was enough. In fact, I have on several occasions been taken for my own hired man and asked if the boss was in.

P. A. M. Cloete's house was on a hill above the famous Constantia Valley which at one time belonged almost exclusively to my family. They still have one farm there – Alphen – but the vineyards have gone as the town, with its rates and taxes, has crept out towards it. Land now valued for building sites makes agriculture impossible. This was all vineyard country, and some of the best South African wine, equal to any in the world except the best French or German wines, is still made here. Constantia, named after the farm where it was grown, was a heavy after-dinner wine, produced by my family and in demand all over Europe at one time. It was drunk at all the Courts – in England, Germany and Holland. The last request made by Napoleon as he lay dying at Longwood was said to be for a glass of Constantia. The wine was so famous that this might be true. The vines from which it was made were pulled out by the wife of an ancestor who did not approve of drinking, though how she got into the family is a mystery.

There is another story about this wine. When my Uncle Montrose was staying with the Duke of Northumberland at Alnwick Castle, the butler informed his Grace that he had discovered a bin in the cellars with the name Cloete on it. The wine was brought up. It was Constantia and the bottles were marked 1792. The date was moulded into the glass. The Duke gave my uncle the last six bottles after having sampled a couple. Most of them had turned into a dark liquid with a thick sediment that tasted vaguely of syrup of figs, but some had kept a little of their character even after all that time. My uncle gave me a bottle which I gave to my cousins at Alphen – Alphen had been part of the old Constantia estate – where it belonged, so it went home again after nearly two hundred years and twelve thousand miles of travel over the sea.

The story of the old South African families resembles that of the West Indian colonists and the Americans of the deep South. The abolition of slavery ruined them all. They were either unable or refused to adjust themselves to the new conditions. At one time my family owned over two hundred farms between Cape Town and Paarl, whose value today would run into millions of pounds. My great-great-grandmother never left her home unless she drove in a coach drawn by six grey horses with postillions and outriders in uniform. My great-grandfather had a valet for whom he had refused six hundred pounds and for whom, when the slaves were liberated, he received thirty-seven pounds, less collection fees, as compensation.

Then, like the old plantation families of the Southern States, the Cloetes and many others gave up. Their world was ruined, everything was ended, but they continued to live just as well as they ever had, importing race horses and foxhounds from England and entertaining in their big houses, by the very simple procedure of selling farms till they had no more to sell.

Groot Constantia, the farm where the famous Constantia wine was produced, was only sold in the eighties to the Government as a show place and experimental vineyard. We visited this old family home, with its great rooms, its kitchens and sculleries, its dungeons where the slaves were locked in at night, as tourists. But at least it had been preserved.

Groote Schuur, Rhodes' old home and now the residence of

the Prime Minister, belonged to my father's aunt, and he had often played there as a child.

There were two family portraits at Constantia presented by Montrose that I remembered seeing many years ago in the Berkeley Square dining-room. We were also shown my father's old home, Great Westerford. Its garden, with the trees and shrubs he must have played among as a child, is now the garden of a charming block of flats called Great Kimbal. There are still some fine oaks and great camellia bushes left from those old days. In my father's time much of the country now covered with houses was still wild and undeveloped. He hunted jackal with foxhounds over the Cape Flats that are now market gardens, and on one occasion was chased by baboons on the slopes of Table Mountain.

We saw for the first time hedges of blue plumbago that my mother had so often talked about. Wild arums were common, they were called pig lilies and fed to pigs. We saw sunbirds like humming-birds, except that they are unable to hover and cannot fly backwards. Hibiscus, Poinsettia, Oleander, all flourished. There were the famous Cape silver trees – a protea with a silky silver leaf. Almost everything except the oaks and white poplars was exotic as far as I was concerned, though of course the reverse was true, since it was our flowers and trees which were the strangers.

We had been given letters to my cousins Volly and Adrian van der Byl and Piet van der Byl, all of whom were most kind to us and put us up. Volly and Adrian were directors of Van der Byl & Company, a firm which for more than a hundred years had handled a great deal of Cape Town's import/export business. But as the family in general, both Cloetes and van der Byls, preferred hunting jackal and racing, to work, neither businesses nor farms prospered in their hands, Alphen in Constantia and Fairfield in Caledon being the only two remaining family places.

Volly had a couple of pretty nieces at Montclair when we stayed with him, and we went on some good rides in the mountain bush that has now been cleared and turned into a select suburbia. The girls, Betty and Vivian, were very good horsewomen. Their horses – thoroughbreds – had been raced and were not easy to ride as their one idea was to gallop.

We went to Stellenbosch and stayed with another cousin, Colonel Durban Cloete, and his wife Frieda. He had been ADC to the Earl of Athlone and had bought a fruit farm which he named Kelsey, after the plum. He took us out to see the wild spring flowers near Darling which were a carpet of yellow, blue, white and pink in big patches. But the mosquitos were too active to stay long. He had been in the Greys (Scots Greys) and we had friends in common. I helped him prick out some sequoia seedlings that are now big trees.

We stayed at Alphen with Mrs Hugh Bairnsfather whose son, Sandy, had inherited the property under a very curious Will. Henry Cloete, Mrs Bairnsfather's father, had four daughters and no male heir – Nicolette (Bairnsfather), Reneira (Lady Stanley), Deliana (Mrs Southey), and Mary, who was then too young to marry. So he left the place to the first grandson to be born, which must have created an interesting situation for the girls.

Before I went north to Johannesburg I managed to see my old friend Louis Alphonsus Martim again. He had married and was living in a little villa in Cape Town where he had a job as a salesman of some kind. It was no job or place for him and it was not long before he died. The last time I had seen him was in the victory march past Buckingham Palace. He had a DCM and MM and was the bravest man I ever served with – when I was with him I was never really frightened. I never saw him after this, but seeing him brought the war back to me.

What had I learnt in the war? Surely so great an event must have produced some tangible results, have affected the character, made some change in the personality of those who had survived it. For it was no ordinary disaster, swiftly over like a fire, an accident or even a shipwreck. There had been, between the intervals of fear, much time for reflection. Too much time. Sometimes time seemed to be the only thing we had, yet on the other hand there was the knowledge that there was very little time for many of us. Another of the great paradoxes with which men are sometimes confronted. In ordinary civil life these do not occur, or if they do they are less apparent. There, too, we are set in a frame of life and death, but the death is not so obvious nor so frequent, not a companion at every meal. In peace-time death does not walk at your side, it does not creep like a woman into your sleeping-bag.

So there were lessons. The first of these was the appreciation of the greatest relief known to man, the cessation of fear. When there was a silence after hours of shelling, when for a few moments or hours it was possible to rest. Then there was the knowledge that death was easy. This had come to me as a great surprise when I thought I was killed. Pain was the only thing that need be feared. There was the strange knowledge that men were just meat, like beef or mutton. That men could be carved up into joints like carcases in a butcher's shop. I thought of the pile of arms and legs I had seen in the corner of the field hospital when I was wounded for the first time. Man was just a container, just a skin filled with blood that leaked out of him like hot wine when he was punctured.

And that the fundamental realities – the necessities of life – were food, rest and women, in that order. A galaxy of starlets would be safe from hungry tired men. If each carried a medium rare beef steak in her hand, the men would snatch them and lie down to sleep. The time for women would come after that for, in principle, they had only one thing to offer and that was useless until life had been renewed by food and rest. The one thing which they dangled before men like a carrot in front of a donkey. Endlessly, tirelessly. In the cities, in the pictures of the magazines, in the advertisements, as if men lived for that alone. As if life was nothing but a going to bed – getting into as many beds as possible in the shortest possible time.

I also knew that I had been tested, tempered like steel by fire. I still mistrusted men who had not shared my experience. I had learnt that the two great facts of a young man's life were love and war. That no experiences would ever equal them.

CHAPTER 4

A NEW START

WE had been told how dusty the trip to Johannesburg would be, so Eileen bought a brown linen dust coat and wore gloves when we went to the dining-car. The warning had been right. The red dust, fine as talcum powder, seeped into everything, even into closed suitcases.

The trip through what seemed to be, after Europe, an empty land took three days. We went through no real towns, just wayside stations and whistle stops where we picked up water for the engine. We saw no buck or wild animals and few domestic animals. Some flocks of sheep that were the colour of the soil, a few black-and-white Friesland cattle, native cattle, some goats, and that was about the lot. There were scattered homesteads here and there with trees round them. We saw a few cars on the country roads and some Cape carts with two horses plodding along to some unknown destination.

I made the best of it trying to entertain and amuse Eileen, but it was not easy. After the lush fields of France and England this was a depressing spectacle.

When at last we reached Johannesburg, we went to the Langham Hotel where we spent the night. The impression Johannesburg – or Jo'burg – gave me was that a new city was being superimposed on an old mining camp. Many of the buildings were still made of wood and corrugated iron. The tempo was feverish, hectic; at once exciting and depressing in this city of gold with yellow mine dumps like miniature hills scattered among the houses.

Next day I went to Mr Owen, the General Manager of the Transvaal Estates and Development Company, my new employers. Their not very impressive offices were in Main Street, a not very impressive street. But Mr Owen was very pleasant and told me I was to report to Ivan Pentz, the manager of a very big farm called Roodekuil, some ten miles from Warm Baths in the Waterberg, a small town about a hundred miles north of Pretoria.

I was to receive a house, a servant, a riding horse and a salary of twelve pounds a month, considerably less than I now pay my gardener. Mr Owen asked us to dinner at his house where we met his wife – a new one – and his daughter, Peggy, a tall, blonde, really lovely creature of nineteen with whom we later became great friends. At the moment it occurred to me that this was the kind of boss's daughter men met and married on the films, though most bosses' daughters weren't like that.

As I write it seems to me that there is a lot about pretty women in my life. The truth is not that I have only met pretty women or that all my geese are swans, but that unless a woman is pretty she makes little impression on me. But the pretty women and good horses I have known I seldom forget. It is a serious character defect, I suppose, to be so prejudiced in favour of attractive people though they are, in fact, less likely to have a chip on their shoulder and as a rule are easier to get on with.

After another night at the Langham Hotel we went to stay with my cousin, Albert van der Byl, at Irene where he had bought an enormous estate from the son of Count Nelmapius, an Austrian, who had been one of Paul Kruger's friends and had made a fortune through being given the dynamite monopoly – a very fine concession to have in a mining country. My cousin became a second father to me and never failed to help me with my many problems, though of course up to this time he had never seen me. But my father had been kind to him as a boy.

He told me of his early struggles. He had started farming at the Cape in the Bredasdorp area, running two farms – Nagwacht and Sandown. They produced wheat, wool, race horses, ostrich feathers and salt butter. It used to take them ten days to reach Cape Town over the mountain passes to sell produce and get stores for the farm. They went twice a year, combining business with pleasure and visiting their numerous relatives on the way and going to the races and dances.

This trip – because by a most curious chance I am now writing on a portion of Sandown which I bought without realizing it was part of the same farm – now takes two hours.

Because he was dissatisfied with conditions at the Cape, my cousin moved north and took over the Irene estate, which was running at such a loss that everyone advised him against buying it. But he bought it and for six months let it run on in the same way while he studied the situation. At the end of that time he had made his plan and reorganized the whole place after firing every manager and foreman on the property. He was saddled with an immense mortgage which he paid off in ten years by hard work and skilful farming, and built up what is now the Irene Township lying almost midway on the railway between Johannesburg and Pretoria.

It was a very big estate of several thousand morgen (one morgen equals two acres approximately) where he was dairy farming, milking three hundred Friesland cows and breeding large, black pigs. It was an important operation and quite the biggest farm I had ever seen. The family consisted of Bertie, then about sixty-five, his wife Ethel who had been a Myburgh, a son, Henry, who helped his father, his wife Evelyn, and two small sons. There were also two van der Byl girls, neither married, Dorothy who lived at home, and another who was a nurse in Johannesburg.

The house was old-fashioned, ugly but comfortable, built about 1880. The dining-room walls were covered with horns – Bertie's hunting trophies. Buffalo, kudu, gemsbok, blesbok, eland, impala, reed buck, water buck – the lot, in fact. I was very eager to hunt and envious of these heads. Bertie had a herd of blesbok and allowed me to shoot a ram. My first buck. I shot him behind the shoulder at a hundred and fifty yards and killed him with one shot. The camp in which these buck ran adjoined the Pretoria/Johannesburg road and eventually poachers killed almost all of them, shooting from their cars.

The house at Irene was surrounded by enormous blue gums and beef woods (Casuarinas), in which thousands of doves nested. The bare trunks of these great trees rose in sculptured columns to a canopy of leaves overhead so thick that it shut out the sky except where it was pierced here and there by sharp arrows of sunlight that flecked the ground which was carpeted with violets. This part of the garden gave the impression of a cathedral, even having something of its quality. Instead of the organ there was the endless melancholy murmur of the doves and the swift ripple of the water as it ran over the stones of the masoned furrows. Such light as there was seemed to be tinged with green. The scent of the masses of violets that flowered in the shade perfumed the air, and the whole effect was one of mystery and romance which left an indelible impression on my mind, so much so that forty years later I used it as a background for a love scene in *Rags of Glory.*

Though the springbok is South Africa's national animal and the protea its national flower, the dove should be its bird, for surely no one who has lived there can ever hear a dove again without thinking of the country.

After a couple of days at Irene I asked the van der Byls if I could leave Eileen with them for a few days, and took the train north. A dull journey over monotonous country covered with scrubby thorn and patches of ploughed land. The soil was black or bright red in unequal patches, or chocolate-coloured where they merged and was known as turf, one of the richest soils in the world if it got enough rain. When dry in winter it cracked, contracting into crevasses that were sometimes nearly a foot wide.

The springbok flats were an open plain with patches of thorn scrub and a few big trees – flat-topped acacias, syringas and *vaalbos.* There was no open water and the area had not been farmed till boreholes were sunk. The water table was some two hundred feet down. The turf soil was of great depth and immense fertility. If it rained, very big crops of mealies were reaped year after year without fertilizer, the plants often growing twelve feet high. If it did not rain, which was often, there was no crop at all. Monkey nuts did well in the red soil. When wet the flats were all but impassable to wheeled transport of any kind. It was even difficult to ride or walk over it if the ground cover had been destroyed by ploughing or traffic of any kind. It was the most glutinous substance I have ever encountered, forming great balls of sticky mud on one's feet, a horse's hooves or the wheels of a vehicle. At one time, and that not so long ago, hundreds of thousands of the buck which gave the area its name roamed this veld. There were some left but they could be counted in dozens rather than thousands, if one saw them at all. Riding over the flats was dull – a vast grey-green sea devoid of any interesting features.

To the north lay the Waterberg, once a land flowing with milk and honey, with big trees, heavy bush and a spring in every kloof. Rightly named the 'Water mountains', and at that time full of malaria. Bad farming, consistent over-grazing and burning the watersheds had dried up the range so that it was, shortly after we got to the flats, declared a drought area. The summer rains, instead of soaking into the bush-clothed mountains like a sponge and coming out again in springs in the foothills, ran off them in torrents with every storm, carrying valuable topsoil with it and cutting *dongas* in the flat land below them. This is the story of much of Africa.

Land on the flats was expensive, or at least we thought so. It ran up to £9 a morgen, but one good year – and they got one good year in three if they were lucky – would pay for it. All bush clearing was done by hand with bush pick, spade and axe. There were no bulldozers and the clearing of the land had to be added to the cost. Most of the farmers on the flats were ex-soldiers. Major Doyle headed their community, though we knew very few of them as our paths seldom crossed.

Warm Baths was a small town with natural hot springs which were known to the old-time Boers who used to come here for curative mud baths. These medicinal springs had been developed into a swimming pool and baths for sick people. The water was very tiring to swim in, but the setting was beautiful in a walled garden surrounded by flowers. There was one hotel, two churches, a couple of general stores, a blacksmith's shop, a doctor, a lawyer and a visiting dentist. The population was probably about a thousand souls or less. It was on the great north road and the main line, and was the centre for the Waterberg farmers. A dull, hot, ugly little town not unlike those shown in Western films, but for a while it was our metropolis.

It lay a hundred miles north of Pretoria via Pienaarsrivier, once considered one of the worst places in the Transvaal for lions, several travellers having been killed there in the old days. The country was scrubby thorn-bush, grazed out except under the bushes where the cattle could not reach the grass, varied by big flat-topped *kameeldoorns* – camel thorns – a tree much favoured by giraffes. *Kameel* in Afrikaans means camel, which the early Boers, never having heard of a giraffe, called this animal which must have once roamed here with buck and zebra.

As I travelled up-country I had stared out at the dreary grey-green landscape patched with bare soil under a sun-bleached burning sky. It all seemed very romantic, the beginning of the real Africa not yet fully tamed by man or plough.

The big rough-barked thorns must have been hundreds of years old. I have seen one after being away for twenty years and been unable to detect any change in it, their growth being estimated at an inch a year. There were groups of aloes which in their season had dull, pink, bell-like flowers, and occasional tall aloes, four feet or more in height, with candelabra blooms of red or orange. Birds in plenty. Bush shrikes, black with brilliant scarlet breasts and a beautiful liquid call. Finches, little brown ones with red beaks – *rooibekkies* – finches with sky-blue breasts, purple finches, long-tailed widow-birds. Weavers, orange and black or yellow and black, that built their hanging ball-like nests near water. Hoopoes, hornbills, crows, hawks, eagles and vultures. There were partridges and pheasants – really francolin – guinea fowl and khoran – bustards that rose screaming when put up and which were protected as royal game. Doves by the hundred cooed and in the evening came, just as darkness was about to descend, on swift wings to drink at any open water such as a dam or storm flood water after rain.

To the south were the Magaliesberg with Pretoria cupped in the hills.

This was the country we were to live in for the next few years. I did not take it all in at once. At this time I only knew I had left Eileen behind at Irene while I went north to establish some kind of home for her.

I was met at Warm Baths by a four-wheeled buggy with a native driver named Johannes. He drove me to Roodekuil, a distance of about ten miles, most of it over company property and as flat as the palm of my hand. Some of it was bush, but there were big patches of sand and two thousand acres of cleared black land divided into rectangles of sixty-four acres each. I thought of the springbok that had lived here. They are one of the few buck, like the gemsbok, which can do with very little water, even none at all where there are succulents or a heavy dew.

Ivan Pentz, the manager, gave me lunch, detailed a servant to me and came down with me to the house I was to use. It was quite large but gloomy and called Toowoomba. It is now a Government experimental station.

I had my army kit with me and set up my bed, wash-stand and folding table, got out my sleeping-bag and told Frazer, my house boy, to make some tea. He came from Nyasaland, now Malawi, and had been an Askari in the East African Rifles. Pentz had lent me some stores and cooking utensils to go on with. Next day he sent down my horse, a rather common light draught animal. Because he was black I called him Zulu and became very fond of him. He was a very good-tempered willing horse, but never a good ride as his shoulder and pasterns were too straight. He was very much the type of animal that is used for stock in Wyoming. Though I do not care for cold-blooded horses, Zulu did me well.

Mounting him, I rode down to the dorp about five miles away to explore it and buy what I needed. I had also been given a Scotch cart, a very strong two-wheeled springless affair that was pulled by two oxen. The red one was called Bloem, and the red one with a white face, Bles. I remember their names because they were the first oxen I ever handled.

Into this cart I loaded my purchases. I bought a complete set of bedroom ware. It was made of white enamel and decorated with very large pink roses, and included two chamber-pots. I bought a double-chain mattress which I later mounted on four flat boxes, and a number of paraffin crates, the kind that hold two four-gallon tins set side by side, for furniture. I bought candles, two lamps, a hurricane lantern, paraffin, two brooms, a dustpan and a feather duster made of ostrich feathers instead of turkey tails. I was much struck by this – most exotic, I thought it. I bought two Morris chairs and four bentwood kitchen chairs, two kitchen tables – one for the dining-room – some crockery, glasses, knives and forks, blankets, sheets, pots and pans, and some food – bully beef, herrings in tomato sauce, sardines, flour, potatoes, tea, coffee, sugar, salt and pepper, a bottle of Rose's Lime Juice Cordial, a bottle of cheap brandy and a supply of cigarettes. We loaded the Scotch cart and the store said they would send up the rest later in the day.

A few days later I bought some cross-bred hens and a cock in the market. I brought them back, their legs tied, hanging like bunches of flowers over the front of my saddle. They made the place look more homelike when as soon as I put them down they started scratching in the dust round the house. When any of them got broody I would sit them and breed some birds of my own for eggs and the table.

Toowoomba was a very ugly house, expensively built of hand-wrought red granite blocks, with a tin roof, set in what had once been a garden. There were twenty-four dying orange trees and some big peppers which even gross neglect will not kill. The rooms were square set on each side of a narrow passage. The house had not been cleaned for years. The lands were full of weeds and the fences down. It was altogether a melancholy spectacle. I wondered what Eileen would make of it.

I must say I was very depressed and wondered if I had not jumped out of the frying-pan into the fire. I was very alone in this country. I had relatives but they were strangers on whom I had no real claim. The country, although I felt its call somewhere in my blood – I did belong here – was inhospitable: hot, arid, harsh, comfortless, and the people uncouth. I spoke neither kitchen kaffir nor Afrikaans – in fact, there was nothing to recommend the place except that it was one more ambition achieved. I had always meant to get to Africa. Which once again seems to prove how careful one must be about directing one's will and projecting one's personality into a definite but unknown future. This would seem to be the white man's curse. His real burden is anxiety, his urgent desire for tomorrow, when things will be better, so that he is often incapable of enjoying today however pleasant it is.

It will be wonderful to get that raise, wonderful when I can make love to that girl, wonderful when I can buy that gun. None of them is wonderful, at least not as wonderful as the thoughts about them were. The raise is quickly spent, the girl is like other girls, the gun, though beautifully chased, shoots no better than the old one.

Again I wondered how would Eileen react to all this? I thought of the comfortable bedroom we had left. Her big walnut dressing-table by the window, her fitted cupboards that I had designed with special shelves for all her clothes and hats and shoes, with mirrors on the inside of the doors, so that she could see herself front and back. The carpets, the big four-poster, the white enamel stove that burned so brightly in the winter, the bookcases, the chintz curtains. And I looked at what I had now. A bare, not quite clean, wooden floor, a double chain mattress mounted on four low crates, an arrangement of paraffin cases set one on top of the other along a wall to hold clothes. A few six-inch nails driven into the wall for hanging things. Of course, when our stuff came it would be better. Some books, pictures, weapons – the old friends that I had been brought up with or that we had collected would make a difference.

Frazer and a couple of the farm boys scrubbed the place out with Jeyes Fluid and cleaned the windows. We white-washed the rooms and I rearranged the furniture. The bed on its boxes, more boxes against the wall, a dressing-table of planks set on boxes, and that was the bedroom, with a wash-stand that was a twin to the dressing-table and held a tin basin, jug and soap dish. There were also the two enamel chamber-pots, the only other convenience being a small structure in the garden with a seat set over a hole in the ground.

In another room I put a kitchen table and the four bentwood chairs. This was the dining-room.

I took a walk round and within two hundred yards of the house put up a pau – a giant bustard. The place had not been farmed for years – it had gone back to nature.

It took me four days to clean things up, and once I had got the place as shipshape as I could I wired Eileen to join me. I borrowed a light trap and a couple of mules from Pentz and went to meet the train in a mixture of excitement at seeing her again and trepidation as to how she would take this really horrible little dorp, as it was then, and the acute discomfort of Toowoomba. No running water, no toilet, packing-case furniture. No carpets, and a black cook whose English was vestigial and whose repertoire limited to curry and rice – which he called 'cully and lice' – roast meat, fried meat, boiled meat. Fried and boiled eggs, potatoes, tea and toast. He did, however, make quite good bread. The kitchen stove was wood-burning, the wood being dead trees dragged in from the bush by a pair of oxen.

I was early, as I always am, and had a long wait for the train.

CHAPTER 5

ANOTHER HOME

AT last the train came in. It was wonderful to see Eileen again as, although it was less than a week since I had left her at Irene, we had never been apart for a night since our marriage.

Eileen was very good about settling in and she soon made a home out of this barrack of a place. She made cushions for the Morris chairs out of a kind of tartan cotton used by the Shangaan women for their kilted skirts. We stuffed the cushions with seed cotton. She also sewed up the mosquito nets which we needed badly. I had just draped them roughly and they were far from adequate.

I bought a dining-room table and big armoire from a farmer who was selling up. The armoire took to pieces, sides, bottom, top and back being pegged together with dowels. I also got a fly-netted meat safe which we hung on the south side of the house by a No. 8 wire. Meat cost 6d a lb, boys' meat 4d. But it was difficult to keep in the hot weather. The farm boys got meat sent down from the main farm where they did their own slaughtering twice a week. They often hung it till it went black and was, to our point of view, rotten – a long way beyond being high. I believe in this state it contains some enzymes or amino acids that are valuable if they do not kill you.

Milk they allowed to go sour and thick in calabashes that were never properly cleaned and so contained the necessary culture to start the next lot. They also drank kaffir beer, a thick porridge-like liquid made of kaffir corn (millet) and water. A few mouthfuls of the corn was chewed by the women who made it, their saliva being the starter. It had a pleasant sour sweet musty taste and a low alcoholic content. I often drank it as it contained a lot of vitamins. They also ate wild spinach and other field herbs, but their basic ration was white mealie (corn) meal. Each boy was entitled to 3 lbs per day, which was more than he could eat. It was cooked by the cook boy in a three-legged iron pot. This was half filled with water and brought to the boil. When boiling, the meal was added and mixed with a kind of large wooden swizzle stick. When the meal was ready they squatted round the pot and, moulding the meal into lumps a bit smaller than a cricket ball, ate it with their fingers.

Cotton was my crop. I was given implements – a disc plough, a disc harrow, a spring tooth harrow, a planter – and told to get on with the job, which I did. I did most of the planting myself and have done so ever since, as the boys are quite happy riding up and down the rows with empty hoppers. Cotton is a dull crop to grow. It suffers from some hundred and fifty known diseases and pests and a number of unknown ones. Boll weavils; stainers and many others. In addition I had army worms which completely cleared the grazing land. These are black-and-yellow caterpillars about two inches long that advance like an army, eating everything they come across and leaving the veld as bare as a tennis court. By burning some of them, discing in others, and with the help of the birds – ibis and storks that accompanied the worms – I saved the best part of the crop.

The cotton plants resemble small shrubs on woody stems and grow to a height of thirty inches or so and then flower. The flowers are quite large and yellow. Then come the seed pods that contain the cotton. When ripe they burst open and the field looks as if it had been snowed on.

I had a good driver called Philip for the plough and harrow. All the work was done by oxen. Philip used a sixteen-foot whip set on a sixteen-foot bamboo whip stick and he could crack it like a pistol shot. He seldom hit an ox. The oxen were yoked in pairs and the wooden yokes fastened to trek chains. The position of the oxen was never changed. A pair of fast and intelligent oxen were used in the lead and the strongest taken for wheelers.

I was also given four or five cows with calves for my own milk. The calves were kept away from the cows till milking time, and then when the boys had taken a couple of pints from each, they were allowed to suck. Quite often a boy would be milking with one hand and pushing the calf's nose away with the other. If the calf was not with her, some cows would not let down their milk. These were not dairy cows but half-wild ranch animals that had to have their hind legs tied with a *riem* before their udders could be touched. The *riems* were dirty, the boys' hands were dirty, and the milk bucket hard to keep clean. It was not very hygienic, but the dirt we consumed was, as it were, natural dirt. Dust, dry cow dung from the *kraal*, sweat from the milkers' hands. All impurities which the human body had been conditioned for millenia to resist. There was no DDT in the milk, no antibiotics were fed to the cows. Still, when we strained the milk through a cheese cloth the residue was somewhat surprising. Even though it had been strained I once found a tick in my cocoa.

When the cotton crop was ripe and the snowy seed bursting from the bolls came the picking. Piece-work by women who were all pregnant or carried children, their black button heads bobbing on their backs, or were both pregnant and carrying a child. They had a trick of leaving their babies parked on a cradle skin between the rows, which meant jumping them if I cantered down from one end of the land to the other. The women were very hard to deal with as they were inclined to put stones and earth into the sacks they brought to be weighed, and so each had to be emptied on the spot as soon as it came off the machine, as they were on piece-work and paid by the pound.

This carrying of babies on their backs, naked baby skin to naked mother skin, seemed a very good way for their lives to begin. It certainly gave them a sense of security. In thirty-odd years I do not think I have ever heard an African baby cry. When hungry the mother simply swung the cradle skin round and the baby drank its fill. They were usually walking before they were weaned.

The picked cotton was put into wool packs – enormous bags that held 500 lbs. It was fastened at each corner to a wooden frame and packed by a heavy boy tramping it down. Then the bags were sewn up.

I found fifty-odd women very difficult to handle and I complained to Pentz who sent me down a boss boy, the son of a chief, who soon had things running well. But I was very glad when it was over and I got rid of my women and girls, some of the younger ones being rather embarrassingly friendly. At that time there were no laws against miscegenation as far as a white man and a black woman were concerned, though the reverse could mean death for the African, for the white woman, even if she had enticed him, could always claim rape. This was the same situation as existed in the Southern States of America until recent times, though there has never been a lynching in South Africa.

Our twenty-six boxes, crates, trunks and canvas bags turned up at last. With a few pictures, silver and ornaments the place took on a more homely look. Eileen made curtains for the windows out of kaffir sheeting. These few things that we had collected or that had been given to us by our parents were a link with the past. The household gods that gave us continuity. Today, fifty years later, I still have some of them – survivors of moves and changes.

I got some straw mats and skins for the floor and had picked up a few more bits of furniture at sales. But we still had no transport other than my horse and the Scotch cart drawn by the two tame oxen, Bloem and Bles.

The bombshell now fell. A wire from Lady Wolseley to say she was coming to stay and giving the time of her arrival. We were in no condition to entertain visitors. My salary was £12.10.0 a month, my pension was about the same, so an extra mouth was a consideration. In addition she was quite a personage – the widow of the Commander-in-Chief of the British army. Still, we could not stop her as we did not even know where she was. I bought her an iron bedstead and mattress, got some more paraffin boxes for furniture, and on the appointed day inspanned my two oxen to the Scotch cart in which I had set up a deck chair, and with my most respectable-looking farm boy to lead them set out for the station. I rode Zulu, no doubt the most primitive mounted escort she had ever had. She was used to Lancers.

I met the train, loaded her and her luggage on the cart, and we set off home along the dusty red road. She stayed a month and I think actually enjoyed it as a change from the parties and protocol she had had elsewhere. If she was surprised at conditions she never showed it and took it well, having been on several campaigns with her husband. But even on active service generals live rather differently from young farmers in the bush. We breathed a sigh of relief when she left. It was a far cry from 52 Berkeley Square where we had met her and she had said she would come and visit us, to the actual visit which at the time we were sure would never take place.

Her stay strained our finances and keeping her in food was a problem. One meal I remember particularly. We had Irish stew which Frazer had sprinkled liberally with Keating's Powder instead of pepper. Keating's was about the best insecticide in those pre-DDT days and was made from powdered pyrethrum flowers. The pack it was in was similar to that of the pepper so he was not to blame. Fortunately it is only poisonous to insects.

The only friends we had at that time were Mrs Scott, her young daughter Roberta, her husband and his father. Old Scott was well off and owned quite a big farm near the mountains which his son ran in a lackadaisical way. He was a sick man, never having recovered from the war in the East African theatre where he had picked up blackwater fever and other tropical complaints. He was lucky to be alive. Mrs Scott had a big car and often took Eileen home with her or for drives, which made a change from a life that was really most monotonous for a woman and uncomfortable at that.

I now had to think about some form of transport. Everyone had a motor car and because of it everyone was in debt. The answer came quite by accident. Mrs Scott took us for a long drive one weekend and at a place called Pyramids, because of the shape of the hills, I saw a little donkey cart drawn by two snow-white donkeys going along like a bat out of hell. They were cantering and galloping in a most amusing manner. I found out to whom they belonged and bought the whole outfit, after a bit of haggling, for thirty pounds. The donkeys were mares and I got a young jack thrown in. From them I bred up a nice little herd during the next ten years. They were the descendants of donkeys that Cecil Rhodes had imported from Egypt and which had been allowed to deteriorate to such an extent that there were very few pure bred ones left. Mine was, I think, the last herd in the country when it was dispersed. These donkeys were very fast and would never stand. To go through a gate they had to be tied while the gate was opened. Then they had to be tied again before it could be shut. They did over eight miles an hour and I often passed both mules and horses on the road. Later, when I had bred enough, I used to drive a team of four and they looked very pretty, snow white with blackened hooves. With some mealies in them and grooming, they were a very pretty sight.

The foals, like all donkey foals, were woolly when they were born, but being white they looked like angora rabbits with long legs. A donkey mare takes the jack again within a few hours of foaling and the jack pursues her till he catches up with her, often savaging her neck quite badly. She reciprocates by kicking him in the chest, but eventually gives up, and all the time the bewildered foal gallops beside his mother.

I had one foal killed by mules. I did not know then that mules would kill foals and calves, chopping them with their hooves. Because they cannot have foals themselves they seem to hate all young things. I had a stallion later who would serve donkey mares. The offspring is a jennet, much smaller than a mule but like one to look at. The mule is produced by a donkey jack and a horse mare. The Boers get a stallion to take donkey mares by deceiving a colt foal. They take him away from his mother and put him on to a donkey. She brings him up and he thinks he is a donkey. In the Zoutmansberg there were, after the Boer War, mules produced by runaway horse stallions and wild zebras.

My jack when he grew up had some amusing habits. One of them was to bang at the door of the outside Johnny with his hooves until it was opened, and there he would stand waiting to be fed toilet paper which he adored. It disconcerted visitors to hear this savage knocking while they were busy.

The cart was a miniature Cape cart, the axle about eighteen inches off the ground. I was delighted to have transport at last.

I was now looking for a second horse for Eileen. A neighbouring farmer called Thornhill said he had one for sale and he took me out to his farm to try her – a 14.2 grey Basuto type five-year-old mare. She went very well as we rode all over his farm. He only wanted a fiver for her; this was cheap. She was worth at least £10 but I thought he wanted a good home for her. Next day a mounted boy rode over, leading her. When he had gone I put a saddle on her back and got up. I did not stay long. She put me over her head and I landed bang on my bottom, the ground being as hard as concrete. I tried again and was put down again. She was one of those horses that go well in company but do not like going out alone.

I then got Lange, the Roodekuil stockman, to break her. He said he would do it for a couple of quid. He was a bigger, heavier man than I and a fine horseman, but she put him down too a few times before he tamed her. Lange, who did the slaughtering for boys' meat at Roodekuil, tried to make a whip out of a bull's penis but it did not work. There was some trick he did not know because many years later I bought one in Martinique. He also had a curious thing happen while I was there. His little boy of four tried to drown his sister of two in the horse trough. An example of sibling jealousy that I found interesting.

One day walking about the veld with a gun I found a big liver-and-white pointer dog. He attached himself to us at once and I called him Shot. I was very upset when his owner found I had him and came to claim him.

Reg Langebrink, who had taken over the management of Roodekuil and was a heavy man, eventually bought the grey mare from me and did not have much trouble when she felt his weight on her back. He was a first-class horseman. He had an Arab mare of 22 that I sometimes rode, and a very good ride she was. Reg was a connection of mine, his mother having been a Cloete.

Thornhill also gave me a brindle Boer bull bitch pup about six months old that I called Helen and became very fond of. But one day Reg called in his pick-up truck to take us to his place for lunch and she jumped out and broke her hip. I was in a terrible state and in tears. Luckily a mounted policeman came riding by and I asked for his gun to shoot her. He was not allowed to hand over a weapon but he dismounted and shot her while I held his horse. It was not a happy lunch for me.

At that time the country districts were patrolled by mounted police (SAMP), and very smart they looked with khaki helmets and brown polished leggings and belts. Their horses were a good type of charger with a bit of blood, bred by De Beers in Kimberley.

I lost Frazer now as he married a town girl who was certainly a prostitute. I missed his military manner – we had understood each other very well. A much less sophisticated boy called Kleinbooi replaced him. His cooking was mediocre but we liked him. He was very good-tempered and cheerful.

Snowdrop, one of the donkey mares, foaled, dropping the most beautiful little long-haired pure white donkey it is possible to imagine. We had some Johannesburg friends to lunch that day, Tommy Clapham and Laddie Rissik among them. Leaving the room, I went to fetch my little donkey. It was then about twelve hours old. I carried him in my arms and he galloped round the table on tiny white hooves – they had not darkened yet.

By this time I had some dogs. Duchess, a great Dane bitch, I bought from Mrs Struben of Lynwood, a West Highland, a

Doberman and a very nice pointer that I trained to retrieve called Fifi. She was a wonderful watchdog and slept in the bedroom.

I next grew a crop of monkey nuts (groundnuts or peanuts). They grow underground rather like potatoes and are pulled, holm and all, and set out in heaps to dry. The holm is excellent cattle feed but very fragile when dry. The plants grow to a height of about a foot and have yellow flowers. Once dry and free of earth, the nuts are packed into bags for marketing.

On going to the village two days running for some reason, I saw on the second day an old white horse tied up at one of the stores. I had seen him there the day before and I was sure no one had fed or watered him from the deep hollow in his flanks in front of the hip bone. So I went in and asked about him. He was for sale but no one wanted him and no one had bothered to take care of him. So I bought him for a pound. He had been a very good horse once and I fed him up so that I could use him at a walk and slow canter on the lands. I could also shoot off his back. He had been trained to a rifle. He must have been over twenty years old from the length of his teeth and his general condition. He soon became a great pet and followed me like a dog. I called him Tetrach but was afraid to let Eileen ride him in case he fell.

We had some trouble with tombo fly. They laid eggs in Fifi's ears and we had to wait until the maggot got big enough to pop out. They also lay in laundry hanging out to dry. This was how one got into Eileen's skin on her side below the ribs. We had to wait for this one to mature too before I could pop it out. It was a little larger than a blowfly maggot but Eileen was in no pain.

Eileen got an infection in the calf from a tick bite which I cured with Cooper's ointment – a cattle remedy that I had found to be very good for sores on cows. She also got tick fever, a very unpleasant fever that it takes four to six weeks to get over. Ticks were very bad and we had to dip the cattle every week.

Dogs got biliary (redwater), a tick-borne disease, but this was easily spotted. They went off their food, their noses were dry and their urine red. The disease destroyed the red corpuscles in the blood which were passed out. When the dog's lips were lifted the gums were white as the teeth. This was cured by an injection of Tripan blue, but the dogs generally got an abcess where they had been injected, probably because I did not know that I should have sterilized the skin first with alcohol. However, I never lost a dog with it.

When shooting in the Rooiberg area I once got covered in seed ticks, smaller than a pin's head, which sent me nearly crazy. This is the first stage, they have three, in the tick's life cycle. I only killed them by wiping myself over with a rag dipped in paraffin. Another experience I had was to find when I undressed a big tick in my navel. So I filled it with Keating's Powder and it died and fell off. One day going into a disused shed I was covered with fleas, my khaki trousers literally black with them almost as soon as I crossed the threshold.

There were quite a lot of snakes: puff-adders, cobras and boomslangs. There were stories of mambas but I never saw one till I went to the bushveld.

Eileen was very good and uncomplaining, but this wilderness could not mean anything to her as it did to me. I soaked it all up like a sponge. South Africa was at that time not anathema. It was a British dominion with a governor-general and British troops stationed in various parts of the country, and I was home at last.

The vast horizon made me want to get on a horse and ride towards it. I wanted to hunt, to camp under the stars, to sink myself into it. Much of this was, of course, due to the way I had been brought up with stories of Africa, to what I had read – Rider Haggard, Livingstone's Travels, Du Chaillu, Selous and the works of other explorers. But I think it went deeper than that. It was in my blood as well as my brain. My family, father and son, had been here almost three hundred years. They had been born and died here, had hunted in these wilds, had fought in the Kaffir wars, had in their time been rich and powerful, and though all that was only a memory now it still was part of my background. We were not newcomers nor had we taken land from other people as the American settlers had taken it from the Indians.

I was by now completely fascinated by this arid semi-desert. I had grown into it.

CHAPTER 6

THORNYCROFT

A CHANGE now took place. Thornycroft, a derelict farm about two miles away and also belonging to the company, was taken over by a farm manager called Harrow and I worked under him. He was a serious, humourless man who knew his job, but I never got on with him. He lived with his wife, his mother-in-law and a small child. The women were terrified of natives, which was quite unnecessary in those days, and never went for a walk without carrying a .22 rifle. When riding over the veld, which was heavily bushed, I sometimes came across the women. Mrs Harrow was afraid of being raped, an almost unheard of crime, though this fear was not uncommon. Eileen and I called it 'Rapitis'. I was not afraid of leaving Eileen even for a few nights as I had to do later on. She had a gun and the dogs.

The Harrows kept no dogs, which struck us as odd. He was my boss and I have never liked having a boss living too near me. I have always been a hard worker but like to work my own way and in my own time. Anyway, this situation did not last long as Mr Harrow was promoted to a bigger place in the north where I have no doubt he did very well. It is impossible to imagine him failing. Any failure he had could only be attributed to an Act of God, not of Harrow.

To work both farms I had two spans, that is eight pairs, of sixteen oxen each, a three-furrow disc plough, a harrow and half a dozen cultivators, together with such hand tools as bush-picks, hoes, spades, picks, axes and crowbars.

My driver, Philip, trained his teams to work without *voorloper* (a boy to lead them). They turned inwards to the left when he shouted: '*Kom! Kom!*' To start a team the driver cries: '*Loop!*' To slow them up and stop them he shouts: '*Woe kaai!*' and gives a long slow whistle. Driving oxen is an art in which the Boers and certain natives excel.

My work was boring in the extreme. Getting up before dawn to wake natives who were sleeping like dead men rolled in blankets in their huts and getting them out. Setting a boy to cook the mealie porridge in the big black three-legged iron pot, sending out herders to find the grazing oxen and get them inspanned before breakfast. Then when I had the boys started, the implements moving up and down the rows, and the boys weeding with hand hoes, I could go and get my own breakfast.

In a job of this kind there is very little to occupy the mind. There are some wage sheets to keep, a few stores to check, but the rest of it is pure routine, over-seeing of the simplest kind – foreman's work – just a matter of getting a gang started and keeping it going. There was not even any hiring and firing; this was done from the head office of Roodekuil of which both Toowoomba and Thornycroft were subsidiaries.

There were incidents that broke the monotony. I saw a large python in a deserted kaffir village, a story no one would believe when I told it. But I saw him all right – about two feet of him – nearly as thick as my thigh, going through the long grass. In the same village I picked up a biggish Bushman digging stone. These are almost round, somewhat flattened at the top and bottom, pierced by a hole so that they resemble a gigantic ten-pound bead. The Bushman, now almost extinct, used to fit a stick into the hole at one end – the top – and insert the fire-sharpened bottom into a buck horn. With this instrument they dug edible bulbs and roots out of the iron-hard ground. When they trekked they took off the stone, ran a thong through it and slung it over their shoulder.

These people were the original possessors of the country we now call South Africa and were crushed between the black Bantu tribes coming down from the north and the white man working his way up from the south. There are a few thousand half-breed Bushmen left in the Kalahari and a few families of pure Bushmen in South West. I was told by a man who was ranching on the borders of Angola that not so long ago they still shot an occasional Bushman, as they were continually killing stock. He said the police knew about it but let it go, as some policemen had been killed by their poisoned arrows. I do not know how true this is, but it seems possible. The same man informed me that lions were very bad where he was and that he ran big herds of donkeys for the lions which, since they prefer donkey meat to cattle, now left the horned stock more or less alone.

In the north lions and leopards interfere with ranch operations, and I have many friends who have shot lions in the way of business. Some, like Tony Combes, have lost a limb in their encounters. He had shot eight lions, the ninth he wounded but did not kill. It charged him and his gun boy ran away. He was a powerful man and wrestled with it, putting his hand in its mouth and twisting its tongue, which is the correct procedure in such a case and which delays matters for a few minutes. In the meantime his picannin, who was some way behind, took the rifle from the gun boy and ran up and shot the lion at point-blank range. Combes' life was saved but he lost his left leg. He now uses poison both for lions and leopards. The leopards take a lot of calves and often kill more than they need, quite wantonly. Crocodiles Combes poisoned by hanging poisoned meat on branches that overhang the water, just clear of the surface.

Much later I met a man who had a coconut plantation on Harbor Island in the Bahamas who had lost the use of his left arm through an accident with a wounded lion, and in the game reserve I met the famous ranger, Wolhuter, who was carried off by a lion and, feeling for its heart with his left hand, drove his hunting knife into it, between the fingers, with his right. A game ranger's job was one that I would have liked, and when I heard there was a vacancy I put in for it, but was turned down.

While at Warm Baths we had a locust invasion. At one time they literally blackened the sky, hiding the sun, and their weight broke the branches of the trees on which they slept at night. I was riding a big chestnut thoroughbred sent up by the van der Byl girls to see if I could sell him, which I finally succeeded in doing, but he was the stupidest horse I ever rode and took as much room to turn as a battleship. When the locusts came – the advance guard as it were – I had a lot of trouble with him as he refused to face them. They were coming from the north and I had to ride into them to get home. They drove at us like a rain of bullets. Then he started to bolt and the locusts hit my face so hard they drew blood. I managed to get him to walk at last, but he was going nearly crazy with locusts creeping all over both of us. It was impossible to go faster than a walk because of the force of their impact. It was just a matter of going slow, but my chestnut was black with sweat when I got him back. Eileen had shut all the windows but a lot still got into the house.

They came for three days and ate every green thing – the leaves off the trees, the crops, the grass itself. The only crops that seem more or less immune to their attack are sunflowers, monkey nuts and cow peas. The locusts were accompanied by swarms of insectivorous birds – storks, egrets, bee-eaters, shrikes, and tiny insectivorous hawks. The natives collected the locusts in bags as they rested at night, killed them by drowning and spread them out to dry. They are very fond of them and so are cattle, horses, pigs and poultry. I tried a few roasted over an open fire on a piece of tin and they were not at all bad. The hens, of course, ate themselves full, almost to bursting point, on the live ones that landed in the yard.

The natives also ate white ants. When they were winged and went on their nuptial flight, they piled up in small brown drifts against the windows of the buildings. Like the locusts, white ants were not at all bad when fried. It was quite a job sweeping up the white ants' wings which they lost once their purpose was accomplished.

Whole lands of mealies (corn, maize) disappeared beneath the locusts' jaws. One could hear them chumping. The swarm reached Johannesburg and, getting into the offices, created a panic. A large locust is over four inches long, and the girls went into hysterics, bringing all office work to a standstill till the windows were closed and the locusts killed. That was a day that the little typists of the city got a taste of Africa. Many pairs of stockings were ruined by the locusts' spiky legs. There were interesting stories of screaming typists with locusts half the size of mice crawling up their legs and getting into their panties. Under such conditions even the most modest girls appear to have lost their inhibitions.

We could get away for the weekend once a month or so and went to stay with our new friends – the Strubens at Lynwood in Pretoria, the McLeods and Cloete-Smiths in Johannesburg, the van der Byls at Irene. Not being very social I did not mind whether I went or not, but it made a break for Eileen. So I got her away as often as I could. If friends came down for the day, they would take her back to town with them and someone else would bring her back the following weekend. I missed her a great deal when she was away, but felt it was only fair to give her a change – some gaiety, parties, dancing, theatres, pictures, good food, shops, and women to gossip with. Our living conditions were adequate but no more. There was food of sorts, we had books from the Pretoria library – they sent them to us by post. The bath was filled by our houseboy with four-gallon paraffin tins of water heated on a fire outside. The sanitation was primitive.

Eileen sewed, she wrote a lot of letters, she read, she did a little cooking. Sometimes we drove our donkeys up to see Reg and Margery Langebrink at Roodekuil. Sometimes Mrs Scott came to fetch us in her car and drove us home again. Our windows were not fly-netted and the flies were very bad. Sometimes at night the ceiling was black with them. We used sticky flypapers but they were soon full. There were moths of all sizes from micro moths to things the size of small birds banging into the oil lamps and singeing their wings. Flying beetles, large and small. A few snakes. I caught one by the tail as it was going down a hole in the floor. I called Eileen to bring me some string. She tied it round the snake's tail while I held it and I fastened it to a chair. Then I got a longer string, pulled it further out and broke its back with a stick.

Another time there was a medium-sized cobra lying extended on the top of our big silver tray – a wedding present. It was a very hot day and it was cooling off. I shot it with my .22 – a shot I was rather proud of. Another time I nearly walked on a puff-adder as I stepped out of the house. These are nasty snakes, very sluggish, that strike if stepped on. They are very venomous with long retractable fangs which lie flat along the sides of the mouth when not in use. They are vipers and rather prettily patterned in grey-black, touched with white and yellow on the belly. They are viviparous, bringing forth their young alive. The babies are born fully equipped with fangs and poison glands. Puff-adders are thick, heavy-set snakes and are said to reach six foot in length. I have never killed one more than four foot long.

Both our homes had been ugly, functional, rather like the barracks or small police posts. In neither was there enough water. It all came from windmill-driven pumps. The boreholes were a hundred and fifty to two hundred feet deep. The towers were fifty feet high as they had to be to pump water from such depths. The water flowed into circular concrete reservoirs holding 30,000 or more gallons and was piped from there to the house. When the reservoir was full the wheel was turned off by bringing the tail up against the wheel instead of its sticking out at right angles to it to keep it into the wind. This was done by means of chain and a ratchet with a handle from the ground. The gears of the wheel had to be checked and greased now and then, a job I hated as I do not like heights, and both hands were required to do the work.

There was nothing in the life here to suit a good-looking young woman in her twenties. I liked it and should have liked it even wilder and rougher. Had I not been married I should have gone north to Rhodesia or Kenya.

When Duchess, our great Dane, was a year old we took her with us to stay with my cousin Gavin Graham and his wife Hester, on their farm at Naboomspruit. Duchess was quite quiet with stock, but went mad when she saw Gavin's large black pigs. This, I think, was hereditary, the great Dane being descended from the old German boarhound. Great Danes had not yet been spoilt by the Kennel Club and in no way resembled the herring-gutted animals that one now sees in the show ring. They were big wide-chested animals, weighing a hundred and fifty to two hundred pounds.

Gavin had a big vlei (marsh) on his farm where there were quite a lot of reedbuck. We went hunting one day, Gavin and I and three local Afrikaner farmers. It was very heavy going trekking through half-dead knee-high reeds. We saw a few buck and I shot the only one. When we got up to it we found I had hit it in the head. 'What a shot!' the Afrikaners said. 'Oh,' I said, 'I always shoot buck in the head so as not to spoil the meat.' Of course I had shot in front of the buck and it had jumped into my bullet. Just a lucky fluke, but my local reputation was made.

Ypres, Gavin Graham's farm, was one of the best in the northern Transvaal. He had been a flying ace with the RFC with fourteen planes to his credit. He was a distant cousin and his wife a first cousin, the daughter of my Uncle Peter Cloete from the Eastern Province, a very pretty blonde girl and a fine horsewoman. I rode with her a lot. The farm being well watered was very snaky, and I nearly rode over a really big cobra one day. But one can't have everything, and if a place has a lot of water it also has a lot of frogs, mice and other small animals which makes it ideal for snakes. The Grahams had two small girls of six and

My grandfather P. L. G. Cloete
of Great Westerford, Cape Town

My maternal grandmother,
Mrs. E. Park née Fairlie

My mother

My father ca 1880 in Persian uniform

eight – horrible children – who eventually grew up into charming young women. Gavin was ranching with Sussex bulls and had a good grade herd of cows, but later gave up ranching and became for a while the watermelon king of the north, sending away his produce by the trainload.

While we were there I found a nice little black blood mare that I thought would do for Eileen, so I sent her to Irene for a few days and rode the mare home – about a hundred miles over the mountains – in three days. I slept out two nights and spent one in the hotel at Nylstroom. Actually the mare was not up to my weight and I had to be very careful with her over the mountains and lead her over the bad places. In the end Eileen did not like her so I railed her back.

At home in Warm Baths we were sometimes picked up and taken to parties on neighbouring farms. I did not take my donkeys out at night having no lights to my little Cape cart. Certain features of these entertainments were amusing. People with children brought them, and they were either left to sleep in the cars or, if very small, put in a bedroom with the coats, where they were in some danger of being either sat on by a courting couple or smothered by the coats of latecomers who did not see them. We danced outside to the music of a gramophone and by the light of a fire and the moon, with the trees black above us. The food was a braaivleis – barbecue – of lamb cutlets, sausages and steaks with home-made bread – everyone made their own bread – washed down with beer, brandy and coffee. There were usually a lot of dogs waiting for titbits. House dogs and visitors' dogs. Sometimes there was a dog fight over a bitch, or a man fight over a girl, which livened things up.

It was all very simple, very primitive, bucolic and at the same time enjoyable. The women and girls in fresh store clothes, unless they had made their own dresses with patterns from the *Farmer's Weekly*, and the men in clean khaki shirts and trousers. The women talked food, clothes, servants and babies; the men of crops, horses, cattle, hunting and sport. Not much of women. They talked prices, of course. Mealies (maize) was about ten shillings a 200 lb bag, a working ox, say five years old, was worth £10 at the most, a tolley – a young two- to three-year-old steer – £7, a slaughter ox so fat it could just walk fetched £14. A boy's wages were around thirty shillings a month, a very good man might get £2. House servants £5, though a good cook in Johannesburg got as much as £14 to £20. A riding horse was worth anything from £5 up. £10 for a good farm horse unless it was salted, that is had recovered from horse sickness and therefore immune to it. A salted horse could sell for £50 or more.

Our big weekly excitement was the English mail, which reached Warm Baths on Wednesday, and we always drove in to collect it. Letters from Eileen's parents, from mine, from friends. We were both good letter writers and kept up with people we knew at home, for England and France were still home to us.

Our little donkey cart used to create quite a sensation trotting down the street or tied up at the post office or the hotel where we went to read our mail and have tea. I fed the donkeys well and kept them clean and groomed. I was very attached to them.

Life was still colonial with few real changes in the last fifty or even a hundred years except for the near extermination of the wild game. Few natives could read or write. At night they sat round their fires beating their tomtoms and singing. Some were even dressed in sacks with holes for the head and arms, most wore sandals made of old motor tyres. There were no tractors, there were not even a lot of cars. All farm work was done with spans of oxen. The poorer farmers used horses and Cape carts to get about. Except in the town there was no electric light; we used paraffin lamps and candles.

I was managing to do fairly well on my salary and pension, even saving a little so that we had some cash for trips to town or clothes for Eileen. I had bought a very nice little German .22 with a magazine and now had a 32/40 Winchester and a twelve-bore shotgun as well as my .45 Webley in the way of arms. Not that there was much left to shoot. An occasional steenbok, guinea fowl, pheasant or partridge, but nothing was thick on the ground and it had to be hunted for.

Duchess came into season and I took her to Lynwood, the Strubens' place, and had her served by her own father, a very fine dog indeed. She had a nice litter of pups which I sold for a fiver each. Before they were weaned a stout trek Boer woman came up to the house and said she wanted a pup. She had seen that Duchess was in heavy milk so she knew I had pups. I said she could not afford one. I also asked her how she would feed it. Instead of answering she opened her blouse and exposed an enormous breast. It appeared that she had a young baby and enough milk for the baby and the pup. But I was not having any of it and I doubt very much if she had even a pound in cash.

These trek Boers, as they were called, nomads living in their waggons, were poor white landless vagrants. Their parents had been ruined by the British policy of burning farms in the Boer War (1899–1902). They moved over the land in wagons, grazing a few miserable animals – scrub cattle, sheep and goats – as they trekked. With the industrialization of Africa they have disappeared, but then, in the twenties, there were any number of them. Some were the result of their ancestors' fecundity – the old Boers had very large families and Roman Dutch Law made it necessary to divide all land equally between all the children when the father died. Even the biggest farm can only be subdivided just so often and almost any division at all will make it uneconomic to run since each section must have access to water. So long corridors are cut through the veld which later become eroded and silt up the spring to which they lead.

Civilization eventually caught up with the trek Boers. They were among the world's last free men but had to make great sacrifices to achieve their freedom. In winter they hunted, often poaching to make biltong (sun-dried meat) which they sold. In summer some of them made chairs with reimpi seats. The only things they bought were coffee, sugar, mealie meal, some soft goods for clothes, and ammunition.

One way and another I had a lot of dogs at Thornycroft. I fed them on mealie meal, milk and meat scraps when I could get them. Among them was a cross-bred Dane Greyhound – Diana – that was given me by a road ganger who was camped on the farm. She looked exactly like a greyhound and showed no trace of her Dane mother. She was always hunting and galloping into barbed wire fences which cut her to ribbons, so that I finally gave her to a man who was going to the relatively unfenced north and wanted a hunting dog.

Neethling, the man who gave me Diana, was a great hunter and poacher with a passion for dogs. He lived with his wife and half a dozen children under canvas and had fourteen dogs of various kinds, including a bulldog, that he kept tied to trees in all weathers. I was surprised that they survived, but they seemed to. He always wanted me to hunt with him, but I could hardly poach on my employer's property. He had a grade Hereford cow that gave fifteen bottles of milk a day – a surprising amount for an animal with so much beef blood. Cows then were described by the number of bottles (whisky bottles) of milk they gave. A five-bottle, ten-bottle or twenty-bottle cow. He also had a very fine brown shooting pony called Tommy that he wanted to sell me. He was a wonderful horse and steady as a rock under fire. You just dropped the reins on his withers and he stood. Then, as soon as you had shot, he would gallop after the wounded buck, following it without any help and running to the flank to give you the chance of another shot, rather like an American quarter horse. I would have bought him except that he was lame with a corn on his near forefoot. Later he was sent to the veterinary school at Onderstepoort where they cut out the corn, effecting a complete cure.

Instead I bought a little bay mare on the market at Warm Baths for £7. A Jewish dealer offered me £7 10s for her as I led her out of the ring and I refused it. He said: 'You are wrong to refuse it. Just look at the profit you are making – 10s on £7 in less than an hour. That's how we Jews make money; we turn it over.' I said I did not want to sell the mare because I fancied her. She was a pretty little thing, not up to my weight but very tame and quiet and might do for Eileen. But I could see the dealer's point. My approach was sentimental, not practical, as it was to Swartkloof, a farm in the mountains about ten miles from Warm Baths that I had taken a fancy to. The owner wanted three thousand pounds for it which was, of course, far beyond what I could afford, but I toyed with the idea. It was a very wild farm facing south and looking out over the flat land towards Pretoria, and backing up into the mountains which were reached through the black valley that gave the farm its name. This sinister poort was only lit when the sun was vertical, but going on through it the mountains opened up into a large quite wild cup, and further back was an even wilder farm, the home of hundreds of baboons, that could not be reached except on foot or horseback. There was a group of magnificent Marula trees at the foot of the mountains, which would have been the site of my homestead, and there were numbers of other large flowering trees and bushes. The place could have been turned into a park by grazing it extensively with donkeys and goats. The donkeys would have grazed the long grass down and the goats eaten the scrubby bush and cleaned the trees as high as they could reach standing on their hindlegs, creating a browse line.

I have always preferred beauty to good farmland. The trouble here, however, was lack of water. I did have a borehole put down by a dowser and driller on a 'no water, no pay' basis, but what he found was too little to be of any use. Had we found water I could have raised a bit of money somewhere and borrowed more, but I doubt if I could have made a go of it. My Jewish horse-dealing friend would certainly never have looked at the place, but it had everything I liked except being a viable proposition.

But it was strange to think that in my father's time the Waterberg was a range flowing with milk and honey and malaria. It had been a malarial death trap during the Boer War and now it was drying up.

Once while on a picnic at Swartkloof a cow ate Eileen's raffia handbag, and when we got back from a walk she was blowing scarlet bubbles of lipstick blood out of her mouth.

By this time I had, in addition to my own donkeys, the use of the headquarters' American spider and four mules. They had evidently been named by a militarist and were called Maxim, Machine Gun, Aeroplane and Zeppelin. I was now being employed by the company to inspect outlying properties they held in the district and to report on them – the condition of the fences, dams and homesteads.

It was a very pleasant opportunity for making long drives into the country with just Pete, a Cape coloured driver boy, for company. Eileen, who did not care for camping, stayed at home. With the dogs and a gun she was safe enough, but some women would have been afraid to be left. On the other hand, others would have liked camping in the bush. This is something I never got tired of, especially with animal transport. To lie looking up at the stars, seeing them pinpricked in the dark blue night through the black tracery of branches, and listen to the night sounds – the cry of a hunting jackal, the call of an owl, and the steady munching of the mules as they ate mealies spread out on bags on the ground in front of them.

On one occasion when we rested on the bank of the Crocodile River I made one of the best pots of tea I have ever tasted. After tea I walked upstream and round a bend in the river found about three hundred mine boys from a new development washing, cleaning their teeth and doing laundry. No wonder the tea had body.

I had only one adventure on a trip of this kind. I was fast asleep beside the spider but was woken by a smell of smoke and, jumping up, I saw a big bush fire bearing down on us. It was coming downwind towards the road on which we were camped, on a wide front. We could not get away from it as it stretched for miles in both directions. There was only one thing to do and we had to do it quickly – that was to back burn a break for ourselves and get on to it. But we first had to move the mules who were becoming nervous. They were tied by riems to a rope stretched between two trees. I held them while Piet stretched the rope on the other side of the road. As soon as he had done this we led the mules over. It all went well till Maxim, who was the most nervous, tried to bolt and dragged the riem through my hand, cutting it almost through the palm. But I held on and we tied him with the others. Then, starting from the road, we lit a fire along it with torches made of dry grass. It burnt slowly against the wind. As soon as it was about twenty yards wide we went upwind and burnt downwind again towards it, giving us an area of five or six acres that was safe from fire since there was nothing left to burn. We then manhandled the spider on to the burn and moved the mules back over the road again. That took some doing as the ground was still warm and there were patches of smouldering twigs; scattered game and cattle dung were sending up little columns of smoke. But we managed it and then we set fire, again with the wind, to the veld on the other side of the road behind us where the mules had been standing. We were now safe enough and settled down to wait, standing between the mules, talking to them, pulling their ears and petting them till the fire was past us. There was a lot of smoke which made breathing difficult for a bit, but we put wet handkerchiefs over our faces, and the mules, apart from a lot of snorting and pulling at their riems, stood it pretty well.

Next day we reached Rooiberg which was on our route. There is a tin mine here with a very ancient history. Tin is supposed to have been taken from it hundreds of years ago by both Arabs and Chinese. The road approaching the mine was so dusty – the red dust, as fine as flour, lay four inches thick – that it muffled the sound of the mules' hooves and the wheels of the spider. I soon lost sight of my cattle, my reins disappeared into the red mist. I found that the only way I could drive was by looking at the telephone wire over my head and watching the leaders' ears, which were just visible.

We had a meal at the hotel, rested and watered our mules, and pushed on to camp that night at Krantzkop, an enormous cliff where vultures must have nested by the hundreds for centuries. The whole cliff was chalky white with their encrusted droppings and, as the sun went down, became tinged first with pink and then with red, brilliant mauve and purple. It was a wonderful sight. There were very few vultures left, even then. The poisoning of carcases for jackals had killed off most of them all over the country. That is to say there were still vultures but they were scarce, whereas at one time almost as soon as anything was killed they were there by the dozen.

The mules were still nervous as the hair on their fetlocks had been singed when we led them over the smouldering burn, but no actual damage was done to their legs and we set off next morning in good shape. My map and directions were vestigial. The roads were rough tracks, sometimes less – just a spoor of wheel marks where at some time within the last few months a wagon had passed. I came across a family of trek Boers, a man, his wife and half a dozen children. I gave them some coffee and sugar. The tow-headed children were as wild as buck. They would not approach us but peered at us from behind trees. However, I got some directions from the man and found the farm I was looking for. Next day I went on and found the farm I had to report on. It was being run by two brothers – Labuschagne by name. Among the biggest and most powerful men I have ever seen, they were living under primitive pioneer conditions over seventy miles from rail or even a store. One of them had just brought in his wagon with some bags of seed cotton. These bags weigh two hundred pounds and he picked them off the bed of the wagon the way I would pick up a parcel. I checked the fences and the dam which was nearly dry. They were filtering their drinking water through a cloth but seemed quite happy about it. It would rain soon, they said, and if not, if things got really bad, their neighbour ten miles away had a strong spring.

Exploring the mountain, I found a small piece of sulphur. It looked like a bright yellow nugget. I burnt a piece of it to be sure. I reported it to the office and sent in the sample. As far as I know there is no sulphur in Africa, but there was some up there somewhere.

Then with my business done, I said goodbye to the giants and their wives and children, inspanned and reached Rooiberg again that night.

I now realized it was January 28th and that tomorrow was Eileen's birthday. I was still forty miles from home. This, in the days of motor cars, is an hour's run, even on bad roads – and the roads here were only tracks – but it is a long way with mules after a few days in the blue on short rations, but I made it. I made it four hours' actual driving time with two hours out for rests and outspans where we watered the mules and allowed them to roll in the dust. This refreshes a horse or a mule rather in the way a shower refreshes a man. By great good fortune at Halfway House – halfway between Rooiberg and Warm Baths – I found a present for Eileen. A tiny baby monkey that I bought for five shillings and put into one of the mules' feed bags.

There were no further adventures on the trip except when one of the wheels hit a stump and the jerk smashed the riem that tied the leaders' swingle tree to the *disselboom* (pole). They nearly pulled me out of my seat as the draught was transferred from the traces to the reins. I just managed to stop them and, having made the repair, we pushed on home.

CHAPTER 7

A BROKEN LINK

WE called the monkey Edward. He was a vervet with a brown coat that in some lights seemed to be tinged with green. When adult the males become beautifully coloured with a sky-blue scrotum and rose-pink penis. Edward was a sweet pet. He had a light chain attached to a thin belt round his waist. The chain was fastened to the box in which he slept. We took him walking loose with the dogs in the bush and he followed, airborne most of the time as he kept up with us leaping from tree to tree. He was fond of climbing the pepper trees and hanging from their branches. These trees, which grow to thirty feet, are drought resistant and look a little like weeping willows. They have small red berries on them that look like peppercorns but are not edible.

Edward was well fed and never teased, but one day for no reason he bit Eileen's neck quite badly. He had also developed a habit of jumping into the middle of the tea-tray as Kleinbooi brought it on to the stoep.

After these events, which proved, as I had been told but not believed, that vervets were unreliable even if never teased, I swapped him for a black donkey mare with my neighbour Charlie Pentz. We often visited Charlie and his wife Hedie, and I sometimes rode into Warm Baths with him. He had a Basuto pony but said I rode too fast. He was a retired civil servant who had bought a small farm, all black turf, the best mealie land, on the advice of his brother Ivan, who had been running Roodekuil when I first arrived. He was a small, very nice man and a hard worker. His wife was a big, very good-looking dark woman. They had a boy at school in Pretoria.

We saw something of my cousins the Cloete-Smiths in Johannesburg. There were three girls. Helen, who became a close friend, Margorie and Dotsy – a small, very pretty blonde. There was a brother whom I never got to know well. They lived in a house built of corrugated iron dating from the time Johannesburg was a mining camp. They had very little money though their father was a contemporary of all the men who had made fortunes in the seventies and eighties.

But he had been a very religious man who did not believe in money and never bought a share, which was rather hard on his family. At one time Helen told me they did not even have the money for a stamp in the house.

Other friends with whom we sometimes stayed were the McLeods – Louis Rose and Trixy. McLeod was a big, immensely stout man, who was then editor of the *Rand Daily Mail* and had been the editor of *Punch*. They had two very pretty daughters, Betty and Barbara.

We also saw quite a lot of my cousin Molly van der Byl who taught riding at Roedean in Johannesburg, and of Peggy Owen, my boss's blonde daughter. These girls all came to stay and Eileen visited them. Sometimes alone, sometimes, if I could get away, with me.

One thing I had not been prepared for were the storms. Sometimes the lightning was continuous and one crash of thunder merged into the next. There is, I believe, the highest rate of casualties from lightning in the world in the Transvaal and also a very high rate of pneumonia from the sudden fall of temperature when the rain comes. It can drop from 90° to 60° in a matter of minutes. We had one strike of lightning so near the house that the shock made Eileen drop the tray she was carrying. Years later after I had sold it my farm Constantia was struck and burnt to the ground. If we were working with a span of oxen and a storm came up we always outspanned them to get them away from the trek chains which could attract lightning. Whole spans of oxen were sometimes killed in this way. Fortunately Eileen was not frightened of storms, though some of her friends hid in cupboards or under beds. Nor was she frightened of insects. We had plenty of all kinds, also tarantulas, large hairy-legged spiders and scorpions. So though in one way it was dull something was always going on. Visitors, spiders, snakes in the house, boys with cuts and wounds to be dressed.

Then one Wednesday when we got the mail there was a letter from my mother to say my father had died. I was not surprised; he was seventy-three years old. My mother said he had not suffered and that was surely all that really matters. He and I had been too alike in many ways for us to get on. I often wish now that I had remembered more of his stories.

I can only say this about my father. That they do not make his like today. His world was different to ours. The sexes had not been levelled up by female suffrage, women competing with men in business and associating with them in their affairs. Women did not smoke or drink, marriage was regarded as permanent. The men wore moustaches, the women's hair was long, and they did not shave their armpits. Today, if he had lived, my father would have been a hundred and twenty years old. Ten such lives put end to end would reach back into Saxon England. His going left a blank space in my life. Another string that held my life like a balloon to my childhood had been severed. This is the life process, the slow elimination of all ties till, if we live long enough, we float alone in the meaningless space of age. Children may make a difference – having none, I do not know. But since they are projections into the future I do not see how they can affect the past except in terms of continuity. All they do is to make us links in a chain, whereas the childless are the end of one – the final products of an endless series of reproductions.

Though I had not expected to see my father again, his death still came as a shock. I had not even known he had been ill. He died of diabetes. Insulin had not yet been discovered.

My father had had a very great influence on my life. I would have liked to have loved him, but as I got older he talked to me less and I could never get close to him. The thing that struck me as terrible was that a man should live as he had and be unable to pass on the vast amount of worldly knowledge he had accumulated in his lifetime. He was a rationalist, an agnostic, and I certainly followed him in this. Had he been religious I might have been. I often wonder about this.

I remembered things he had told me as a child. Never to run downstairs with my hands in my pockets or a pencil in my mouth. Always to be careful to pay back small sums I borrowed. Never to touch my genitals, which I did not do till I was eighteen when, as a soldier, I chose masturbation in preference to going with tarts as I was afraid of venereal disease or nice girls because I was afraid of making them pregnant. He gave me the run of his library. He taught me a lot about philately, though in the end he sold my stamp collection, which I had amalgamated with his, because he said they would all be mine one day. I remember some of the stories he had told me of his life. Of how he had driven a tandem up the steps of St George's Hospital at Hyde Park Corner. Of how he had dived off Waterloo Bridge into the Thames for a bet. Of how, when he was new to London, he had eaten five peaches at a dinner-party only to find later that they were hot-house grown and cost a guinea each. Coming from the Cape he was used to eating fruit by the basketful if he felt like it. Figs till his lips got sore, peaches, apricots, grapes.

He had held a commission in the London Scottish and I had his claymore. He had had a racing stable at Newmarket, a yacht at Cowes, a house in Queensgate.

His brother, my Uncle Broderick, was a great racing man who with Paradox had won the Two-Thousand Guineas and the Grand Prix in Paris. Paradox finished second in the Derby in 1885. Melton won, but it could have been declared a dead heat if in the previous year there had not been a dead heat with St Gatien and Harvester. The judges decided they could not have two dead heats running. (Broderick later, in 1911, won the Oaks with Cherimoya.)

So that when my father's crash occurred the Cloete name was very much in the public eye. My parents had been in the jet set of their day, going in Court dress to levees at Buckingham Palace, meeting everyone, knowing everyone. They gave big parties and intimate parties at which my father sang, playing a banjo, while my mother accompanied him on the piano.

He was a great raconteur. He told very good stories about his life, his adventures and people he had known – many of them vastly exaggerated. This may be why I never tell stories, am in fact allergic to them except when I write them.

My father had oil interests in Persia and had received a decoration from the Shah. He was possibly the first man to see the importance of oil. He had had the first ice factory in Kimberley. He was, in fact, a man of great vision, and was what was in those days called a company promoter. Today they are called financiers. Had he not messed things up he would perhaps have been a millionaire.

Till recently (1972) I did not know anything about the crash except that he had gone bankrupt, had been imprisoned for six months, changed his name from Cloete to Graham and gone to the Continent to live – first in Antwerp and then in Paris. I did not even know the nature of his offence or the details and dates of the case.

Now, thanks to material sent me by Miss Thelma Gutche, I have some of the particulars, which are as follows:

Extracts from *The Star* – 15th March 1891

The Cloete Family in London

Capetown, Thursday (Special). There was a fresh washing of dirty linen at the meeting of the De Kaap Gold Mines, Mr Laurence Woodbine Cloete presiding. It appears that a large sum of money had been lodged with the Development and Investment Company, which one shareholder said consisted practically of the Cloete family. Mr Cloete was requested to resign the Chairmanship of the Company. At the Knysna Concessions meeting, Mr L. Cloete, who is Chairman, did not attend, and was not proposed for re-election as a Director.

Mr Woodbine Cloete

The prosecution of Mr Woodbine Cloete does not appear to bear any relation to Rand matters. He was charged at the Marlborough Street Police Court on Tuesday with fraud. Counsel alleged that the accused had made the acquaintance of Mrs Page, of Cadogan-place, and, persuading her that he was engaged in promoting several valuable companies, obtained cheques from her at various times, amounting altogether to £16,705. All the companies were said to be bogus. The evidence of the liquidator of one of the companies was taken, and the case was adjourned.

Extract from *The Star* – 21st May 1891

The Case of Mr Cloete

Mr Lawrence Woodbine Cloete had appeared for the tenth time before the Marlborough-street Magistrate, to an adjourned summons at the instance of Mrs Annie Page, on the charge of having defrauded her of £16,705. In the course of the inquiry, Mr Peter Lawrence Van der Byl was examined. In his evidence he stated that he had lived at Paarl, near Capetown, and was till lately a member of the Upper House of the Colony. He remembered Mr Cloete coming to the Transvaal in 1876, in order to have a thorough look at the country. Grants of land, he explained, were at about that time granted without the Government surveys now required and without title deeds being issued. He knew the Johannesburg goldfields quite well, and all the concerns in the Witwatersrand district.

Is that district a well-known gold-producing district? – Oh, yes; as thoroughly well known in England as in the Colony.

And, in particular, are the Johannesburg goldfields a good property? – Yes; I myself negotiated to get a bit of the property.

Are you prepared to say that the properties in the district are gold-producing, if properly worked and engineered? – Yes; but everything lies in the management. At first, of course, there must be a considerable expenditure without any return.

Have some of the present best companies in that district taken years to develop? – That is so.

Do you happen to know the output of gold in the district? – The return last month was something like 53,000 oz. A year or two ago the out-put was not a third of that amount. The out-put is increasing monthly, and the last return, I think, is one of the best. I know something of this, as I was one of the first on the fields.

Should you say that London quotations were any criterion as to the value of these properties of which we have been speaking? – Not at all. It is not right to infer, from the fact of there being no quotation in London, that a property is necessarily valueless. Of my own knowledge there are many good companies in South Africa which are not quoted in London. I saw Mr Cloete in January, 1889, and had a conversation with him as to the value of some of the gold properties which have been mentioned. Mr Cloete seemed very sanguine as to these properties; he perfectly satisfied me that he had full confidence in the mines.

And did you concur in his conclusions? – Yes; because I am fully satisfied that, if these properties in Witwatersrand were properly developed, they would yield a good dividend yet.

Given a property in the Witwatersrand district, near to Johannesburg, if that were properly worked and sufficiently financed, what would be the prospect? – The prospect would be perfect, and would open up an excellent investment.

At this stage the case was again adjourned, Mr Besley intimating that he would have two or three more witnesses to call.

Mr Van der Byl omitted to state that he was nearly related to the accused, and had been closely connected with him in several of his financial schemes.

Extracts from *The Star* – (Johannesburg) 1891

6th June – Paragraph announcing that Cloete was committed for trial in London for defrauding Mrs Page.

7th July – *The Cloete Case*

London: Mr Matthews, Home Secretary, replying to a question in the House of Commons last night, said that he abstained from intervention in the Cloete case when the superior court had sanctioned the withdrawal of the prosecution. Sir George Campbell gave notice to call attention to the matter later on.

1892

19th January – *Well-Deserved Sentence*

London. Woodbine Cloete and Macpherson were sentenced yesterday, the former to six months and the latter to eighteen months hard labour.

23rd January – *Woodbine Cloete*

London. Woodbine Cloete and his clerk Macpherson have both been found guilty. Sentence was deferred.
(Nothing discerned thereafter.)

From the evidence and from the little my father told me he appears to have chanced his arm and been caught off balance. There are a number of psychological factors to be considered. What was his relationship with Mrs Annie Page who claimed he had defrauded her of £16,705? Then there was the question of my mother who, he told me, could have saved him had she been nicer to some man. How much nicer? Nice enough to go to bed with him?

In May 1891 the question of gold on the Witwatersrand was brought up in court. How incredible this seems today.

Then, of course, there is the matter of his changing his name and bolting to the Continent instead of riding out the storm. Some of his friends would have stuck with him and with his ability he could probably have made a fresh start. Many men have done it since and are millionaires today. But that was yesterday. Eighty years ago. He was a proud man and it broke him. So I never really knew my father, only the shadow of the brilliant, gay, business and society man he had once been.

He had committed no felony. He had simply been careless and left too many details to others. He had trusted his luck too far and now it was all over. He was dead.

CHAPTER 8

A MAN ALONE

An event now took place which was to change the picture. I heard that Frank Struben, with whom we stayed quite often at Lynwood, was selling some of his pedigree Sussex cattle at the Rand Show and was sending the rest down to his bushveld ranch for which he had no manager. I obtained two days' leave and went to Johannesburg to see if I could help him with the stock and get the ranch job. I was a stock man. Cattle and horses were what interested me. He gave me the job and I gave notice to the Transvaal Estates and Development Company.

Frank Struben was a tall, handsome, somewhat quick-tempered man who had been a gunner in the war. He owned Lynwood and a lot of other property in the suburbs of Pretoria, as well as the ranch, and was a wealthy, though land-poor, man. His father and uncle had been the first to discover gold on the Witwatersrand in the seventies and were the real pioneers of the Reef. The Strubens had two children – Roderick and Rosemary, both very nice. Roderick spent some days on the ranch with us and we were very fond of him.

A few years later Frank bought a plane and had a crash which left him paralysed. He had bad sight and never should have flown.

The ranch was a big place. Sixteen thousand morgen, that is to say over thirty-two thousand acres. It had no house and poor water facilities. It was carrying about a thousand head of cattle of all ages. Frank drove us to the ranch in his Buick over very rough roads after we left the great north road at Hammanskraal. I asked Eileen if she could take the isolation and she said she could.

As Eileen's parents wanted to see her and were prepared to pay her passage, we decided that she should go home while I packed up and built a new house in the bushveld. I saw her off at the station in Johannesburg and returned to Warm Baths.

I then hired two wagons and packed everything into boxes,

My mother in Court Dress, 1880

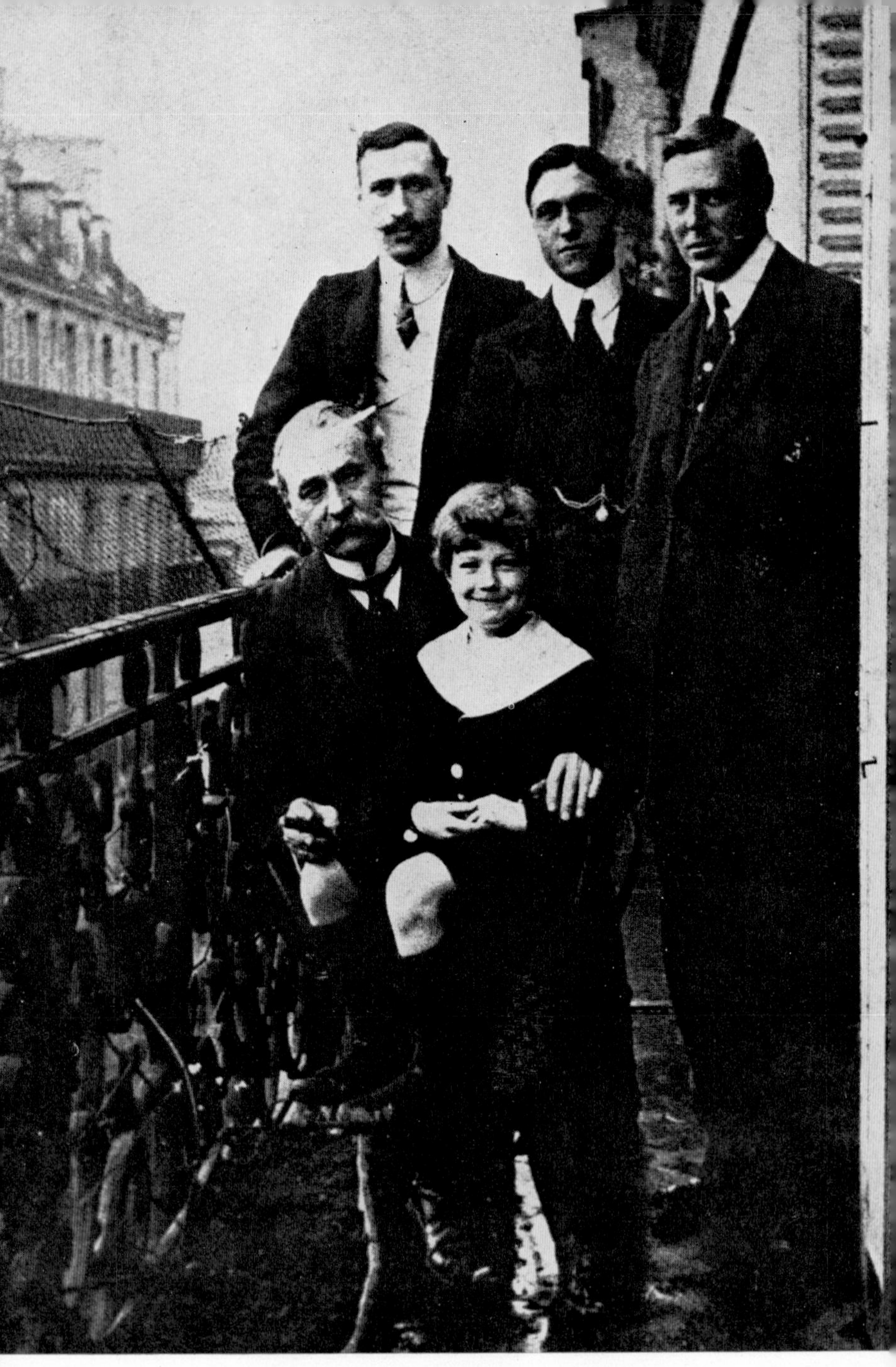

Self and Father with three of my brothers
(l. to r. Lovel, Jim, Lance) in Paris, 1902

crates, barrels and bundles. By that time we had accumulated quite a bit of rubbish – oddments of furniture, big red kaffir pots, animal skins and native weapons. The donkey cart I tied behind the leading wagon, the dogs were tied to the pole of the donkey cart and under it. Tetrach and the bay pony I had bought were tied behind the second wagon. The donkeys ran loose and off we went – south – along the great north road. The first night I slept beside the wagons on the roadside. Next day when we came to Hammanskraal we turned west till we came to Silberman's Post at the Salt Pan and then north again till we reached the house site Frank Struben had chosen. There was a borehole here which gave permanent water but not too much of it. After five thousand gallons it gave out and one had to wait a few hours for the sponge to fill up again. It was seepage water, not a spring. The depth was about two hundred feet.

I now set about making Kimberley bricks. I forget how many thousand we needed, ten or twenty, I think. They were made of clay-like earth mixed with water and tramped to a dough-like consistency. This material was then shovelled into forms, nine by nine by eighteen inches, each block being equal to six ordinary bricks in size and of course much quicker to lay. As soon as the form was full and had been tamped down it was lifted off and filled up again.

The blocks were laid in parallel lines and left to dry in the sun. They took a month or so to cure.

While the bricks were being made we laid the foundation of the house by casting a large concrete floor, the size of the whole house – like a dance floor – completing it with a red granolithic finish and even building the chimney, which was double – one side for the kitchen and the other for the sitting-room fire. The idea was to prevent white ants getting into the bricks from underground, but it was only partially successful. When all this was done we built our walls on the big slab, embodying the chimney. The house had four rooms and a bathroom but no lavatory. There was a bedroom, a spare room, living-room, kitchen, bathroom, and a wide stoep which was netted and ran right round the house. The windows were metal and the roof galvanized iron. On top of the roof where it came to a point there was a kind of widow's walk from which to watch for bush fires. It was reached by a ladder.

While we were building the house I lived under canvas in a couple of bell tents with my furniture piled up and covered with a bucksail. The kitchen consisted of our wood-burning stove with its chimney lashed with wire to the trunk of a big tree, and some piled-up boxes for stores and provisions.

An old English carpenter was left with me to do the fancy bits and Frank came down for days at a time to supervise the building, which went very well and fast. I still had Duchess, the great Dane, and Fifi with four dog pups. She had been served by Scott's Spanish pointer which I had found to be a wonderful worker. One of Fifi's pups was a beauty – pitch black like his father. The others were liver and white like their mother, or black and white. The black one I was going to keep. He unfortunately came to a bad end when he was quite small, by licking a very heavy iron skillet that was hanging on a tree. It fell on his head and killed him – a very uncommon sort of accident because, as a rule, puppies can stand a lot of knocking about.

But the pups caused me trouble and might have lost me my job because once, when Frank Struben was spending the night, I heard great yells coming from his tent and saw him rush out in pursuit of one of the pups who was galloping with flopping ears into the long grass.

'What's up?' I shouted.

'He's got my teeth.'

My God, I thought. 'Don't chase him,' I said. 'Don't make him nervous.' I followed slowly and there he was, sitting down near an antheap looking at my boss's dentures which he had deposited on the bare ground. It seemed that Frank had taken them out of the glass in which they had spent the night and was about to put them in when the pup rushed into the tent – it was the one I generally used – and seeing such a pretty shiny plaything on the box beside the bed, had picked them up and run out with them. When it was over it was funny.

It took about four months to complete the house. During the whole period I never had a drink. I had a gallon of brandy with me but thought it a mistake to open it when I was so lonely. And it was lonely there, particularly as I had never been alone before. School, the army, marriage, and now this. There were the boys, it is true, but they were not company. There was no other white man to talk to when the carpenter left except my neighbour, Barnard, who had a very good farm at Silberman's Post, the two storekeepers at the post – young Russian Jews who were friendly and hospitable but too hard worked to be able to spare much time – and a Danish couple who worked the mine at the Salt Pan. They were all eight miles away. The mine was an extinct volcano that looked just like any other isolated *kopje* till you rode to the top. Then to your astonishment you looked down into a crater five hundred feet deep which was full of water. This water was pumped out and processed to extract salt and caustic soda. At one time every kind of game must have come here for the salt because the whole crater was networked with old game paths. A wonderful sight it must have been.

Later when staying at Naboomspruit with my cousins, I saw another salt lick on a farm called Magiliquin's Eye which I thought of buying. Here a whole hillside of reddish clay had been licked away over hundreds of years by game for its mineral content which I was told was a mixture of salt and arsenic. We camped on this farm and Eileen and I slept on a newly excavated grave, this being the only place where the ground was soft. The farm was all rocks and stones and rose to a cliff where one could look down a thousand feet into the low country. It was named the Eye of Magiliquin because the Magiliquin River rose here. As usual in Africa, if there is good water there is no soil.

Barnard, my nearest neighbour on the ranch, was an old-timer, a Boer War veteran, a bachelor who lived well and drank hard. He had piled up two cars and gone back to a Cape cart and two salted horses. The horses, he said, would always get him home when he went to Pretoria, which was about thirty miles from his place, a first-class farm with sweet grass and lots of open water.

On the ranch which Frank had named *Ad Astra*, I had a curious experience. One night I dropped my shirt on the ground by my camp bed, instead of hanging it to the tent pole, and in the morning when I wanted to put it on it was gone – only the buttons were left, neatly arranged. The white ants had eaten the whole shirt.

I had Boer neighbours who lived ten or fifteen miles away and came out of curiosity to see what I was like. I was a Britisher to them and since I spoke practically no Afrikaans communication was difficult. Some were real poor whites, inbred to the point of harelips, cleft palates and club feet. Many of the earlier Bushveld stocks were very inbred. Since they were without option or choice in the matter and nature pressed very hard on them grouped in tiny family communities, survivors of disease and war, fearful of exposing themselves to long journeys and by nature solitary – to a Boer of those days another man's smoke was anathema – they mated with each other, cousin marrying cousin and then their children marrying again, generation after generation.

They came and sat. They sat in silence for hours on crates in the shade of a tree and I gave them tea to drink. I would not open my brandy for anyone, except in an emergency. But they had curious ideas. They offered me a share of what they shot if I would let them poach on the ranch. They were surprised when I said no. Then, because I was alone and my wife away, they offered me first a donkey mare and later a goat. All in complete good faith, these animals were the local prostitutes. Later I had some trouble with poachers and caught one on a Sunday. He was convicted and fined. But another, in order to find a steenbuck he had wounded, set fire to the veld and burnt out about five thousand acres of our best winter grazing.

To work the farm I was given three horses – two chestnuts that had been cast and sold off by the artillery – Ginger and Orator – and a grey called Peter. Greys often seem to be given that name. Later I bought a splendid little bay Basuto-Arab stallion that I named Pasha. I have ridden him thirty miles in a day and he has come back full of life and still shaking his head and fighting for the bit. I used the heavy silver Mexican bit that my uncle had used when he was ranching there, on his brother Broderick's place, Sabinas, with an enormous two-inch port. It was not, as some people seem to think, cruel, as it only had to be used once. After that you could ride with a piece of cotton for reins. I have a preference for stallions because, though army tests in Egypt and India proved geldings to be their equal, I found that they have more personality and if they suffer hardship come back more quickly.

The working of the cattle consisted chiefly of counting them and dipping the various herds. These were divided into the main breeding herd of about four hundred cows running with twelve bulls, the heifer herd – three hundred or so – and the oxen and tollies, about three hundred. The numbers of these herds varied continually, drafting them from one herd to another was an important part of the stockman's job. Picked oxen for slaughter were drafted out of the ox herd for finishing off. Heifers ready to take the bull were put into the breeding herd. Old cows and queens (cows that are barren and grow pig fat) had to be culled from the breeding herd. The weaned calves were drafted to their respective herds – young oxen to the tolly and ox herd, the females to the heifers.

These stock figures are very rough and there was a great variation in the counts. Sometimes I would be fifty or more short as parties would get away from the herders who, working on foot, had to drive them through these big five-thousand acre, heavily bushed camps. Often they missed some of the animals, and of course there were those that had died.

About twenty of the old cows had bells on their necks. This helped us to find them, as they were very often grouped in family parties. Weaned heifers, when old enough to go into the breeding herd at two years old, often found their mothers again after an eighteen-month separation. For the first few days after weaning I had the calves in a camp near the house and they made an endless din lowing for their mothers.

We had fourteen pedigree Sussex bulls – three to a hundred cows and a couple of spares. I found one bull to be a bachelor by nature. A Ferdinand who would have no truck with any female and we sold him. Frank then sent me two beautiful young bulls he had bought at the Rand Show. I kept them stabled and grazed them carefully to condition them to our veld, but we later lost one. He got red-water and died. The other was also sick but I nursed him and pulled him through, largely by feeding him milk, eight gallons a day, which he drank eagerly.

Apart from counting cattle I knew many of them by sight. Those of odd colours and markings were easy, but many of the red ones – and ninety per cent of the herd was red – I knew by their faces and horns. Some cattle with Afrikander blood have a tendency to grow their horns downwards. Soon after I got to the ranch I found one whose horns were growing into his cheeks, so I sawed off the tips with a tenon-saw and had no more trouble.

I now had all the riding I wanted and seldom went out in the car or on foot without a gun, usually my .22. But the riding was spoilt by not being able to ride good horses. Pasha was the only one I really liked to ride, and shooting was no pleasure when I had to shoot for the pot if I wanted anything in it. I shot what game I could but it was scarce and shy, so that all I brought in sometimes were go-away birds, bush parrots, doves or a hare. The go-away bird, the curse of African hunters, is the grey lourie, a slate-grey, crested, long-tailed poor relation of the parrot. They go about in small groups and as soon as they see a man they give their cry which sounds like 'Go away . . . Go away and away'. All wild animals know this signal and immediately move off.

Binks, my new Alsatian, retrieved well and jumped from the pick-up as soon as I fired. He was very upset if I missed. He was a splendid pup, black and tan like Reine, and the son of Itis, a fully trained German dog belonging to Bob Gwatkin. He disappeared one day, shot, I think, by one of my neighbours.

Part of my work consisted of visiting the dams and drinking places, which I did about midday, to look for sick animals. Cattle in good health at this time of day have eaten their fill, drunk and are lying down chewing the cud. A working ox needs eight hours' grazing, eight hours' sleep and can do eight hours' work. The sleeping or rest times include cud-chewing and it is easy enough in a bunch of two or three hundred head to pick out any sick animals. They tend to stand with their heads lowered, their coats are dull, their eyes staring. Being wild cattle there was not much one could do beyond getting sick animals into a kraal or run, dosing them with Epsom Salts and dressing any sores or wounds they might have. One day I found a cow that had eaten a steenbuck skull and driven the thin needle horns right through the roof of her mouth so that the points stuck out of her nose. She was easily fixed up, the skull top and horns withdrawn and the wound disinfected with Kerol. But if she had not been found she would have died of starvation. This eating of bones and garbage is due to a mineral deficiency and is called pika. I wanted to feed the stock bone meal but Frank said it would cost too much. I maintained that it would have paid off.

If I had been allowed to I could have made the ranch pay, but Frank was insistent on having lands cleared and plenty of mealies grown for silage. This pushed up a big labour bill when, if we had just stuck to cattle, we could have managed with the squatter labour at no cost except for rations. I wanted to cull the herd; culling it fifty per cent down to two hundred picked breeding cows and two hundred picked heifers. This would have given us ample good quality grazing and enough water. Then I wanted to select the best bull calves, not cut them and sell them as grade Sussex yearlings to up-country ranches who could not afford pedigree bulls. Their sires were pedigree and their dams selected hardy cows. I had a bunch of them ready and even prospective buyers for them at £10 a head – very good value for what they were, that is, very suitable animals for up-grading herds in rough country. Much hardier than pedigree bulls and the loss if one died was £10 as opposed to £40 to £100.

I had the young bulls tamed and rung. Copper bull-rings come hinged, and one open end has a sharp point which is pushed through the septum of the nose; it is then fastened with a small screw. The operation is painless. There is no blood as the ring only goes through gristle.

But Frank would have none of it and made me castrate them, which upset me as some were real beauties. The third part of my plan was to buy in native oxen six or seven years old in poor condition from the nearby reserves, run them for a year and sell them. They would have cost about £7 and sold for £10 to £12. The losses would have been less than one per cent as this type of beast was very hardy, the weak ones all having died long ago. But this was squashed too. Rather than grow mealies for silage, I would have put the money we spent on agriculture into bone-meal and medicinal licks. However, I was not the boss so I did what I was told but lost a lot of interest in the operation.

It was not a good ranch, the soil decomposed granite with some rock outcrops verging into sandveld near the river. This river, called the Sand River, was dry except in the rains, but we pumped water from under the surface into troughs to form one of the watering points.

There was some black soil that grew sweet grass in another part of the property, and this is where we cleared the lands. It was good soil if it rained, but the rainfall was very unreliable. Most of the veld was long, harsh grass, almost useless except in the early spring. There were four scoop dams, one trench dam rather like a silo which the cattle approached from either end, and the windmill near the homestead. I sometimes had to replace the leathers on the windmill pump, which meant pulling up the rods with a pulley and detaching them one at a time till we got the last one up with the valve. This had to be done when the leathers wore out. As each rod was detached those left in the borehole had to be held with a clamp so that they did not slip down to the bottom where only an expert with special tools could get them out again.

When there was no wind I had to use a small petrol engine to pump, and I had a lot of trouble with it. Difficulty in starting, belt slipping, and other problems which, not being mechanically minded, I found hard to solve, though I always managed in the end. I made a number of low earth-walled dams that held about two foot of flood water near the borehole, and I think this helped to keep up the water table, since it was sunk on a sponge formation.

The country was heavy thorn-bush of several varieties – black sweet-thorn, appiesdoorn, wag 'n bietjie, suikerbos, and a big area covered with rooibos. The coarse dry grass often came up to my stirrup irons and the country was so closely bushed that if you could see more than three hundred yards you pulled up your horse to stare. I have worked in heavy bush and on flat plains and dislike both. The one gives you claustrophobia and the other agoraphobia. I like rolling downland with patches of forest and vlei, which is what I got later at Constantia. I do not think I ever went out on the ranch without tearing my shirt or trousers on a thorn, and ten years later my wife was still picking them out of my shoulders and back.

I used to ride four horses. There was always one tied up ready saddled so that when I came in I could just snatch a cup of tea and go off again. I suppose I averaged the best part of five hundred miles a month in the saddle. Much of the time it was so hot that if I dismounted the pigskin saddle burnt through my trousers when I remounted. I solved this problem by putting a sheepskin over it and fastening it with a surcingle. If I worked on the lands repairing an implement I had to put my tools in the shade or they became too hot to pick up.

I always rode with dogs, with my Alsatian Vixen alone if I was working cattle, or with more dogs if I was just riding along the fences and firepaths to check them. At one time, with pups, I had twenty-three dogs. Fifi, the pointer with pups, the Dane with pups, a West Highland, a Doberman and Vixen. I had got Vixen when I lost Mr Binks, as we called him, again from Bob Gwatkin who had sold me Binks. Vixen was nothing like as beautiful as Binks but turned out to be one of the best dogs I ever owned. I soon trained her to cattle. She would work by following the directions of my hand when I waved it, drop when I whistled, and attack when I said 'Sah!' I once drove a mob of breeding cows, some of them with very young calves, nearly five miles through heavy bush with her alone. Any stockman knows how hard new-born calves are to drive. They can run almost from birth but they are both fearless and stupid. They have not the sense to run away from a dog but stand on trembling legs and face it. Meanwhile the mother turns too, and generally charges.

German shepherd dogs are wonderful at their work, tireless even in the heat. Their double coat of guard hairs and under fur provides them with insulation. Intelligent beyond belief, faithful and courageous, they are, if of the right working type, the best dogs a man can have. Vixen never left me and slept on my clothes by the bed, which was nice in winter as they were warm to put on in the morning. This bitch would even separate bulls when fighting because I would not go near them. When each bull weighs the best part of a ton a bull fight is something to keep away from. At Roodekuil when two South Devon bulls fought in a *kraal* and a horse got in their way, one of them just got his horns under the horse and threw him over the wall. But Vixen would attack their heels, biting first one and then the other till, instead of standing face to face, they stood back to back. Then I could go in between them and separate them with a stock whip.

The dip through which we passed the cattle every week to control the ticks was a long cement bath about three feet wide and ten feet deep at the entrance, the point where it joined the race. The cattle were driven into a large *kraal* – this is the same word as the American 'corral' – and from there into a race. Once the race was full some poles were put behind the last animal to stop them backing out, and they were driven forward by twisting and even biting their tails. When they reached the end of the race they had to jump into the water to which had been added a carefully checked mixture of arsenic. They went under as they jumped and then swam till they found their feet on the ramp and went into the drying race, where they stood till most of the dip had dripped off them and run back into the tank. While they stood there they were hand dressed with a mixture of axle grease and Stockholm

Tar, under the tail between the legs, as the dip never reaches the ticks here, since, when the cattle jump, they clamp their tails down, and between their legs and on the udders of the cows, and in the ears. Ticks will kill cattle in this area. I have seen cows with holes I could put my fist into eaten out of their udders, and ticks by the hundred encrusted round the edges of the wound.

There are many varieties of tick – blue tick, red tick, bont tick, spinose ear tick. The red tick carried red-water fever – the Texas Fever of America – which was brought to Africa with stock purchased during the Boer War. Khaki weed, the Mexican marigold, also came in with forage and so did black-jack from Australia. The heart water tick – this is a fatal disease against which in my time there was no vaccine – is the bont tick, a very beautiful arachnid, dark brown in colour, ornamented with patches of green, gold and creamy white. It has a very hard shell so that one can hardly smash it with one's nails. Dipping does not kill the ticks; it does not touch their vital parts since their heads are buried deep in their hosts. What happens is that by continuous dipping arsenic is absorbed into the animal's skin and the tick comes in contact with it as it bores its way in.

For red-water fever in those days we injected trypan blue subcutaneously. The symptoms are lassitude, loss of colour to the tongue and membranes of the mouth and round the eye if the eyelid is lifted and, naturally, the red water itself. This organism attacks the red corpuscles of the blood, destroying them, and they are passed out in the urine which changes its colour from yellow to red. They are unable to live in a blue light and the injection of trypan blue has the effect of changing the colour of the blood. With a bit of luck if you get it in time you may save the animal. It is much easier to deal with dairy stock than with ranch cattle. One sees them twice a day, they are near home and easy to handle. They can be stabled and nursed as they are not wild, whereas ranch cattle have to be caught and thrown before anything can be done to them, which is naturally bad for an animal that is already sick.

Today they have new vaccines that are almost a hundred per cent effective. Not long ago my bull mastiff had such a bad attack, and it came on so suddenly that he fell down and could not walk and would certainly have died if he had not had expert treatment at once. I saw the blood smears under a microscope and the vet described them as classic, as bad as any he had ever seen, and in each red corpuscle there were three or four groups of bacilli literally destroying them as you watched.

The main trouble on the ranch was lack of water, and drought. This area had a summer rainfall, that is to say it only rained in the summer, of sixteen inches. But if it came too late, and sometimes it only came after Christmas, we lost great numbers of cows which died calving and many calves that had been born starved as their mothers gave no milk. To some extent we remedied this by taking out the bulls and running them separately till the end of March or April, which meant that the bulk of the cows would then calve in late December or January, but then this left us weaning the calves in the dry season before the rains came again the following year. The gestation period of a cow is two hundred and eighty-two days, nine months approximately, and the calves are generally weaned at nine months. As a rule the cow will not take the bull again while she has a calf at foot.

Our calving average was quite good for ranch conditions – about sixty-eight per cent – but we went down on our calf losses as we lost twenty-five per cent of all calves born from various causes – lack of water, and lack of good grazing for their dams while they were raising them, tick-borne diseases, and a few from accidents and vegetable poisoning from certain plants.

The stock was based on native cattle which had been graded up with Afrikander bulls and, more recently, with Sussex. The Sussex is a nice, hardy, beef animal, dark red in colour with a white tail, but for our conditions it was too quick maturing. In very hard conditions one needs animals which do not grow out too fast for, once they have done growing, they have done. For instance, the Sussex, Shorthorn, Hereford, Aberdeen Angus have all been bred for baby beef. They grow very fast for two years and then stop. In consequence, if in those two years they suffer a setback they will never grow out and remain runts. Whereas an Afrikander or native beast can stand still for two years and then, in a good season, grow out fully. The same thing happens if a native heifer calves too young. She will not take the bull again for some years and will end up a big cow, whereas what we call an improved breed heifer will be completely ruined. In addition, these African breeds all have humps of various sizes in which they can store fat. They are, after all, the indigenous cattle of the country – the famous Afrikander – merely representing the improvement effected by three hundred years of selective breeding on the animals Van Riebeeck and his successors bought from the Hottentots when they settled at the Cape. I have always found that animals that approximated most nearly to these original types did the best under any but the most ideal conditions.

When we weaned the calves, we castrated, earmarked, branded and dehorned them in one operation. The calves were caught and thrown, castrated with Budizzo pinchers, a bloodless operation which, by compressing the cords to the testicles, causes them to atrophy without doing any damage to the scrotum, a remarkable invention by an Italian doctor that must have saved the livestock industry many millions of pounds, particularly in hot countries where any wound becomes fly-blown almost at once.

The dehorning was done with large two-handled shears with a cup-like blade that cut a convex pattern close to the calf's skull. The earmark was a nick taken out of the ear to give us a check on its age – one year lower left, next year upper left, next lower right, next upper right, next left tip, next right tip. We could in this way draft our stocks according to their age and get rid of any that showed no sign of growing. And finally the branding. The irons are heated in a fire of wood and dry cow dung. The calves are caught and held and the iron is pressed down on the skin. It must just take. As you press you feel it break through the outer-skin, and as soon as this happens the iron is lifted. This burning kills the sebaceous glands of the hair so that none will grow through the imprinted design. Should the burn not be deep enough the brand will be blurred, whereas if it goes too deep a painful wound is inflicted that will leave a bad scar that may become infected.

A rope is not used in Africa. Instead the animals are caught in the *kraal* by means of a *riem* looped about a long stick – a *vangstok*. The loop is put into the animal's legs as it runs, by running beside it. As soon as it is taken up the stick is dropped and the *riem* is pulled tight. A helper joins the catcher and other boys get the animal round the neck. If it is a bull or a savage cow it must now be pulled backwards to prevent it turning, while a second *riem* is thrown over its horns. This *riem* is then run through a heavy wire ring that is thrown over a big post set in concrete in the *kraal* and the animal is slowly worked up to it till it is snubbed up quite tight to it. But for calves, once they have a *riem* on them, they are easily thrown by putting one's hands under their bellies and seizing their legs, one in each hand, and pulling them over so that as they fall they knock the wind out of themselves. One can then hold even a big calf by grasping the top hindleg and pulling it hard while the right leg is pushed under the hindleg, that is, the one that is nearest to the ground, forward as far as it will go. This forms a kind of scissor lock and was taught me by Major Doyle, who was an Australian. He also taught me to use a stock whip. He was a fine performer with a whip and could demonstrate what I think is called the Sydney Flash, where the whip is cracked four times – once in front and once behind on each side consecutively. I never learnt this, but I did learn to use a whip behind me, a very useful crack if an animal is trying to rush past you.

I learnt much of this in that first six months while I explored the farm. I got lost several times and once had to sleep out, but by degrees I got hold of the place. Since I was alone I had nothing else, apart from the building, to do. It was a strange life. It came much nearer to what I wanted. If it had been a little wilder still, with a little more game, it would have been ideal.

Looking back on the ranch, I see it as another milestone, a decisive turning point in my life. It was for those days a good job. Twenty pounds a month, a car, a five-year contract, a share of the profits, if any, and a share of the increase of the cattle profits, or no profits. It was the beginning of some sort of security. It was, though I did not know it then, the place where I saw the Africa about which, later, I was to spend my life writing. It was also another ambition achieved.

The first had been the army. Then marriage to Eileen. Then Africa. I had always wanted Africa. Then cattle. Ranching was almost, but not quite, the equivalent of the American cowboy-and-Indian stuff. The next ambition was a place of my own. That was to come too, and to end. Somehow, more than most people, it seems to me my life has been divided into sections, each chopped off from the one that preceded it, and yet each complete in its way. In every case it would almost seem that as soon as a thing was done, as soon as tomorrow began to resemble yesterday, and I could see no change but a slow consolidation of the existing situation, I have smashed the mould.

In every case I have said when I began, how wonderful it will be when I have the job done – when I have built the dams, bred up the herd, finished the house, planted the orchard, made the garden – but the day that it is done, the day to which I had looked forward so much, to where I had hoped to sit back and rest and think what a wonderful job I had made of it, things lost their savour and had, as far as I was concerned, ceased to live. Having breathed life into something, when it lived by itself without my aid, it was dead for me. The cord of creation was cut.

This must be my temperament. It shows in my books. As soon as one is done I start another. The old one is nothing. I never even look at it again. I forget the plot and the characters. It is the new one that is important. The new one that is going to be good, really good. I have no explanation for this. I have no doubt it is quite common. It must be the mentality of the ne'er-do-well and the hobo. I think I could easily have gone that way, become a beachcomber, because I can live on very little and have no great desire for possessions.

I should have liked to have lived as my ancestors did, in a very big way, with large farms, horses, servants, vineyards and the rest, but half cock does not interest me and, failing at one extreme, I think I should be reasonably happy at the other, provided I had a roof over my head, enough to eat, and lived in a warm climate. I expect the one thing that has saved me from this fate is my inability to live alone, and it is very hard to persuade a woman that the simple life is admirable. There have been, I think, very few lady hermits. Saints, yes. But not hermits.

In addition I must have some kind of drive, which I deplore, that makes me work. This is probably an example of that facet of the nordic white man's character which has driven him to such prodigies of labour all over the face of the earth. It is this energy which is the real white man's burden. His inability to rest, or leave well enough alone. Everything must be improved, developed, exploited. I have even come to believe that we are all unhappy, that none of us could remain sane in the world we have created without alcohol, tobacco, aspirin, Luminal, tea, coffee, books, radio, TV and films. Remove these various methods of anaesthesia for a month and the result would be a universal breakdown in our urban populations.

I am inclined to think that only those whom we call uncivilized can be happy, that is to say, can enjoy life, since they live as men are meant to live, in close touch with the elements and with some degree of natural conflict and danger. The surroundings among which they live are natural to them, they are the background of their evolution, and they move in a society where each man has his specific place and work. They are each a part of a whole – a family, or tribe, or both. This view must be qualified, however. To be content these people must not be obsessed by fear of ghosts, taboos, gods, and the mumbo-jumbo of the witch doctors.

I have lived in great cities for long periods but have always been forced to return to the wilds because I found no contentment there, no rest, no God – not my kind at least. Whereas in the country I was continually seeing His works. A hen hatching her chicks, a calf drinking from its mother, the flowering of a tree, the glitter of the leaves in the moonlight, all bring me nearer to this necessity. Not to God perhaps, since God cannot be defined, but to His works, and here, on this ground, surely I and the most orthodox Christian of any denomination whatsoever must agree. I like to look at the mountains and the sea, at the trees and flowers and birds. I like to move and work among them. They are the works of God. But I do not believe that God made Rockefeller Centre or that he takes a personal interest in my welfare.

Coming to Africa and going to the ranch where I should be on my own were challenges, chances to be taken to see what I could make of them. This testing of one's own character has always been important to me. In the army, in towns, among people anywhere, one is moulded by them, influenced; only in the bush is one alone pitted against reality, the earth, the sky, space. There is no watch time here. The slow march of the seasons are the clock. God, or what I call God, is here and only here and on the sea where one can feel part of all life, of all living things. There is silence except for the sound of bird calls, of jackals in the night, of cows, of distant cocks crowing from an African village. There is time to think.

I thought of the decisions I had made in my life so far and their effect on the 'ifs and mights'. The first when I was five was not in my hands – that was when the Picks, an American couple, wanted to adopt me. Had they done so I should have been an American.

Next came my refusal to be confirmed at Lancing, a difficult decision in a religious High Church school. Then at Burlington House where I gave up the Sandhurst exam which I thought I would fail in, though later it turned out they passed everyone, and instead took a temporary commission. This lost me two years' seniority, though I got a regular commission in the field in 1916. Had I been a regular the casualties were such that by then I should certainly have been a major instead of a lieutenant. Then on the very day I received my temporary commission in 1914 my father broke the news to me that my name was Cloete not Graham – that he had changed it after he came out of prison.

This was the turning point of my life and the cause of the drive to succeed, regain my name and put it on the map.

In September 1914 in Aylesbury when I refused to let the senior officer with whom I shared a room get into my bed, I made an enemy which probably saved my life as the Battalion left me behind when they joined the BEF and were killed almost to a man at Loos in 1915.

In 1916 when I refused to obey an order by the Brigadier to turn out my men in the line. They were sleeping after three days' fighting and he put me under arrest. I was not court martialed but I might have been.

In October at Le Transloi with the 6th Yorkshire Light Infantry where I gave up after I had been shot through the chest. I could have gone on and been a hero, but I could also have been dead. I felt having been over the top six times in two months without a wound I was expecting too much of Mr Luck, as I called fate, if I went on. Mr Luck and Mr Death were our companions in the battle of the Somme with fifty per cent casualties in every attack.

Another quite involuntary decision was when in hospital at 10 Palace Green I fell in love with my nurse, a VAD called Eileen Horsman. Discharged from hospital, I decided to give myself another breakdown and go back. I succeeded by living on whisky and aspirin for four days and never going to bed.

In 1918 when I left my regiment and transferred to the Household Battalion. It was composed of the Household Cavalry dismounted. I did this to get into the London Command – they were stationed in the Combermere Barracks at Windsor. When we were disbanded (and) the King said we could join any regiment we wished without loss of seniority and the way was open for me to go to the Indian Cavalry, my ambition since the age of six. Instead I went to the Coldstream Guards, also at Windsor, so that I could stay near London and Eileen.

This decision saved my life, as when I was wounded again in five places, being in the Brigade of Guards gave me a choice of hospitals and I went to Sister Agnes – King Edward the Seventh Hospital for Officers – where I received the best treatment in England.

When convalescent I proposed to Eileen. We were married in Brighton on October 30th, 1918.

My next decision was to change my name back to Cloete from Graham with my Uncle Montrose's help.

Then I decided to sell up in France and came to South Africa.

Now I had given up the safe job I had and taken on the management of Frank Struben's ranch on the Pretoria bushveld.

This was what I liked, making something out of nothing, putting my imprint on it. Clearing the lands, driving fences straight as a bullet through the bush. But there was a paradox – I was destroying the wilds that I loved, taming them to the plough, binding them with barbed wire. This area was primeval in that no white man had ever worked it. Savage tribesmen had fought across it, none bothering to keep it. It was relatively waterless and the grazing was poor except in spring. There were few big trees, and the ones that still stood, Hartekoal mainly, great white giants, were dying. If it had been a little lower, two thousand feet instead of three thousand, it would have been Baobab country. The impression I got was that once, perhaps a hundred or more years ago, it had been better watered. Most of the big trees, if there had been any, as I suspected, had been burnt in bush fires and only the Hartekoal, as hard as iron, had withstood the flames.

This six months alone was a wonderful experience. Painful at times, for there was such beauty in much of it and beauty cannot be taken alone. Not by a man or by a woman, or even by two women or two men. Beauty, if it is not to hurt, must be felt by a man and a woman who love each other, who are one, and can see it standing hand in hand. Yet this bushveld country was not beautiful in the true sense. It was dry and harsh, covered with scrub rather than trees, though there were patches of thorn which, in the spring, were bright gold with their mimosa-like flowers. There were vistas here and there that were grand, and some of the autumn colours in the red Boekenhout, the Rooibos and the Tamboutis were lovely. But there was mystery, the mystery of wild, untouched, untamed country. With the evening approaching the whole African world became much more than beautiful in the pale roseate lilac light, with the shadows of the sparse trees cast on the foothills like black pencil stripes a hundred yards long. The perspective of everything changed. Distant hills came forward so that you felt that by stretching out your hand you could touch them. Bushes grew into trees. The light deepened from pink to mauve to purple. The giant Mexican agaves turned from grey to pink. The mountains were blue on the horizon. They lay there in their folds like a woman's scarf against the sky. It was the time the Zulus describe as 'the hour when all things are beautiful'. I looked forward to this half-hour – the light lasted no longer.

There is a great stillness. The birds have already been to water. The day is over and the night has not yet begun. Somewhere a girl from a native village is singing – shrill, sweet, the full-throated song of a natural woman, a girl who has come from her lover. A jackal calls its slavering maniacal laugh that others take up. They have begun hunting now, the night is near. The night when there is no peace in the forest and the hunted tremble. An owl calls. A night ape – swift, big-eyed, the woolly fairy of the bush – flies as if it was a bird from tree to tree, quite fearless of the camp. The firelight, which hardly showed before, now becomes prominent – the very centre of life. The cooking fire, the protection fire. Unconsciously I draw nearer to it. It is not cold but I hold out my hands to the flames. How many men have done this for how many hundred thousand years . . .

It is not cold but it is lonely as the black bowl of the African night descends. Very black at first and then slowly the stars pierce it. Only one, two, three – the great ones. And then suddenly the rest, the diamond galaxies, the necklaces and decorations of the firmament are there, reducing man in the scale of things, peeling away the falseness in him as if he were an onion being stripped of skin after skin. Somewhere a tomtom throbs softly, a little drum. But to the white man alone in the night these are not men who play, men who lie with their women in the huts a mile away. They are part of the mystery, as he sits alone on his kerosene crate with his dogs by the dying fire, looking at his hands in the glow. His white hands that are red with conquest. And sometimes he wonders if his skin is not his burden, if, instead of its being a blessing, his whiteness is not a curse.

CHAPTER 9

THE BUSHVELD

THE ranch was in what was known as the Pretoria bushveld, twenty miles from rail and seventy from Pretoria. At one time alive with game, it was now more or less shot out. There were small buck – steenbok and duiker – a few kudu, ostriches, wild pig and jackal. This was all that was left of the wildebeeste, zebra, giraffe, lion and leopard that had roamed here within the memory of man. There were no baboons. Monkeys (vervet) I saw a few times, and a fair number of birds of various kinds, including such game birds as francolin, partridges, quail, plover and guinea fowl – khoran, royal game – but I shot them too, they were excellent eating. I often had to live on what I could shoot as we had no refrigeration and in that heat meat turned at once and milk would not keep twelve hours.

I lived mainly on egg flips – milk with fresh eggs whipped up into it – as I was often too tired to eat, and even at night the temperature seldom dropped below ninety in the summer months. Up to ninety heat is bearable, but after that one begins to feel it. At ninety candles bend in the candlesticks and end up in a 'U' with their wicks pointing to the table. We used to lay our candles flat in the daytime to avoid this happening. When you went out into the sun the heat struck at you like a blow which you had to brace yourself to resist. I never sweated. It was too dry, the sweat dried before it left your body. You could feel the moisture being dragged out of you by the parched air. It seemed to attack the very pores of the skin as if it was thirsty. The country itself was real ranch country, semi-desert. The foliage of the trees was olive-green and grey, with patches of greenness near the dams. The grass was always, even in spring, yellowish or khaki coloured. The dams were filled by flood water in the rains, and dependent on the rains, so that if they did not come they dried up and the weaker animals got stuck in the mud and died there unless they were pulled out. And even then they generally died after the experience.

Fires were a perpetual hazard and one of the big jobs was making fire breaks round the whole estate. There were over forty miles of break which we kept clear of grass by dragging large trees with spans of oxen, one following the other, along the boundaries. We made a double road and then, in the still of the night, burnt the grass between them. We chose the night because at night the wind is less capricious and, if it is still, there is little chance of its suddenly springing up. It was a pretty sight to see the short grass burning, controlled by natives with rough brooms made of bushes with which they beat it out if it looked like spreading too far or went too fast. We had one or two bad fires, and very terrifying they were, with the leaping flames in the tree-tops, clouds of smoke and the fiercely burning grass so that there were, as it were, two fires at once, one on the ground and one above it. The smoke rolled in great clouds and the fire crackled and roared, soaring up in great pillars when it came to some particularly inflammable tree. I got to be able to estimate the distance of the fire by the smoke. You could not see the smoke roll until it was relatively near, about five miles away. Then, at a mile or so, you could hear the fire roaring like an animal. When there was a fire I collected the boys in the pick-up and we tried to burn back to it upwind as it came downwind towards us. This was where the tragedies occurred when the terrified buck and hares galloped out of the flames only to be met by those we had kindled. For days after the fire had passed trees were still smouldering and the cattle and game dung sent up little pillars of pure blue smoke.

Cattle are very stupid in a fire, for though quite capable of smashing through a fence, they will bunch in a corner and allow themselves to be burnt to death. This is particularly true of improved breeds and grades who are unable to adapt themselves to new conditions. On several occasions I have had to gallop to the fire, drive cattle away from it, and even cut a fence to get them through. There was no danger in this provided the horse did not fall, for, unless there is a gale blowing, a good horse can get away from a fire quite easily.

And this was the life I was going to bring my wife to. It was isolated, lonely, with a strong element of pioneering that suited me very well and to which she had agreed before she left for England. But six months at home might have unsettled her, especially as she had been presented at Court in a white satin dress with a train, ostrich feathers in her hair, borrowed jewels and all. This was my Aunt Mary and Montrose's idea, and Eileen dressed for the Palace at their house, in Berkeley Square. The whole thing, in the context of the world as it was even then, was somewhat absurd, though everyone, as they say, had been through it. For a girl, like a white wedding, such a function had a certain glamour, though at this period in the world's history it served no useful purpose. In the old days when Europe was full of Courts, being presented meant that as a visitor a woman had the entree to all of them through the British Ambassador.

I had all this in my mind when I met her in Johannesburg. I was very excited. I had been alone for six months, seeing hardly a soul. I had built a house. I had packed and moved everything and not even a cup had been broken. Everything was in order, even the pictures were hung, and I was rather proud of what I had accomplished.

I took a nice room at the Carlton Hotel and arrived about an hour early at the station. There were a lot of other people meeting the Cape Town train. I knew a number of them. When the train came in I saw her, looking more beautiful than ever. I went to meet her but found her surrounded by friends. Some had come over on the boat with her, others were the people who had come to meet the train, knowing she would be on it, and before I knew what had happened I found that they were all invited to a cocktail party.

It was nearly midnight before we were alone. My welcome, my stories and all my news had by that time fallen rather flat. It was, though I only realized it subconsciously, the beginning of the end. She was glad to be back. Oh yes, she was glad. And to see me – yes, very glad to see me. She had been presented, as I knew. My uncle and aunt had given her the dress and she was much more full of her experiences than interested in mine. Everything was fine except that everything was not fine. Not for me at any rate. Still, I would no longer be alone. Perhaps on the ranch in the bushveld we would at last really get to know each other. That was in '28. We had been married ten years and Eileen was still in a sense a stranger. A beautiful woman but an invention, a product of my own heart and mind.

We spent the next night at Lynwood with Frank and Maisie

Struben and then drove down to the ranch. Eileen seemed pleased with the house. It was a vast improvement on any we had had before, being better lit, altogether brighter, and having a proper bathroom with a bath and wash-basin in it. The other convenience remained outside in the home paddock about twenty yards from the house, where later I kept my young bulls.

Life began again now and took on a new pattern. We went to Pretoria once a month for two nights, staying with the Strubens, to do our shopping, and returned with the Ford truck fully loaded. We had friends to stay with us – generally girls and women whose fathers or husbands brought them down one weekend and fetched them the next. They were company for Eileen and she liked having them. We got books from the Pretoria Public Library, and I then made the curious discovery that all Jonathan Cape's books were readable. Being out of touch, getting no papers except the *Farmer's Weekly*, I had to devise some system of choice beyond that of taking any new book written by a writer whom I liked.

My work settled down to the routine of riding round the fences, dams and pans, looking for sick cattle, checking their condition and doing a general supervising job. The dipping took up four days of the week. I made some new dams with scrapers. They were large scoops resembling wheel-barrows without wheels that were pulled by two oxen. The ground was first ploughed and then the scrapers were forced into the loose earth till they were full and then driven to the bank where they were emptied. A slow, tedious process, but one which worked well and economically, provided time was no object.

We cleared about a hundred acres of land by means of a stump jack. This worked like a car jack – a spear thrust into a tree would lift it out, roots and all, like a tooth. It was then dragged away by a team of oxen. I found that so much time was wasted getting the trek chain loose from the tree when it was in position, owing to the difficulty of getting oxen to move backwards, that I had some quick-release hooks made by a blacksmith which came loose at a touch on the retaining ring.

I did not enjoy riding much owing to the heat and the fact that I could not afford to take the risk of anything difficult or interesting in the way of horseflesh in case I got thrown, as I was often ten miles from home and no one knew where I was. I assumed the herders would have looked for me and found me in a day or two, particularly as I always had dogs with me which would either have stayed with me or gone home and led someone back to me. Another trouble was that this was horse sickness country and to be safe all riding had to be done when the sun was well up and before it grew too late in the evening, that is to say, in the heat of the day. This was what the old Boers said and they were right, because by following this advice I never lost a horse. But the work would have been much easier if it could have been done very early in the morning as soon as it was light. If I could have started at five in the morning I would have finished my rounds by ten instead of setting out at that hour.

The evaporation was enormous – seventy inches at least. This meant that six foot of water was lost in a dam once the rains stopped. So the dams went down very fast. Drought was our most serious problem, weakening the cows so that they died in giving birth or lost their calves soon after birth. I once heard a calf bellowing in the bush and rode towards it. I found it in a clearing surrounded by vultures which had blinded it by pecking out its eyes. I went back for a rifle and shot it. I also found a cow down with the vultures grouped round her. They were tearing out her entrails while she was still alive. I had to shoot her too.

In a drought even the wildest animals came up to the homestead as if asking for help. They even licked the iron tyres of the waggon in the early morning for the dew which had condensed on them. They stood about lowing. Their coats were dull, their eyes staring, their heads were down. Our usual procedure when the dams went dry was to water the stock at the Sand River on our boundary. It was a big job to pump water by hand for a thousand head and we only managed it by watering every second day, which reduced the number to five hundred. And then in this particular year even the river-bed failed. Quite desperate, I found water about fourteen miles away – a big dam in the river that was very deep. The water was impounded by a high concrete weir. I drove the herds down here every second day and averaged a loss of thirty head every twenty-four hours. Cattle were dying quicker than I could skin them, and the track to the water was marked with bones stripped clean of meat by natives, vultures, jackals and native dogs. It is a very painful thing to handle drought-smitten cattle. They moan and stagger as they walk.

They are strung out with the bulls and strongest cows leading, the weak in the dust at the back of the herd. But suddenly, when a mile or so away from it, they smell the water, their heads go up, and those in the best condition force their way to the front at a trot which turns into a canter and finally into a mad gallop. When they reached the water they charged right into it, swimming about with their mouths open. They drank so much that I could not get them back till it was dark for fear of foundering them in the heat.

This went on for a fortnight and then the drought broke, but it was not an experience I would like to go through again.

Since those days of water shortage I have never been able to completely fill a wash-basin. It was a traumatic experience, the homestead being surrounded by lowing cattle tamed by drought.

But to offset these horrors there were wonderful days of riding through the silent veld along the narrow cattle paths, watching the stock and birds and game. Often the only way one found a sick or dead beast was by seeing the vultures circling. Vultures in the sky were always a bad sign and they would just as soon eat a sick or wounded man as a steer that was down. They were the repulsive scavengers of the veld.

Vultures were revolting but once up in the air they were magnificent, sailing in on motionless wings in ever-widening circles and then falling like stones on their prey when they saw it. It was strange to think vultures were always there, patrolling the upper air beyond the range of man's vision but able to see the slightest of the tragedies that took place on the veld beneath them. Once there had been hundreds of them, but now the most I ever saw together was twenty-two. There is one interesting fact about vultures. They cannot just fly off the ground. They have to run and get the air under their wings, taxiing like a plane before they can become airborne.

There was a pair of king vultures, big black ones, the kind that the ordinary griffon vultures fear, that I often saw, and whose nest I finally found on the top of a big flat-topped thorn. I climbed the tree and cut a hole through the thorns so that I was quite near the great platform of twigs on which the hen brooded her two eggs. When I extended the handle of my whip she attacked it with her beak and opened her enormous wings.

At Hammanskraal, Dr Hagner had a depot for wild animals

that he was collecting for various zoos, so one day as we passed I asked him what he would pay me for the vulture hen. He offered one pound ten, which was not nearly enough. I'd have tried it for ten pounds. My plan was to throw two nooses round her neck and pull her off the tree with two groups of boys. In this way she would be able to attack neither, and then, while they held her, I would wrap her in a bag, tying her wings and feet, and then put her in the truck and deliver her. But I am glad I did not do it. I was never very keen but I wanted the money. At that time I always wanted money – I had so little.

These king vultures are the only ones that nest in trees regularly. The griffon vulture will only use trees if there are no cliffs at a convenient distance. In Natal we found a whole colony of vultures' nests in a group of tall trees. In this they resemble baboons who prefer to live among the rocks of the mountains but will, where there are no mountains, make their home in a big wild fig or other tree.

Food presented some difficulties as I could grow no fresh vegetables, and so we only had them for a few days each month after we got back from town. Fresh meat was the same. We had it for three or four days and after that we had to eat canned meat or the poultry I bred for the table. I shot a buck or some birds every now and then, and if I had an animal so sick that I did not think it would recover, I slaughtered it for the boys and took the liver, tail, kidneys and tongue for ourselves. This may not sound very hygienic, but it did not kill us and was at least fresh meat. There was always milk and generally plenty of eggs.

There were surprisingly few adventures. Actually a life of this kind is much safer than that in a city where one is continually exposed to traffic accidents and robberies. Snakes are much less dangerous than taxis and there seem to be few other dangers on the veld. One is isolated from infectious diseases. I did get veld sores on my hands – a skin disease due to malnutrition – but I got over it by increasing the percentage of vegetables in my diet and by taking our yearly holiday at the sea. Instead of going north to my cousins at Naboomspruit, we went to stay with the Stanleys at High Commission House at Milnerton, in the Cape. Reneira had brought back a grey arab stallion from Ceylon, where Sir Herbert, or HJ as we called him, had been Governor-General. Reneira, who had been before marriage an Alphen

Cloete, was one of the most beautiful women I have ever seen – tall, slim, with honey-coloured hair and the golden eyes of a Weimaraner. I enjoyed riding on the beach, which I had to myself, and going out with the girls and their governess to look for micro-flints made by bushmen in the sand dunes. HJ's ADC was a Grenadier, Laurence Holbeach, DSO, MC, who became a great friend.

I had some adventures with cattle. On one occasion I was cutting a big bull we had thrown. He was tied by the head to a post, with his hindlegs lashed together and held extended by a strong game *riem* held by three boys while I worked. Suddenly I heard the *riem* snap. I had just time to drop the burdizzos and raise my right arm to cover my eyes when his two legs, still bound together, hit me. They cut my forearm almost to the bone and the force of the blow threw me fifteen feet across the *kraal*. I was out for ten minutes and a bit shaky when I came to. I went into the house where Eileen bandaged me up, had a drink, and went back to finish the business. But after that occurrence I sank a big stone in concrete with a chain and a ring to hold the hindlegs of anything big that I had to throw.

Cattle are quite easy to throw once they are tied up. A *riem* or rope is passed in a loop over the body behind the ribs. This is then pulled tight and the animal will fall. It won't stay down, so, as it goes, a boy jumps to its head and holds it down on the ground while another takes its tail and passes it between its hindlegs and holds it taut. We usually made our own *riems* by cutting up a heavy skin into a single long strip about three inches wide, starting on the outside and going round and round until the centre was reached. This strip of skin, thirty or forty feet long, was now passed over a strong branch and threaded through a piece of wood that had been fastened to a large stone, so that it resembled the handle of a flatiron. The strip went through this handle and over the top of the branch twenty or thirty times till finally the stone weight hung about waist high. A long stick was inserted into the handle and the *riems* were twisted up by a boy walking in a circle, till the stone was in the air and he could turn it no further. Then he withdrew the stick and the stone came down, untwisting as it fell. He then repeated the twisting process. This went on for three days or so with frequent rubbings of fat. When the *riems* were cured and ready for use they were stretched between two trees and cut into eight-foot lengths.

Game *riems* were stronger as they were made from wildebeeste hide which is much thicker than any ox skin. They were generally used when something particular was being done. But a *riem*, like a chain, is only as strong as its weakest point, and as they were often attacked by white ants, mice or rats, they needed continual watching.

The other interesting experience was with a very wild cow who had a dead calf in her. We brought her up to the *kraal* and I got the calf out, my arm covered with vaseline almost to the shoulder as I worked inside her, a very unpleasant and difficult job that took nearly two hours in the boiling sun. The calf was very dead and had to be brought out in pieces. Then, because I thought the cow looked so bad, I gave her half a bottle of my brandy. But when we let her up she was far from weak. She charged, and I was only over the rails of the *kraal* a fraction of a second before she hit them.

Then one day my neighbour Barnard sent me a message. Would I come and help him draft and cut some of his young bulls? He was feeling under the weather and was a bit old for the job. I said of course, and went to his farm in the truck with my gear – boys, burdizzos, ropes, *riems* and what have you. He took me to the *kraal* and I saw what he wanted. He had not cut anything for three years. There, milling around, were about fifty bulls each as big as an elephant. Luckily he had got another neighbour to help as well, a Boer called Piet Marais, and between us, with my boys, we did the job. But it took two days and at times was quite ticklish as such big bulls are very hard to hold by one leg, which must be done to prevent them charging, while a second rope is thrown over their horns. To make things harder, Barnard had been using Angus bulls, and some of their progeny were hornless. It is much easier to hold a beast by the horns than the neck as the leverage is much greater.

We now fattened some cattle for the Rand Show. It takes about ninety days to fatten a wild beast. For the first ten days they only lose condition, being quite unaccustomed to being tied. They tame slowly but finally will allow themselves to be groomed. At first, to get them used to it, a brush is attached to a stick and passed over them for hours till they stop kicking and plunging, out of sheer exhaustion. We did not win with them but did fairly well and sold them for a good price. In those days fifteen to eighteen pounds for a prime beast was high. Today the same animal will fetch fifty pounds or more.

I sometimes bought back some of our prime meat from the butcher who had taken our stock, and I have never eaten better meat. Steaks you could cut with a fork, with a wonderful flavour because they were four-year-old steers and not baby beef, which to my mind has no taste.

One surprising thing about the bushveld here was the large areas where there was no sign of life – dead areas, where not even any insects were to be seen. The trees were stunted *rooibos* and the soil shallow decomposed granite. In all the years I was there I do not think I ever saw a buck or a hare in this part of the ranch. For a month or so the grazing here was not bad – just after the first spring rains. But after that the grass grew too tall and harsh for anything to eat it.

We did not have many pets but I once caught and raised a young steenbok, a sweet little thing that pattered round the house on tiny hooves and used to sit on the sofa beside me when I came in. But when winter came and we lit the fire, it seemed to fascinate her, for she rushed into it and was so badly burnt that I had to kill her with a poker. Then I had a baby ostrich that I took when I came upon a nest of newly hatched chicks. This was rather a foolhardy thing to do as both parents were there. The chicks scattered when I rode up but I marked one, jumped from my horse, stuffed it into my shirt and galloped off. I had it for a month and then one of the dogs killed it. We did not like ostriches as they ran through the fences, smashing the wire, and if they hit an iron standard they not only bent it but wrung it so that I could not straighten it out on an anvil.

Then I got a wonderful idea about ostriches. Once when we were very short of food and I had seen a cock nearby, I decided to kill him. An ostrich was, after all, a bird, and I thought it should taste like a big chicken. That was what it looked like. So I got on a horse, took my Winchester, and went after him. They are not easy to hit as they fluff up all their feathers when they run which makes them seem much larger than they are and one is inclined to shoot at the feathers. It took three shots to bring him down and one more to finish him off. I then had to cover him with branches to keep the vultures off while I rode home and sent a boy with a pair of oxen to drag him in. He must have weighed three hundred pounds. We got him back, and the black-and-white plumes I had looked forward to getting proved to be miserable scraggy feathers covered with small grey lice. However, there was the skin – I had him skinned – and the meat. Meat like chicken breast, at least twenty pounds of it.

I must say it took a bit of cutting, but I was sure cooking would cure that. After two days on the stove it was still like rubber, so hard that even the dogs could not eat it. So all I ended up with was the skin, from which I made a despatch case, a pair of leggings, four cushions, and two belts for girls I knew. The belts came much later. I knew no girls then.

But the food problem was interesting. I shot little birds – doves, starlings and bush parrots – and we had them in a pie. Game birds, of course, when I could get them, but always sitting with a .22 rifle as I could not afford shotgun cartridges. One day we had a treat, or it should have been one. I heard the dogs barking and they had a leguaan at bay. This is a very large lizard, about four feet long, that weighs up to thirty pounds and has quite formidable jaws. It resembles the iguana of South America. I killed him with my whip handle and brought him home. By a fortunate accident someone had just sent me a new *Wide World Magazine* and in it I had read about iguanas being edible. This was good enough for me. So I cut off the tail and cooked it like a fish. It was superb. I had never had anything better.

There were very few adventures with snakes. It was really too dry to be a snaky farm. My houseboy, however, did get struck in the heel of his shoe by a puff-adder one morning as he came down the front steps. It did not hurt him and he killed it. And on another occasion I saw a *boomslang* – a tree snake – in the branches of a thorn tree just by the kitchen door. This tree had a lot of weaver birds' nests in it, and when I shot the snake he vomited up about seven young birds before he fell to the ground. The weaver birds had other enemies even so close to the house. Among them was a grey hawk that would flash down and literally tear the nests to pieces to get at the young. Finally I shot him too.

I once saw two mambas in the act of mating. One was black and the other emerald green. They were twined tightly together, writhing, festooned in a small tree. I left them alone. It was a long way from the house and a gun and mambas are too dangerous to fool about with. I always had a snake bite outfit on the farm with fresh serum in case of accidents, and later on I did save one of my oxen that had been bitten. I saw and killed a few other snakes – one a cobra that the Siamese cat, Mitzi, was attacking. I had to shoot past her to get him. I had his skin tanned by the monks at Marianhill and wore it as a belt for many years.

There is a story about Mitzi. In one afternoon she killed thirty-seven half-grown Rhode Island chicks, and I thrashed her with a *sjambok* till she nearly turned on me. This is one of the few occasions I have lost my temper with an animal, but I could see how people could go beserk and flog things, even men, to death. I was suffering from strain at the time, tired from overwork and hard-up. Thirty-seven pure bred half-grown chicks meant a lot to me then. Lack of money makes people very hard.

There were more snakes near the homestead than elsewhere because the frogs in the big dam attracted them, and so did the mice and rats in the stables and outbuildings. The frogs made a wonderful chorus in the night – an orchestra. There were tiny ones that had vocal sacs nearly as big as themselves, medium-sized frogs and giant bullfrogs.

One day one of my neighbours came up in a great state – his riding horse had been shot by poachers who, using a spotlight attached to their foreheads, had thought it was a kudu. He asked me to co-operate and write to the police to try and check the poaching. But it was very hard to do. My native herders would do nothing. There had been mysterious disappearances of natives who had interfered with the poachers within the last ten years in that area. Murdered? How would I know. I only know that they disappeared, and that they were afraid.

I now laid on hot water to the bathroom by building a brick stove outside with a fire box made of a forty-five gallon steel drum set longways and another similar drum set vertically for the water. I took a pipe from it into the bathroom and fed it from my reservoir with a ball-cock to control the flow. It worked well as we had plenty of wood, and the water soon heated up to almost boiling-point.

Frank now wanted a fence driven miles through the bush. I did this using my old army prismatic compass and worked with a special boy called Ben, Frank had sent down from Pretoria. Ben was one of the few Africans I have ever met who could sight a straight line. A straight line is not part of the Bantu culture. Their huts are round, their *kraals* are round, and even their thinking tends to be circuitous. The fence, with heavy anchor poles every four hundred yards, 14-lb standards every eight yards with four iron droppers in between, cost us £37 a mile to lay. Today it would cost £200.

One interesting thing we did was to train spans of oxen for work. This was quite a performance. They were driven into the dip race and then coupled by a collar of *riems* fastened to a heavy iron swivel. Then they were let out and off they went like mad things, sometimes falling down, sometimes running into a tree by trying to pass on either side of it which brought them up short, knocking the wind out of them. But after three days they were grazing quietly side by side. The next move was to tie a heavy trek chain to the couple so that they got used to it banging against them. When this first happened they again went off at full gallop. Then we separated them and tied a chain to each ox alone. And when they seemed quiet we got them into a *kraal* and hooked them separately to a tame ox, much larger than they were. This was quite a tricky business. These cattle had long, needle-sharp horns and were as wild as buck. Still, we managed it and soon got them working. Once they were used to this, they were inspanned with the ox to which they had been coupled in the first place. Then they had to learn their names. Every ox has a name and he is taught it with a whip. Every time his name is called the driver hits him. He shouts: Rooiland! Swartland! Bosveld! Bloem! England! Witpens! claps his sixteen-foot whip and hits him. This makes the ox not only learn his name but move inwards away from the whip when it is called. In this way a well-trained span of sixteen oxen can be guided while working without a *voorlooper* (the boy who leads them). And very fine these spans of mature, big, matched oxen look – red, black, red-and-white, or red with white faces, or yellow. The Boers are very proud of their matched spans, and rightly so, because in the old days their lives might well have depended upon them. Some men used cross-bred bulldogs to train their oxen, allowing them to pull them down by the nose and hold them till they were inspanned. I had only one loss among all the oxen I trained. This was a young black ox who was too wild for the yoke. He just flung himself against it, reared up and broke his heart. Blood poured from his mouth, his ears and eyes, and he was dead.

There is one final incident. We had one splendid red-and-white ox that stood about sixteen hands, with horns that spread five feet. He was pig fat but I could not sell him. Each time I got him to the railhead, he broke back and came home. No whip could stop him, no fence or *kraal* hold him. What he could not jump he smashed.

When handling cattle they always turn away from you. That is to say, if you ride into a mob of a hundred or two they all move away, but when a beast begins to be dangerous he faces you. This ox began to do that and then, instead of my chasing him he began to chase me, even making short charges at my horse. Having the greatest objection to being chased by anything, I decided to shoot him. But in order to utilize the meat I had to jerk it, to make it into biltong, as the South Africans call it. Eileen was away at the time, so I had the place to myself. We drove him into the yard with some other tame working oxen (no animal can ever be driven alone; cattle move in herds and panic if separated). I got him near the waggon shed and shot him between the eyes with a .22; then we skinned him, cut him into joints and hoisted them on to the waggon bed and filleted them, cutting the meat from the bones in long strips a couple of inches wide. Now the next problem was to put the meat into something to draw. He was a very big ox and I had no receptacle that would take him. The wash-tubs were much too small. So I decided to use our bath – after all, Eileen was away and she would never know. So we started. The boys came through the kitchen and bedroom with their bloody feet, dripping blood from the strips of meat they carried. I packed it in the bath. A layer of meat, a layer of salt, then more meat and more salt. The salt draws the blood out of the meat at the same time impregnating it with brine which acts as a preservative. After three days of soaking like this the meat is taken out and hung on wires in the shade to dry. It takes about a month to cure and then will keep a year or more. It was by means of biltong and *boer* rusks – dried chunks of bread – and the fact that their ponies could live off the veld, that the Boers succeeded in keeping the British at bay for so long in the Boer War. I have lived on biltong for several days at a time when hunting. One shaves it off in slivers with a knife.

I had only just finished working when Eileen arrived with friends. She had decided to return early. There was the bloody bare-footed spoor in the bedroom and kitchen. The bathroom was a butcher's shop and the bath full to the scuppers with bloody brine. It was not an easy situation to talk my way out of. I did it by saying we had to live, that as any money we made was spent on her, she could regard not having a bath for a couple of days as her contribution. But I see now that I left a lot to be desired as a husband. To start with I was not what she had married. Why should she have imagined when she married a young but penniless Guards officer that she would end up in South Africa with a bath full of blood?

CHAPTER 10

SETTLING IN

A CHANGE now took place, owing to an accident. My cousin, Bertie van der Byl, of Irene, came for the weekend, and when he wanted to go back his car refused to start, something had gone wrong with the ignition and we had to tow him with the Ford pick-up. When we reached Irene he said he had heard of a farm nearby that he thought would just suit us and we might as well go and look at it with him, which we did. Eight hundred morgen (1600 acres), a portion of the farm Knoppies Laagte on the old Potchefstroom Road. It was near Roberts Heights and fourteen miles from Pretoria; to reach it we had to cross two drifts (fords).

The farm had plenty of water and good lands. The house was in fair condition and we decided to buy it. I had some money saved. I also had a little capital from the sale of property in France, and Bertie was sure my Uncle Montrose would help me, so I conceived the plan of running both farms, working half-time on the ranch for half-pay. That is to say, for ten pounds instead of twenty. I still had my pension and this gave me altogether twenty pounds, enough to get by on if we could pay for the place and get a little working capital. Everything turned out well, and I spent alternate fortnights at Constantia, as I called the new farm, and the ranch. The first time I went there to look the place over after I had bought it, I went alone, took some blankets and slept on the floor in my shirt. I woke very suddenly with rather a queer feeling. There was something in my armpit. I had felt it in my sleep and had clamped my arm down hard. I thought for a moment and then realized what it was. I had trapped a mouse and it was scrabbling at me with tiny nails. I whipped off my shirt and shook it out.

I bought a small German plough, a Rudsak, some donkey chains, a lot of buckles, a dressed cow hide, and rivets. Then I borrowed a machine for cutting leather. You just set it to the width you wanted and pulled it along the skin. It cut it into straight, neat strips. Having got all this together, I set about making my harness. I made twelve sets, enough for six pairs, and then started catching the donkeys. There was a fine herd of big, wild donkeys on the ranch, and Frank said I could have my pick at seven and sixpence a head. I collected some beauties, mostly mares, because donkeys are difficult to castrate, and one very fine Catalonian-type jack. He was quite savage when we caught him. So I tied him to a tree without food or water till he would take it from a bucket, and kept offering him a bag on a stick to attack, which he did with teeth and front hooves, chopping at it with his ears laid back. I also stroked him all over with a light stick till he stood still and did not resist any more. This was simply a variation of the Rarey system of horse training. Anyway, it worked, and we found we could handle him quite easily. Donkeys are the most extraordinary animals. You can take wild donkeys – like these – that have never seen a *riem*, inspan them, and they will work at once. It takes a little time to train them to stop when you whistle to them and to start when you shout. But within an hour of having them in harness, they will pull.

I sent this span over to Constantia. I had some good boys there as labour tenants. On this system the men run some cattle and grow crops, for which they pay by working a percentage of the time for the landowner. The terms of this kind of lease vary, but in the one I took over the boys – one adult member of each family – worked for me six months of the year, alternate fortnights for me and themselves, and one woman from the native village on the place came down every day to do laundry, wash the floors and windows, or clean brass and silver. This left my houseboy with nothing to do except cook, do the bedrooms and sweep the house. I had eight families on the farm which gave me four men working all the time. I arranged it so that they took over from each other. Two boys on the lands working the donkeys and a span of young oxen I bought from the ranch and trained. I had one boy in the garden and one with the cows when I got them.

We took Vixen, Mitzi and our cook boy with us every time we moved. I had fixed up my camp kit on the farm – beds, bath, folding chairs and a few boxes and oddments to make it liveable. Eileen was very good about the discomfort. She cleaned and painted up the inside of the house. Eventually we lost Mitzi because we could not wait for her. She was away when we had to go back. She was in season and probably looking for a tom. I had hoped to find her in a fortnight's time when I came back, but I never saw her again. I think she was either shot by a neighbour who, never having seen a Siamese, probably thought she was some kind of wildcat, or she may have been poisoned, as this was sheep country and my neighbours scattered poison along the fence lines for jackal.

After six months I had the place knocked into sufficient shape to move in, and we moved, again by ox wagon. I had bought a wagon of my own, a beautiful custom-made job, for eighty pounds. To move I used my own wagon and hired another from a boy on the ranch called Alfred. A very nice, competent man who was literate and spoke good English. Again I moved without breakages. I put the dining-room table face down on a bed of sacks with furniture against the rails facing inwards, other tables and chairs went on top of the upside-down table, inter-packed, to prevent scratching, with carpets, skins and sacks. China and small objects were wrapped in crumpled newspaper and were put into paraffin boxes. Pictures were packed face to face with newspapers in between, and the whole pyramid covered with a new green bucksail I had bought for the purpose. The poultry went in slatted crates. Vixen came in the car with us. Duchess I had given to the Prides who were fond of her, and I had found homes for the other dogs.

There was a rumour going about at this time that the Chinese were looking for officers with war experience. Very good pay and conditions of service were offered, and if I had not been married I should have gone into the matter. Soldiering again of a different kind under new conditions. Travel and adventure, change, all always appealed to me and it would have been a job I knew. But this was just a dream. I was married, I had just bought a farm, so I put it out of my head and did not mention it to anyone or even think of it again till years later when I was in the Orient. I liked the Chinese I met and made several Chinese friends. The women were most beautiful though they did not like white men. They think we stink. Perhaps we do. The Chinese were the only people who ever gave me a sense of racial inferiority. After all, they invented silk and satin, gun powder and printing while our ancestors were at a very primitive state of development. It is difficult to believe that when Thomas à Becket was killed his underclothes literally writhed with vermin, or that kings moved from castle to castle driven on by the filth and vermin of their occupation. How much more interesting history at school would have been if we had been told some of these facts. Told about chastity belts, tortures, told that the knightly code was a myth and that chivalry was an invention of romantic historians. Told that Joan of Arc was probably mixed with Gilles de Rais, the child murderer.

Once I had the furniture moved and the boys started cleaning up the lands, I decided to go to England for a couple of months. Montrose wanted to see us and was going to pay our fare. Since I had no stock except for the working stock and the few chickens I had moved from the ranch, there was nothing to hold us. When Jean Langeman said she would take Vixen – she was very fond of her and knew her well – my only worry was over.

I do not remember the voyage, and when we got to England we went to see our people and then went on a series of visits to friends and friends of friends.

At one place we stayed with a lady we did not know, a friend of Bunny Small's, and within an hour of our arrival she had lost a valuable pearl necklace. We helped her look for it and luckily found it lying on a garden path. The string had broken.

We stayed with Christopher Turner at Stoke Rochford near Grantham. This was the largest house I have ever stayed in. It covered an acre of ground and there were four floors of it. Four acres of house, in fact. It was so large that to find our way to the dining-room we used to follow the dog, a Scottie. One morning Eileen, who had cleaned her white kid gloves with benzine, put them on the window-sill to air. One blew off and it took me an hour to find it as I could not locate the window from which it had fallen. The house contained some wonderful works of art, full-size statuary, a leather drinking cup that had belonged to Isaac Newton, a falcon carved in wood with all its breast feathers ruffled. There was an enormous Rubens of fat ladies disporting themselves in a state of near nudity, and a lot of family portraits and other pictures. Christopher Turner had a private golf course on which he played with his chauffeur, who described his game as 'all swing and no 'it'.

Another place we stayed was Castle Magendie. I have the spelling wrong but that was the way it was pronounced, like Cholmondeley being pronounced Chumley. This place had a twelfth-century keep in which some English Queen was said to have been murdered and was haunted. In the nineteenth century some young bucks decided to spend the night there but were found dead of fright in the morning – or so the story went. Our room was down a long passage, gloomy with family portraits. The bed was a four-poster, and during the night something pulled the covers off us. A ghost. Why not? There are too many ghost stories to laugh them off and we ourselves have had some odd experiences.

We also stayed with Mildred Tarrant and her parents on the Wentworth Estate which Mr Tarrant was promoting. It was very beautiful with all the houses built of a lovely cherry-red brick.

We went with them to dance where the Prince of Wales was entertaining a party. I had last seen him in France in 1916, but he was much less impressive in a dinner-jacket than in the uniform of the Grenadiers. I did not particularly enjoy being on the dance-floor with him, feeling that Royalty had no place here with ordinary people. It took away some of their glamour. The day after the dance we went to the Derby in a big hired Daimler in which, having a hangover, I felt extremely unwell. I did not care for the racing, though the crowds at Epsom were a wonderful sight. Everything from coach and fours to costers' donkey carts. It was a hot day and there were too many fresh cow pats to make our lunch of cold salmon and chicken with Chablis to drink as pleasant as it should have been. Thousands of people. Thousands of cars. Shouting bookies, tipsters, entertainers, people selling food and drinks – a veritable seething sea of humanity. Men and women of every class and all stations in life out to enjoy this sport of kings.

I forget which horse won the Derby. Though I seldom bet, I had backed a beautiful black called Coldstream, naturally enough being an old Coldstreamer. It was placed, but when I went to collect my winnings the bookie had welshed. I have never enjoyed racing, knowing, as Paul Kruger once said, that one horse can always run faster than another. Nor does the fastest horse always win. Some horses refuse to leave the rest, the horse being by nature a herd animal, and no betting man ever comes out on top in the long run. What I like to see is the paddock where the horses parade round and round. Shining, beautiful creatures topped by brilliant silk-clad jockeys.

We are a racing or at any rate a 'horsey' family, my ancestors in conjunction with Lord Charles Somerset being among the first to import race horses to the Cape Colony.

We ended up our visit by staying with my brother Ronald at the Tower House, Melbury Road. It is now a national monument and is an extraordinary house, quite unique. It was built in 1875, the architect being Norman Shaw. The style was thirteenth-century Gothic, but it had Grecian and Pompeian features. There were panels designed by Burne-Jones, Rossetti, Frederick Walker and many other artists of the period. The house was a mass of painted panels, statues inserted into the walls, painted scenes in ceramic, the tiles depicting gods and goddesses. There was gold leaf everywhere. It must have cost a fortune to build even in those times. Behind the house was a beautiful small, though big for London, garden, filled with rose pergolas, shrubs and flowers.

When we got back to Africa I collected Vixen, who went mad at seeing me again, and bought a car, a big second-hand Nash, from a friend who had made a lot of money and wanted something new and more showy.

I now had to make plans to farm the place. The first thing I did was to concentrate on water and improve my supply by mending a big dam that was breached. For the house and stables I had water by gravity, but I wanted water for irrigation. Then for the farm part. It was no use doing what everyone else round me did. There was no living in growing a few mealies, having some scrub cattle and a small flock of sheep. I had to make a plan for myself, do something new. One thing I knew a lot about was cattle, but this was not ranching country. Then dairy, but what? How? I was too far from town for milk. Cream was possible, but how could I buy the stock, since a good cow cost twenty to thirty pounds? And then there was no certainty that they would be good. A good dairy cow is a gold mine. People do not sell them. When you buy a cow you generally find she kicks, that she only sparks on two plugs, has contagious vaginitis, fights with the other cows, or cannot be kept in by an ordinary four-wire fence. But calves were all right. Calves were like children – given a decent heredity, they became what you made them. So I bought four old Friesland cows that were being culled, just to give a bit of milk to raise my calves, and then set about getting high-quality heifers from the dairies round town. They all sold their calves when they were a week old as they had no facilities for raising them. I went in for Jerseys as far as possible. They were my old love, and one saved a year's keep with them, since they calved when they were two instead of three years old. I bought six Jersey heifers cheap from a drought area – they came by rail to Irene – and it took two days getting them back over fourteen miles of road. But they turned out well. I bought a nice young pedigree bull and more calves, and soon found that things were going quite nicely. No money was coming in but the stock was growing more valuable each day. I ended up rearing twenty-five calves a year, and selling about that number of cows, heavy in calf, to the town dairies or private people who wanted nice, tame, well-bred cows, whose production was guaranteed. I did this by having their milk recorded during their first lactation period, under a government scheme. Once a month the inspector came, checked my milk weights for each cow, and tested them individually for butter fat. I figured that this first lactation about paid the cost of the heifer calf at a week old, which was when I bought them, and her upkeep to calving, so that what I sold her for was profit. It also meant that when I sold her I had a certified record of her performance.

There was, I found, an unlimited demand for cows of this type because there was no catch in them. They had been bred to sell. The buyer could see the milk cows that I would sell next year, my two-year-olds that were about to calve, the yearlings that were just going to the bull, and my babies that I had bred myself or had bought in.

All these animals were very tame. The calves were kept tied in separate stalls, so that they could not suck each other, for five months or so, only being turned loose for a couple of hours to gallop about every morning. At night in winter each had a folded sack over its back held in place by five loops of rope – one round its neck and one under each leg. This meant lifting their legs to dress them up, with the result that you could handle their feet as if they were horses. This stabling was an excellent idea and made dealing with any illness, particularly scour (diarrhoea) which is the greatest curse to calf rearers, easy.

As soon as I bought in a calf or had one born I would dress the navel and cord with iodine, as a precaution against white scour bacteria which finds its way into the calf through this source. But for the ordinary scour I dosed them with aromatic sulphuric acid – a teaspoonful, I think it was, in a cup of water twice a day. I also gave them raw eggs, shell and all, till they were cured. We were somewhat troubled with opthalmia, but, here again, having the calves tied in a stall made them much easier to handle. We used a five-per-cent solution of silver nitrate squirted into the eye, and I devised a soft syringe that could be used quite quickly and even carelessly without any chance of hurting them, by cutting off the bulb of an enema, leaving two short ends of tube, one of which I sealed with a plug of wood. Where the eye had a film over it I used a little cascara oxide of mercury on the eyeball, and if that failed, the powdered skeleton of a large centipede. This worked by friction as an abrasive when the animal's eyelids moved up and down, and was an old Boer remedy.

Opthalmia was much worse in the Bushveld and much harder to deal with, as the animals were wild and so difficult to handle that it was almost impossible to give them consistent daily treatment. We even had some blind cows that managed to live among the others quite well, having adjusted themselves to the life. There was a black one that I never knew was blind till she walked into the pit silo.

One thing I noticed, and I believe it has been confirmed by other cattle men, is that Herefords and white-faced animals in general are more susceptible to opthalmia than others. Whether the eyes are weaker – they always seem weak with their pink rims – or whether the light colour of the face attracts flies or other insects that carry infection, I do not know.

But I had a lot of fun with my tame cows. Sometimes, if someone came unexpectedly and we were out of milk, I would have to go out and get some. None of my cows would get up for me if they were lying down. I had to sit beside them, raise the upper hind leg, getting it more or less over my shoulder, and milk into my jug by holding it almost flat along the stable floor, while the cow chewed her cud and watched me reflectively. Earlier, in France, my cows were even tamer, and I told people how I used to take them for walks with me on the golf course in winter when it was deserted, and how they followed, playing round me like dogs.

Each of my calf stalls had half a five-gallon dip tin built into it under the ring where I chained the heifer. This was not a manger as it would have been impossible to keep it clean. It was a container to hold the feeding bucket and save holding it by hand.

The calves I bred were separated from their mothers at once and fed her colostrum. Cows have this for about a week – it is a thick cream-like substance that cannot be used except for custard and is essential to the calves' health.

The calves I bought in I fed twice a day on full milk for six weeks and then went on to skim milk with an addition of calf meal. After a month I gave them a handful of bran and crushed oats in the bottom of their buckets when they had finished drinking their milk. They soon took to this and licked their bucket clean. I then, after a few days, added a teaspoonful of blood meal which I increased as they got older. The cows in full milk got up to 3 lbs per day, though it took some time to get them used to it. At first they lowered their heads and gave a peculiar low which is characteristic when they smell blood. I increased the amount each day till I reached the required quota. I used blood meal because it was the cheapest protein. I don't know if anyone else used it, but it was very satisfactory. I weighed the milk of each cow at every milking, a drop of a pound or so being a sign of something wrong.

I gave my calves a handful of teff hay to nibble when they were only a fortnight old, and by the time they were six weeks old they were eating hay regularly. I also gave the bigger calves water to drink out of a bucket when they had finished their milk and grain ration. The whole key to calf rearing is keeping the utensils clean, feeding at regular times and stopping them sucking each others ears.' On the ranch I once did a post-mortem on a calf. There we kept the calves near the house loose in a small paddock. I took sixteen hair balls out of his stomach, a couple as big as golf balls. The work with calves could not be left to natives. I fed each calf myself and personally weighed all the milk. My neighbour thought calf rearing a fine idea. He bought eleven heifers and in three months they were all dead.

I ran my young bull with the cows and stabled him with them. Many bulls become dangerous because they are bored and lonely.

He was, however, exercised every day for half an hour on a bull stick to keep him used to it. I still replaced him before he was three because Jersey bulls become difficult as they get older and his daughters were ready for service by then.

It had been my intention to sell milk to the creamery for butter. But my stables did not come up to the regulation standard. Too few cubic feet of air per cow. I thought this absurd as the whole north side of the stable was open.

Defeated in this project, I turned to making butter myself, which was permitted, and sold it to the store in Roberts Heights and some private customers who wanted good farm butter instead of the insipid stuff on the market. The difference lay in the fact that the creameries made their butter with fresh sweet sterilized cream whereas I used sour cream, inoculating each batch with cream from the last.

I bought a very good high-speed Alfa Laval churn, which never took more than five minutes to make butter. I always made it myself because the whole trick is to stop churning in time. This is when the sound of the cream in the churn changes. It begins to swish which means the butter grains have formed. They should be smaller than a grain of rice. The buttermilk is run out and fresh cold brine put into the churn to cool and salt the butter. This is done three or four times till it runs out clear. The butter is then put into the butter worker – a ridged board where it is rolled with a ridged roller rather like a rolling pin, to squeeze the water out. It is then packed in a beechwood form to make a pound pack and wrapped in special grease-proof paper. The butter form and pats must always be kept in water, and to make a good job the butter paper must be wet too.

I had very little sickness with my cattle but nearly lost a very good young cow with milk fever. This only attacks the best and heaviest milkers. They lie in a characteristic position curled with their legs under them and their heads turned upwards and to the left. Their eyes are glazed and their ears cold. They look as if they are dead and will soon die if they do not get attention. I got the vet and he pumped air into each quarter of the udder through the teat, tying it fast with a piece of tape to prevent the air leaking out. In an hour the cow was up and eating and I undid the tapes and milked her. There were no further ill-effects from her illness.

Some friends in Johannesburg left a very nice big, fat, neutered Siamese cat called George with us when they went to England. We had him for some months, and he lay like an ornament on the dining-room table during meals, never trying to touch anything. We were very sorry to see him go when his owners came back.

Then a terrible thing happened. One of my neighbours who put out poison for jackal got Vixen with it, and she died in my arms in one of those spasms that come from strychnine. She had dragged her way back to me and then went into those terrible spastic spells that are the symptoms of this poison. I cried like a baby and did not get over it for weeks. We had been so close for three years, day and night together, with her sleeping on my clothes on the floor by the bed. I replaced her with Bodo, another of Bob Gwatkin's Alsatians about four months old.

I made a good garden with a series of terraces below the house, ending in a big lawn surrounded by wide herbaceous borders. I planted a lot of trees – fruit trees, oaks, gums and, near the house along the circular drive, jacarandas, which do so well in the Pretoria district. The house was comfortable although architecturally uninteresting. It was almost square with a passage down the centre which ended in the dining-room. The front room on the left was our bedroom, the next room on the left was a spare room, and then came the kitchen which communicated with the dining-room. On the right came the first sitting-room, then my study and then the dining-room. The house was surrounded by a stoep which had never been completed, and the wooden posts that held the roof were rotten. So I replaced them with concrete pillars and paved the floor with slate that I quarried myself from a hill nearby. I then planted vines up the posts, and before long the view of the mountains in the distance was framed with a design of vine leaves and hanging bunches of grapes. I put great numbers of roses near the house and built up the west side so that one could walk straight off the stoep on to a lawn, while I lowered the east side to make a really shady spot for the summer afternoons. The house was built on the side of quite a steep hill which made gardening interesting and allowed for a lot of variety.

We had great numbers of visitors. People almost every weekend and we often went away for a night or two. Eileen sometimes stayed away for a week or more, but I could never leave for long.

In fact, I seldom was away for more than forty-eight hours, because if all the stock was well when I left I knew I would still be in time to deal with anything that went down while I was away.

One trouble we had in common to all the Transvaal was what the Boers call *stopsiekte*, a form of constipation due to too much dry grass. The cure for this was an injection of mercurocrome (I do not remember the concentration) intravenously, in the jugular vein. To find the jugular, a thin rope or a rawhide whiplash is put round the neck and pulled tight so that the blood cannot circulate. The vein then stands out and can generally be found after a prick or two. You know when you have found it because, as you use the needle alone, the blood starts coming out of the artery in a steady stream like water from a tap. The syringe is then fitted and the plunger sent home. Once the vet showed me how to do this I lost nothing from this sickness.

I had to dip here just as I had in the Bushveld. And I dipped everything, even week-old calves, taking them through on a long *riem* like a dog on a lead. By doing this they became so accustomed to it that they just ran through without any trouble after a few times, as if they enjoyed the swim. The dip had to be carefully tested with a small chemical set supplied by the makers. A mistake could be fatal as, if it was too strong, it would take the skin right off the softer parts of the animal while, if it was not strong enough, it would fail to kill the ticks.

In view of the present situation in Africa it should be remembered that every farm has all this poison freely available for any native wishing to sabotage a herd of cattle or poison his master. A recalcitrant and sullen labour force in a state of near rebellion is not what one would choose to have in the vicinity of almost unlimited amounts of arsenical and other poisons – dips and sprays of various kinds.

But things were better in those days. The labour was more or less content, provided they were well paid, fed and fairly treated.

My uncle now sent us some good furniture from his house in Berkeley Square. A sideboard and dining-room chairs with the family crest on them that he had had made from an oak beam that had been removed from Winchester Cathedral during some repairs, and had been auctioned. The wood must have been well over a thousand years old since Winchester is an old cathedral and the timbers used were enormous, cut from trees many hundreds of years old. There are even today, in Windsor Great Park, trees that are supposed to have been there in the time of William the Conqueror. They are almost dead but they still put out a few leaves each year.

There was also a beautiful Dutch marquetry chest of drawers with silver handles, and a flat cupboard with a carved front. The carving went right through it in a kind of wood filagree and was the work of Batavian slave artisans in the days of the Dutch East India Company. This piece had come to London from Groot Constantia, which was in the family till the eighties of the last century.

My uncle also sent me some copies of family portraits and a facsimile of the Cape Archives, showing that my ancestor, Jacob, was the first white man to hold land in South Africa. His signature is the first one, and is dated 1656. He came with Van Riebeeck in 1652 and was later murdered by Hottentots.

There were some beautiful silver entrée dishes, mother-of-pearl-handled fruit knives and forks, wine slides and cut-glass decanters. He also sent me my great-grandfather's silver knife, fork and spoon in an octagonal mahogany case that the judge (The Hon. Henry Cloete, LL.D.) carried when on circuit, not liking the cutlery used on the farms and inns where he had to stay. Montrose had persuaded a van der Byl cousin, a great hunter, who lived at Albany, to send me some of his guns – a Paradox shot-and-ball twelve-bore by Holland & Holland, a Greener twelve-bore and a Mannlicher rifle with a telescopic sight. There were a lot of books too – valuable Africana – among them a big book of Danielle prints and a first-edition Harris. All these were later bought by a dealer who must have done very well out of them. This was my second library to go, but that was in the future. There was also a large oil of Montrose himself, three foot by four, for which I had no room, so I cut out the face and shoulders and had them reframed. This would seem to be the solution for large family portraits which cannot be used in small houses.

With all this, the new house, Constantia, began to take shape. It became rather more than just a farm. It was a very comfortable country house. We were digging in. I was there for good. I was thirty-eight.

CHAPTER II

THE LOVE AFFAIR

I MUST describe the farm itself. It ran downhill into a valley bounded by two rocky ridges, then flattened out into agricultural land and beyond that into grazing. The top part of the farm was used by the African labour tenants for both lands and grazing. They obtained water from a strong spring. In one of the rock ridges there were the remains of an old gold mine with adits for entrance. There were the foundations of a stamp block and the remains of the manager's house built in stone. While in operation some £5,000 worth of gold was taken out of the mine. The mineral rights remained with the farm, and when I eventually sold it I retained them. In a small wood beyond the homestead were the ruins of a farmhouse probably destroyed in the Boer War. Another feature was a picturesque abandoned lime kiln used for processing dolomite rock which was plentiful.

With Jack Wood, a miner friend, I took some rock from the pillars left in the mine as supports, crushed it with a hammer, and panned it. We found visible grains of gold. A miner's pan, Jack had brought one with him, is like an ordinary tin wash-basin with a ridge just below the rim. The crushed rock being panned is put into the basin with water which is then swirled round and round and thrown out. The gold dust, which is heavier than the crushed rock, remains caught in the rim.

My water came from a spring with an earth dam which washed away with every rain. I built a strong stone weir reinforced with barbed wire well keyed into the sides. About two hundred yards down I built a small stone tower six feet high to catch dirt that came through the pipe. I could clean out this silt by opening a four-inch valve at the bottom. Some erosion was taking place above the spring and to check it I made a long low horseshoe-shaped earth dam which threw the floodwater out sideways so that it ran over the rocks of the ridges that closed in here. The dip was in good order. All I had to do was to replace the poles of the race and drying *kraal* which had rotted. I mended the high

My mother and hunter,
Cape Hunt, South Africa

My father aged fifty
in the Bois de Boulogne

Self in 1904

Self in Lancing OTC, 1913

stone *kraal* and built my own stables against it open to northern sun, the cows standing at right angles to the back wall. I made stabling for thirty head and twelve calf stalls. I also built a garage of stone with an iron roof. I got my blue hydrolic lime from Roly Cullinan at Oliphantsfontein. He also let me have all the damaged bricks I wanted at a very low rate, two pounds a thousand, I think, so my building was cheap, specially as I used a lot of stone. Except for floors, I used no cement.

Bertie van der Byl allowed me to use Irene as a railhead. We saw a lot of the van der Byls, and one day he took us over to tea at General Smuts' farm, Doornkloof.

I was somewhat astonished at his home, which was an old army mess hut built of wood and corrugated iron. On each side of his front door was a field gun up to its axle in long grass. General Smuts struck me as a man without warmth. A Field-Marshal, a Statesman who helped to create the League of Nations, a guerrilla leader of commandos in the Boer War, the Prime Minister of the Union of South Africa, philosopher, linguist, quite the most important man I have ever met but still not a man I should have liked to serve under. We had tea in what I think was the kitchen, the plates were white kitchen china and the tablecloth was red-and-white-check linoleum. I remember no pictures, just photographs – groups and signed pictures of Royalty. There were several thousand books, but the whole layout and decor was so unpretentious that it was like a stage set designed to prove some democratic ideal. I do not think this was the case. It was not phoney; it was just that the general could not be bothered with comfort or beauty.

Among the many people who came to stay on the farm was Bunny (Percival) Small, an English artist who had often stayed with us on the ranch. He painted a very nice portrait of Eileen and one of me in uniform (now at Alphen). Bunny was a fascinating man, a good painter, though not of the first rank, who knew everyone. While she was acting in Johannesburg he introduced me to Sybil Thorndike (now Dame). She was charming to me when we saw her in her dressing-room.

My life on the farm was a routine. Calf feeding and milking morning and evening, work on the land and dam the rest of the day. I used to push the boys in the morning and let them go slow after lunch. In this way they thought they had got the better of me which made them happy, but I had in fact got a day's work done by lunch-time so anything they did later was a bonus. My head boy was Hermanus. Then came his son Hendrick, a very good man with oxen. Daniel and Piet were good stock boys and milkers, Jim a fine builder with lime and stone. Franz and Lazarus were ordinary workers with no special skills.

My cousin Piet van der Byl sent me some English Mallard from his farm, Fairfield, for my big dam. They bred well in my stable yard and then flew into the water and up the stream in the valley. I have always liked game birds and allowed no shooting on the farm. I had guinea fowl, partridges, pheasants, plover and hares, which increased once they were protected. I had a beautiful pair of secretary birds that rested on the top of a flat thorn in one of the paddocks. The secretary bird, so called because of a plume like a pen behind the ear, is a grey eagle with long stilt-like legs. It kills snakes but also attacks young game birds. But on the whole, however, the bird life was not interesting; the farm was too open for them.

I got some white rabbits from Helen Luxmore Ball. Her father had commanded a battalion of Welsh Guards. Helen was a sweet girl. The rabbits did very well but finally escaped, and I found them popping up all over the place and had to shoot them as they did so much harm in the garden. The Luxmore Balls farmed at Halfway House between Pretoria and Johannesburg. He sold up after a few years but his farm must now be worth half a million or more as not only was it in a wonderful position but he had strong water from the Yokeskie River. My other neighbours were Henry Mellie, who had a big dairy farm at Swartkop near the army airfield, and the Gwatkins at Roberts Heights (now Voortrekker Hoogte). He was a gunner in command of a field battery and bred Alsatians – mine all came from him. Kathleen, his wife, was a wonderful horsewoman and generally won the High Jump at the Pretoria and Rand Shows riding Satan, a white gun horse that no one else could handle. She had a dark brown thoroughbred, Niope, that she used to let me ride. We often went out together. She let me use him because I had good hands, and I think both the horse and I enjoyed our association, understanding each other perfectly. It was a curious coincidence that I should find Gwatkins here, because Norman Gwatkin, a cousin (later General Sir Norman), had been my best man in 1919. When Bob left the army he and Kathleen took over the management of a stud farm in Bethlehem, where Kathleen lost a thumb and finger bitten off on two separate occasions by playful stallions. When Bob died many years later she only lived a few months more. They were childless and very close and happy. It has been my experience that childless people have the happiest marriages and that children, far from bringing people together, tend to separate them. I think men are seldom unfaithful to their wives, only to the mothers of their children.

The farm when I took it over had been rented to a butcher and was badly over-grazed. What this means is that the good grasses have been eaten off to the roots and the bad left to grow and seed themselves. What I did was to burn them off, burning against a light wind. When one does this the grass smoulders without creating enough heat to destroy the humus. The tall coarse grass stems fall burnt off at the foot and lie like a thin layer of straw on the blackness of the burn. When the rain comes the effect is magical, fresh green grass appears and grows so fast you can almost hear it.

I now rested the veld – I had very few stock, just my working oxen and a few old cows and my donkeys – and before long I had a carpet of rooigrass and finger grass, two of the best grazing grasses in the area. I bought a mower pulled by two oxen and a hay rake and made hay. I made two stacks on the French pattern, building them conically round a fifteen-foot pole and capping them with a little canvas hat held in place by ropes fastened to pegs driven into the hay. I grew crops of Rhodes grass and teff. Teff makes a good fine hay crop and is beautiful to look at. About two foot high, it seems to flow like silver water as a breeze brushes it. The lands where I grew my crops were below the house and bounded by a high hedge of clingstone peaches which I sold by the wagon-load at 2s 6d a monkey, this being a big basket. In the early spring it was a wonderful show of pink bloom, with the lands beyond it, and the grazing beyond the lands spotted with clumps of trees. Beyond that were the mountains that changed colour according to the light. So we had a wonderful view from the stoep. The loo was in the orchard and had the same view when the door was open. The seat was often romantically strewn with flower petals – peach, apricot, quince and plum.

Everything was going to plan and I saw myself as fully settled at forty. And then things began to happen. The place was finished, the herd increasing and everything going well, but it had lost its savour. It was finished. There was nothing more to do, to organize. I could only wait for things to mature still further. I am a bad waiter. It is my nature, unfortunately, to drive. So I was bored.

I was now in a very curious psychological condition. I was being driven by some force beyond my control, not so much nervous as ready to jump out of my skin like a horse shivering before a race. But there was no race. I had established my farm. I was building up my Jersey herd. In six generations (only twelve years with Jerseys which breed at two) the calves could be registered as grade Jerseys. But what was the good of a farm and a nice dairy herd with no one to leave it to? I began to see that development was what I liked. Starting something and getting it going. In this I think I was like my father. Once a thing was organized and became easy he lost interest.

At this point fate, or Mr Luck as I had thought of him in the war, took a hand. A number of things happened almost simultaneously. Eileen went to stay with Reneira Stanley at High Commission House in Milnerton. I suddenly began to write short stories and free verse. My Uncle Montrose died. I fell in love and was for the first time unfaithful to my wife. And finally when Eileen came back from the Cape the author E. Arnot Robertson came to stay with us, introduced by Una Long, the daughter of B. K. Long, the Editor of the *Cape Times*. To deal with these events, in the order of their appearance as if they were characters in a play, seems the most logical way of developing the months and years that followed.

Eileen liked parties, dressing up and the protocol that went with government house affairs, so when Reneira asked her to stay she was delighted. I could not leave the farm and disliked social functions of all kinds, so I saw her off and went back to my cows. She was going to be away a month. I missed her very much and to pass the time wrote poems and a short story which I entered for a competition in *Nash's Magazine*. The casting vote lay with Bill Dozier with whom, years later, I was to work in Hollywood.

When Eileen had been away a fortnight I got a letter, not even airmail, telling me my Uncle Montrose was dead. He had died of cancer of the throat. This upset me badly as he had become like a father to me, although he was 6,000 miles away. I wrote to Eileen and thought she would come back, though I did not ask her to, as she knew how much Montrose meant to me. Instead she asked if I minded if she stayed on at the Cape for the races and some other festivities. I said of course she could stay but was hurt that she wanted to. I pulled myself together but felt very alone.

Quite a few people came to see me, some to stay for the weekend. Among my visitors was a Pretoria girl – Monica. She was a tall, slim, red-haired girl with blue eyes. We had known her for several years before her divorce and she had often come to stay on the ranch. The affair began at a dance in Pretoria to which she had asked me. She was wearing a pale green silk dress and very little else, and by her manner of dancing showed her interest in me. On the way back to her apartment I sat on the back seat with her and I realized I had not been wrong. After that she came out to the farm several times, even staying the night, and I went to her apartment in Pretoria. Sometimes we had a picnic lunch in a young pine plantation, making love on a bed of pine needles with the scent of pines in our nostrils as the sun distilled their resin for us. Once as we lay there a little steinbok came by, paused to look at us and galloped off, its tiny hooves clattering on the pebbles of the path.

Eileen had often left me alone with girls on the ranch and farm. I suddenly found her trust in me irritating, and in my present mood said to hell with everything and let nature take its course. It was the first time a woman had shown she wanted me in that way. It would be easy to say the woman tempted me, but the attraction was mutual.

The morning after I had made love to her I sat on the steps of the stoep looking out over the orchard and the lands at the mountains in the distance. I had committed adultery and felt very content. I had never been unfaithful before, but then I had never been in quite this state before: with Eileen away for two months, with Montrose dead, or with a woman who wanted me and showed it physically. A sensual woman as I was a sensual man. It was all new to me. Almost forty but in this way still a virgin. It was something I had heard about, read about, thought about but never experienced before, and it inflamed me. I was mad about her, about my desire being met more than halfway. I had resisted the feeling at first and then given in to it, and a new world had opened up to me. I knew nothing could be the same again. It set in train the events that followed. My near suicide, the sale of my cattle and furniture, my eventual divorce, and probably the fact that I became a writer. But at no time did I feel a sense of sin or even guilt.

As I saw it then and still do, a woman's body is her own. She is not a chattel. This applies equally to her right to abort out a child she does not wish to have. The important and often forgotten factor here being the subsequent happiness of the child. Only a wanted child should be born. If this were universally the case there would be few cases of cruelty to children, some of which even result in their death.

Monica came out several times before Eileen's return. After that things became more difficult, but I managed to see her every now and again in Pretoria while Eileen was busy with the hairdresser or shopping. It is astonishing how quickly two people can make love if they do not undress. I was planning to get divorced and marry Monica, though Eileen was unaware of my intention.

Then Una Long called from Johannesburg. She said Arnot Robertson, the author of *Four Frightened People* and other books, was staying with them and wanted to spend a few days on an African farm. Could she come to us?

We said, 'Yes, of course,' and she came. Her husband, Henry Turner, who was, I believe, on the London *Times*, was on a trip in the north, and she thought a stay on a farm would be a good idea. Arnot was a thin woman of about forty with red hair. She was a fascinating talker. I talked to her about writing and eventually screwed up enough courage to show her some of my work – poems and stories. She took them to her room to read. In the morning I said, 'Arnot, do you think I shall ever be able to write? Is there a paragraph or even a line that shows any ability?'

She said, 'Yes, you have some talent.'

I said, 'Then I'm going to sell up and go to London and see what I can do.'

She said, 'It's a terrible gamble. It's one thing to have some talent and another to become a professional writer.'

It was at this moment, I suppose, I took the biggest gamble of my life. I was uneducated, I had no money. Not in the real sense, just my pension and a little cash.

I showed my work to Louis Rose McLeod, the editor of the *Rand Daily Mail*. I showed it to Sarah Gertrude Millin, the author of *God's Step-Children*. I told them what I was going to do. Both said I had talent but was mad to take such a risk. I knew I was mad but I felt forced to do what I was going to do.

My marriage, though it was not apparent to anyone, even to Eileen, was finished. I was in love, I was tired of farming. I found myself in a state of mixed elation and despair.

Then came the clincher. My Aunt Mary wanted us to come to London and would pay the fare. A few weeks later we sailed from Cape Town.

The only people I remember on the trip were a man called Tony Moon who had been in East Africa, and a very remarkable girl, Betty King, who had a B.Sc. and whose parents owned a big laundry. By now Eileen knew something was up and, reaching England, I went to stay at my club and she went to her parents.

Both Louis Rose McLeod and Sarah Gertrude Millin gave me letters to publishers and friends in London. I was not quite sure about things yet but my plans were maturing.

On reaching London, the letter I had expected from Monica was not waiting for me at the club as it should have been, and easily could have been by airmail, and so I fell in love again with someone else, a very beautiful girl, half Irish and half Swedish, twelve years younger than I. I met her at an artist's party and took her home. She was a good girl, a proper girl, and said she was probably the only one at the party who would not have gone to bed with me. And there had been some lovely girls there – models and women interested in art and artists. But I picked on her and rushed her for the balance of the time I had left in London. I saw very little of Eileen, who was still with her parents.

I went back to Africa alone, telling Yvonne I would return. I left an order at a florists' for dark red carnations to be sent to her each week. In London I always wore a dark red carnation buttonhole. I was heartbroken, romantic and desperate.

Nature was functioning at fever heat in the laboratory that I called my body, driving it with whips and scorpions, knouts and cat o' nine tails. I was ripe for love, overripe, and was searching desperately for a love object. A lot of nonsense is written about people marrying on the rebound. It is not rebound at all. It is simply that the drive for a permanent mating has to be satisfied, and if one fails another is chosen. Coming home alone on the boat I had an affair with a very attractive American girl who was going out to be married to a man in South West Africa. In the end I became terrified as she seemed disposed to change her plans, so I had to behave very badly to her so that she could see what a lucky escape she had had.

I had left my friend Monte Dudding, a very good farmer who had just sold his own place, to run Constantia while I was away, and found it in first-class order when I took over again. I now determined to liquidate my affairs and see if I could get Eileen to divorce me. At one time she agreed and then she changed her mind before the affair was completed. It took some five years of great unhappiness for all concerned before we were finally separated.

There was nothing admirable about the business, nor any justification on my part for my behaviour, except that I had reached an end. I do not think any woman had been more loved. There is something rather special, almost beautiful, about a boy's love, but love seems to me rather like a cup – at the end, unless it is replenished by being returned, it disappears, evaporates, and nothing is left but the dregs. I was married too young. I was twenty-one, and though at first our courses had run parallel, we were now poles apart. Having reached a cross-road we had taken different paths. Eileen was social and conventional. I was neither. I was a gambler, not with money, but with my life – the greatest stake of all. I had always backed myself and ridden hard.

My life had been one long steeplechase in which I have obeyed my father's riding instructions when he taught me to take the big jumps. I have thrown my heart over first and gone after it with a free rein. Over or smash. In love, in war, in all I have done, I have never learnt any other way. But for Eileen, poor girl, it was a great surprise. She had, after all, married a young officer who had metamorphosed himself into a rancher, a dairy farmer, and now was proposing to be a writer. We had had two settled homes, one in France and one here, and now I was going to break up the second as I had broken up the first.

I do not understand the lightness with which many people take divorce. It is a form of suicide, you have to kill a part of your life – in my case eighteen years of it. It is a major psychological operation that leaves a great hole, like a wound, which the years slowly cover with scar tissue. Or perhaps I am the exception. I do not know.

The marriage itself was a mistake. Had my parents not opposed it, had I had a proper home at the time, had we, as so many couples do today, lived together first, it would never have taken place. Part of it was sex, lust, a projection of the will that had impressed itself on me when I was lying in the German wire and thought I was dying. Part was fury, that though I was not considered too young to be killed, they thought I was too young to marry. Part too, no doubt, the natural urge that sweeps through a nation after war, affecting the whole population, and drives them to increase, to replace the dead. Had I been looser than I was and slept around, it might not have happened. Had I not exercised all my will to persuading Eileen to marry me, sending her telegrams proposing marriage every Saturday for months, never leaving her alone, beating down her resistance, it would not have taken place. But she too must have been affected by similar, though to both of us unsuspected, urges. The man she had been engaged to was killed on the Somme a few months before she met me, and always, right through the years we lived together, his miniature, painted on ivory, stood on her dressing-table. She never forgot him. I had never replaced him.

No blame whatsoever can be attached to her. She was a good wife for a different kind of man. A nicer, quieter, more reliable, less sensual man. There were, too, immense differences in temperament. I was nervous, highly strung, a worrier. I was affectionate and demonstrative. She was beautiful – composed and calm. Had she not been I should have sent her mad. In her way I think she was reasonably happy. She had many friends, everyone liked her. In fact, I always thought they liked her better than me, which gave me a feeling of inferiority. Socially, I have always been a failure. Either saying nothing or, if a subject interests me, saying too much.

But there it was, the situation existed and, incised within the situation for which I had no one to blame but myself, I lived – suspended. It was at this time that I thought of suicide as a way out. How simple a path to take. One shot and it would be over.

I regard suicide as legitimate. I feel that a man has the right to take his own life, though I feel it should be done neatly, in such a way as to embarrass no one, and make as little mess as possible. I do not think people should jump out of buildings on to the pavement because of the effect it may have on the people who witness the event, and see him burst like a ripe plum on the side-walk.

To be sure I could not shoot myself in a sudden moment of despair, I locked my ·45 – it was always kept loaded as I have never seen the use of an unloaded gun – in a cupboard, and put the key in a drawer. If I did it now it would not be on impulse. But I was in a bad way. The food, without Eileen to supervise it, was abominable and, although I have often seen this denied as impossible, my hair turned grey. Later on it turned dark again, but at this time it was almost white.

Everything I had done so far was finished, and though driven and committed to a new life I still realized what I was giving up and what a fool I was.

Then Eileen came back and stayed with Roly and Marge Cullinan at Oliphantsfontein. I joined her and we spent a terrible night talking till daylight but could come to no conclusion.

I left her there and went back to the farm alone. I was now in a deep state of depression. On my trip back to Africa I had contracted trench mouth – Vincents Angina, my dentist, could do nothing for me. So I went to a doctor who gave me an intravenous injection of 606 which is used for syphilis and this cured me, as the trench mouth bacillus is a spirochaete and belongs to the same group as that which produces syphilis.

I was rather surprised that I got no comfort from my dogs – their cold noses pushed into my hand meant nothing. Bodo, the Alsatian, and Happy Boy, the Peke, knew something was wrong but could not help. Several girls came to stay, including Monica, but except for her nothing came of it. I was happiest with my cows and spent hours in the stable with them and the calves.

Part Three

A NEW WORLD

ENGLAND AND AMERICA

CHAPTER 12

THE END OF A HOME

HAVING started, I had to go on. When A, B and C already exist, D and E are bound to follow, and I set about breaking up my home. My silver and best furniture I sent by wagon over to my friends Roly and Marge Cullinan at Oliphantsfontein, who said they would keep some of it for me and dispose of the rest. The implements and tools I sold by public auction at the market in Pretoria. There remained the stock. Honey and Treacle, the Pekinese, a pretty pair, I gave to my cousin Lady Stanley, who took them to Rhodesia where her husband, Sir Herbert, was Governor. The two pups, Yo Yo, a minute bitch, I sold, and Happy Boy, my favourite, who used to ride in front of my saddle, was killed by a snake. Happy was lemon and white in colour and a wonderful little dog, always with me. In ploughland he jumped from furrow to furrow. In long grass he leaped like a grasshopper, landing on the top of the grass and bounding up again. In the stables I was always afraid of a cow pat falling on him. Curiously the cattle were more nervous of a Peke than bigger dogs. They were too low on the ground for them to poke at. In fact, I do not think they really knew they were dogs at all.

Monte Dudding took Bodo. The herd, Henry Mellie, my neighbour, said he would take over and give me a percentage of the profit he got from the sale of the milk. He had Frieslands which were rather poor in butter fat, and as my herd average was over five per cent, it would push up his figure. But it was a big wrench, my cows were like children to me, each one a pet. They had almost all been bred on the place or bought at a week old and brought home in a sack with their heads out in the back of the Nash. I had taught them to drink out of a bucket, I had fed them, rugged them at night. They followed me like dogs. I must say I cried to see them go. Ninety-odd head of them strung out along my drive getting smaller and smaller. The last one was a little white and yellow heifer five months old called Butterfly – a favourite.

The rest of the furniture I sold in Pretoria. Monte Dudding took my herd of white donkeys. Those donkeys meant a lot to me and even now, forty years later, I still remember them and many of my cows and heifers.

My collection of guns, including a Greener twelve-bore and a twelve-bore Paradox by Holland & Holland, I had taken to a gunsmith in Pretoria and asked him to sell them for me. When later I got his cheque I realized he had given them away.

I got next to nothing for my implements – the three-furrow disc plough, the Oliver cultivator, disk trek gear, wagon and the rest. I am a good salesman but no good when dealing with my own things. It is hard to sell part of oneself. What would a man do who had had his arm amputated if he was asked what he wanted for it? 'Take it,' he'd say, 'for Christ's sake take the bloody thing.' And there are always buyers ready, the vultures who prey on disaster and call it a bargain. But the working oxen made a fair price.

Nothing was left now. Some camp kit, my heads – the horns of the buck I had shot mounted on little teak shields – and my papers and scrapbooks, the documentary evidence of thirty-eight years of my life. I took them out behind the house, poured kerosene over them and struck a match. After two or three false starts – albums burn badly – they went up in a column of black smoke, a little dark pillar against the blue African sky, all that was left of my friends in the Yorkshire Light Infantry, Household Battalion and Coldstream, pictures of girls, Nancy Wright and others. No one who has not tried to burn an album can realize how difficult it is to do. It had been difficult to make up my mind to do it. It was my past and its destruction had a profound effect on me.

It was a burning of boats, and rather more, for part of me had gone up with the smoke when I destroyed my photographs, whole books of them. War photos. Signed photos of dead men, of girls now married to other men and middle-aged mothers. In burning them I had burnt something of myself, my memories. I had cut the knot of my past with the flame of their burning. Another umbilical cord.

One of the photos I burnt was that of Enid Hopkins, my first love. Another young officer, Wilfred Hewlit, and I had been billeted on her aunt, Mrs Gilbert, in Maidenhead. I still remember this picture. Enid's head was bent slightly forward, with her long dark hair hanging down like a curtain, silhouetting her face. She was a very pretty charming girl of my own age, but her aunt was a dragon and we did not get very far in those unpermissive days. The last time I saw her was when she visited me in hospital in Reading after I had been wounded in 1916.

Hewlit was killed at Loos with almost all the other officers of the 9th Yorkshire Light Infantry. Among them were my special friends Maurice Cambie, Leslie Head, Bradford Gordon, Douglas Jones; so were Gordon Haswell, Ruby Butler, and the two Australians, Knott and Sligh. I survived because I had been left behind to my great disappointment when the battalion went to France in August 1915. But a great piece of luck as it turned out in the end.

I thought about our home. A home was a slow thing. It had a slow growth. It grew round a nucleus of wedding presents, your own possessions before marriage, and your wife's possessions. It grew out of the memories of your old home. The home of your childhood. In each home were to be found the vestigial remains of other, older homes.

I looked round. Each thing I looked at had a history. Given by friends, bought, inherited, each thing represented something other than what it was. They were objects certainly, some of them objects of art, but they were also memories. This man and that woman came up. This place and that place . . . This year and that year. We were there then, I thought. We bought those little brass cannons on our honeymoon. I bought that picture when I was in hospital in Reading. That ivory Buddha in Paris. What was it they said about Buddhas? That you should never use them for anything – not as letter weights or door stops. You should just have them to look at.

This was home. A collection of objects: chairs, tables, beds, chests of drawers, china, silver, pictures, books, that had been integrated into a personality by their possesors. This was home in its final phase, built up slowly – it was now suddenly disintegrated . . . much would be destroyed.

And her clothes. There were lots of Eileen's clothes in the closet. What should I do with them? It was curious how objective one could become at such times. Curious how little – and how much – these things meant. I wondered why she had left so many clothes. Was it part of the pattern of divorce, perhaps symbolic – a sartorial washing of hands?

When I go, I thought, I'll go naked. Naked as hell. I'll take nothing. It is over. It was hard to think of a home being over, of the life that had been lived here being over . . . of beginning again in a brown lounge suit.

But it was clean. I would make a clean start. All I had left now was a few clothes and the car. I drove to the station. In Pretoria I dumped my luggage, took the car to the garage and gave them instructions to sell it. The last thing I did was to borrow a spanner and unscrew the silver racehorse mascot I had on the bonnet – Montrose had given it to me. With the horse in my pocket I walked up the hill to catch my train. I have never driven a car since that morning. This decision could be psychological.

When I left the farm I never looked back at the house. The story of Lot's wife is a true one. It is dangerous to look back.

I took with me a four-skin leopard kaross I bought from Ivy's shop in Pretoria for £13 – today it would cost £300 or £400 – and two unframed Danielle Prints given me by Mrs Carlton Jones.

I had said goodbye to no one. Not even my cousin Bertie who had done so much for me. What could I have said that would make sense to anyone? So I ran for it like a thief in the night. I never even wrote later from London, and by the time I had some measure of success Bertie was dead and it was too late.

I sailed for England on a Union Castle boat, I forget which one. I had gone tourist because it was cheap, and discovered bugs in my bunk. I captured some, put them in a matchbox and took them to the captain, who, as always happens in such cases, suggested that I had brought them on board with me. This is the classic reply. The chief steward, however, said that until I had had bed bugs I had not lived and that it was one of those experiences which complete a knowledge of life. And he also told me how they had got there. On a previous trip they had carried a cargo of British workers for the new steel works, and the bugs had been brought on board by them. Anyway, the cabin was fumigated and I had no more trouble.

I made friends with a big Scotsman, James Campbell – Wee Jock, I called him – and we kept in touch for some years. I attempted to make love to a very beautiful little grass widow

'f in 1916, K.O.Y.L.I.

n Horshan, my first wife

The Farm, Constantia, South Africa

Myself and Eileen with Lumpy, Snowball and Snow Queen
at Thornycroft, 1927

who was leaving her husband and going home. She was part Jewish and tiny and I could pick her up with one hand, but it never went further than that.

There was a Communist on board, a man who, from what he said, was a party official, on his way to Holland. He was dark, thick-set, about fifty, and very highly educated. He talked to me a lot and gave introductions to Communist circles in London. What he said made a great deal of sense. There is, in fact, very little wrong with the Communist manifesto except that it has no bearing on the reality or the practice of Communism, any more than the Sermon on the Mount, a wonderful document, has on present-day Christianity. Many years later I heard at a Catholic retreat, where I was the only non-Catholic, many of the same principles expounded by a very able Jesuit priest, the main difference between the two being that one was religious and the other secular. Communism, though some people fail to realize it, is a secular religion with many dedicated members as ready to sacrifice themselves as there were Christians in Roman times. We, the anti-Communists, have no great ideal. Thousands do not believe in God. Thousands, even in England, have scarcely heard of Jesus Christ. Our anti-Communist attitude is negative, which puts us at a great disadvantage when opposed by a positive belief.

Later on in London I met some Communists and did not like them or their girl-friends. They were not particularly clean and dressed in high-necked blue sweaters and corduroy trousers. They pretended to be working men but their hands were soft, much softer than mine. They had never done a day's work in their lives. At the meeting I went to they were discussing the Italian invasion of Abyssinia, which in those days of innocence seemed particularly horrible. The bombing of villages, Ciano's boasts, atrocity stories.

It did not take me long to become disillusioned with Communism, particularly as they wished to control thought. Russia was perfect. The Party was always right. I did, however, see how bewildered men, tired of trying to think for themselves, abandoned themselves to the party line. Exactly the same reasons drew a similar type of intellectual to the Roman Catholic Church. In both cases thought and worry could be left to others. The priests and the commissars would take care of everything.

A vital factor ignored by all religions is the nature of man. Man is the most savage mammal on the face of the earth. The only animal that kills its own kind; rapes and kills the females and young of its species; that tortures. Man is fundamentally a killer only restrained by the fear of consequences. Man can only be controlled by force. The force of the law or of conscience implanted in him in childhood. This is another advantage Communist countries have. Their use of fear.

My politics have varied depending on my age and relative affluence from neo-Communist to Democratic Socialism and finally to the old-fashioned Tory line. As a young man I believed in Imperialism and the Pax Britannica. I still think the underdeveloped nations, particularly of Africa, will remain undeveloped and that the lot of the peasant mass was better when they were under Imperial rule than it is today.

Now I believe in no political system. Democracy has failed to maintain law and order. Communism is intolerable to people brought up in relative freedom. With the population explosion, pollution and the certainty of shortages of water, food, minerals and even air, chaos is almost certain within the lifetime of today's children. An ecological disaster of one or several kinds occurring simultaneously. Famine, war, pestilence, followed by a rule of force with a leader – 'Fuhrer' – and an élite. There will be no other way of dealing with the enormous half-educated masses that will continue to proliferate until checked by Draconian measures. George Orwell and Huxley will be found to have understated their cases. Only selected couples will be allowed to have children, and the way of life within one hundred years will be so utterly different as to be unrecognizable and bearing no relation to the world of today.

Politically and socially I have been influenced by various novels, such as *The Pools of Silence* by de Vere Stacpoole, dealing with the atrocities of the old Congo free state, *The Jungle* by Upton Sinclair, and the writing of Emile Zola.

It is hard to believe that Darwin's voyage in the *Beagle* took place only sixty-two years before my birth. At that time vast areas of the world were unexplored. Wild animals roamed in hundreds of thousands, even in millions, on the African veld. In the prairies of America the Indians were still fighting off the encroachment of the white settlers who were pushing West.

The American Civil War that ended slavery took place only a little more than one hundred years ago and their battles were fought with muzzle-loading cannon.

History seems to show that men cannot co-operate for long. I agree with Robert Ardrey (*African Genesis*) that man is by nature a killer and the most savage mammal on the face of the earth. His best brains from primeval times to the present day have always been devoted to the development of arms, going from the palaeolithic stone axe to the laser-guided bombs of today.

Man is the only animal that fights without cause. He has destroyed all the large carnivores that once threatened him, is now turning on himself and may, in so doing, endanger the existence of his species or even all life on the earth.

Contrary to the popular feeling, I consider germ warfare preferable to an atomic holocaust. Some people would prove immune and the animal and insect world would remain intact, the soil undefiled, and the general ecological balance on which life depends would remain unaltered.

I do not think human nature has changed much. If there were public executions today in London and Paris vast crowds would assemble to witness them.

In thinking of the past it occurs to me that the noisy world of today is without real sounds – identifiable sounds like the crow of a cock, the barking of a dog, or the music of a barrel-organ. It is also a world without smells, other than the smell of gasoline and its by-products. There are no other smells – good or bad. Women are deodorized and even men have been made afraid of the smell of their own clean sweat which is an aphrodisiac. People have forgotten that each part of the body has its own odour as people of different countries have their own language. For hundreds of thousands of years man has been conditioned to react to sound, scent and sight. These have all been taken from him and the effect of their loss is becoming psychologically apparent in the amount of mental illness in our cities. Man is not attuned to noisy concrete jungles or geometrically true walls and furniture, not attuned to the machine-made precision artifacts which accounts for the high price of hand-made articles and antiques.

On top of this skills are being lost as machines take over. A man loses his pride as an artisan when he works on an assembly line. The skill of the blacksmith and cabinet-maker, even the skills of vaudeville artists as circuses and music halls disappear. The modern child has nowhere to walk, nothing to look at, no animals to play with, no flowers to smell. His hands lie idle in his lap as he watches TV.

It is indeed possible that man has lost more than he has gained. In my childhood there was much misery but there was hope. What is there to hope for today? Only that tomorrow will be no worse than yesterday. Never have so many people been enslaved, so many displaced, and over us all hangs the threat of an atomic war. Even if it does not happen it still remains a possibility. The end of the world has never before been a possibility – something that could happen at the press of a button.

This is probably the cause of most juvenile delinquency, of hippies, of drug addicts and 'drop-outs'. The play *Stop the World I Want to Get Off* was well named for these young people who see no viable future.

CHAPTER 13

THE BROKEN MIRROR

I ARRIVED in England almost blind through falling asleep while sunbathing in the tropics. The sun had burnt through my eyelids and I was in great pain.

But this time it was for real, as they say in America. I had left Eileen in South Africa, sold everything up except the farm itself, and was on my own.

Before we went on shore when the mail came to the ship, there was a letter from my love saying she had married someone else. Had this letter reached me before I left Pretoria, I might have gone back to Eileen. Timing is important in life. But Monica had been the catalyst. If I had not fallen in love with her I would have remained married to Eileen and stayed on the farm. In a sense I owe her a lot, but it was a near-run thing and it would not have happened had Eileen returned to me after Montrose's death. So many ifs . . .

But now the mirror in which I had looked at myself for so long was broken. This was a new man. A very frightened man, filled with energy, fury and all the dangerous qualities of fear. My cap was high in the air. My world was filled with windmills. And I was alone.

I stayed in my mother's flat at Chatsworth Court in Curzon Street till my eyes were well. I might never have left London as far as my feelings were concerned. The ten-year African interlude had ceased to exist.

My mother, poor dear, thought I was mad. But I was getting used to people thinking I was mad, and she was much upset at my break with Eileen. But I had gone beyond the point of no return.

When I left Curzon Street I went to the Guards Club, which was still in Brook Street next to Claridges, and stayed there while I looked around.

Mrs Jameson, Pippin's mother, kept more or less open house for South Africans. She was the sister-in-law of the famous Dr

Jim – Leander Starr Jameson of the Raid after whom Pippin had been named. He had been a close associate of Cecil Rhodes.

Here, at a party in Walton Street, I met Una Long again, and she told me that she and the friend with whom she shared a flat wanted to move and would I like to take it? She only wanted £30 for the furniture, china, glass, cooking utensils – lock, stock and barrel, in fact. I said I'd come and look at it next day.

Also at the party were Dolly Barnard, a wealthy South African whose interest was ballet, and Pippin's sister Tish, a beautiful girl with the biggest brown eyes I have ever seen. They were almost too big. A little later she married a Polish Count with large estates which looked like a very good thing in those pre-war times.

Next day I went to look at Una's apartment, 23 South Hill Park Gardens in Hampstead. It consisted of two rooms, a bathroom and kitchen, with a lavatory on a half-landing. The furniture – two beds, tables, chests of drawers, chairs – was all unpainted deal from Gamages. The girls used one room as a bed-sitting-room and left the other, which faced north, empty. The bath had a temperamental geyser which always sounded as if it was going to blow up but never did, or 'had not so far', Una said. I took over the lease and the contents of the flat. The rent was £5 a month.

When I moved in I had the stairs below the toilet closed with a door which gave me complete privacy from the two floors below me. I bought four imitation Persian rugs at Harrods at £5 each. I had my two Danielle prints framed, and with my leopard-skin kaross on one of the beds soon had the place looking more homelike. I looked out on a small lawn and a very big pear tree.

It was all in the tradition. The writer, the garret – it was a garret apartment. It was the country boy come to town to make good. The only trouble was that I was no longer a boy. And write. Why should I be able to write? I only had Arnot's word that I might. I did not even have a typewriter till a girl-friend gave me one. All my life I have owed a great deal to women, but even she had no confidence that I would pull it off. She gave the typewriter with a kind of friendly irony that I understood. She was a wonderful woman, a person of great reality – and how few of them there are.

To make the decision to come to London at all I must have been suffering from a touch of madness. I had been ready to jump out of my skin almost literally, was being forced by the circumstances of my marriage, my love affair and the fact that having got the farm on its feet I was not ready to continue the routine of work. But there was a vital drive, I felt, though I had little reason beyond Arnot's slight encouragement, that I had a talent, and beyond this was an urge to make my name, and expunge my father's disgrace. There was a drive to take risks and extend myself all out, to measure myself against the great world as in the war. Ambition, fear, desire for change and adventure all had a part in my feelings – so did time. I was almost forty, soon it would be too late.

I had reached another dead end to my life which seemed to have been arranged in chapters, each relatively complete in itself – like the chapters of a book. A wonderful childhood in Paris in its hey-day – the Paris of Renoir, of Manet, of Rodin, of the *Belle Epoque* which, in fact, only ended in 1914. Then came my life at Hardelot and school in England. Then came the war period in which I was wounded and met Eileen. This was followed by the Garden of Eden episode back at Hardelot again. Then Africa and now this: London, with a broken marriage and the crazy dream of becoming a writer.

That my marriage failed was largely my fault. Eileen was a very good wife, kind, patient, brave in the face of adversity. She had come to Africa and lived in great discomfort without complaint till we had established ourselves. My fault for being so uxorious.

Impressions of this period are somewhat blurred. I met many interesting people, mostly the periphery of the artistic world. Painters, writers and their wives and friends. John Pudney, the poet. George du Thuit, an expert on Near-Eastern ceramics and the son-in-law of Matisse. Carol Mosley, sister-in-law of the British fascist Sir Oswald, with whom she had no sympathy. Teddy Wolfe, the South African painter, who had just come back from Mexico and had some magnificent pastels he had done in Tasco, one nude so strong that it looked like an oil. Richard Nevinson, the Cubist painter. I met Cyril Connolly at the Café Royal, where I also met Louise, one of Augustus John's models, and one of the most beautiful girls I have ever seen. A tall brunette who had her long fingernails painted sepia – the first time I had seen dark nails. One weekend I baby-sat for her cat in Charlotte Street. Another weekend I kept Carol Mosley's Skye terrier for her, a charming doormat of a dog.

Perhaps I wrote because not being fully educated I had no great feeling of inferiority. How could I have since I did not know what other people had done?

I think any success I may have had is due partly at least to my lack of formal education. If I had been to Oxford and known more about the work of great writers, I should probably have been too intimidated to enter the literary field.

Not that I regard myself as a writer in the Hemingway, Faulkner, Steinbeck class. I am a commercial writer in that I write for a living and make one. I am by my own definition a first-class second-class writer – neither highbrow nor lowbrow. I have never written anything I did not believe or anything signed with a pseudonym, except my first few short stories.

My formal education had ended when I was seventeen. I obtained a commission in the Yorkshire Light Infantry at that age and was at that time the youngest officer in the British Army. I was seventeen years and three months old. The war was an education. Farming, ranching, riding alone on the veld gave me plenty of time to think. I read a lot. In the war I had seen a great deal of death. Ranching I was struck by the miracle of life. We bred four hundred-odd calves a year.

This combination had a profound effect on me. Life and death. This was the key. To be born, to love, to die. All great events in which we are actually face to face with the miraculous.

The art of a country is the measure of its culture. A decadent culture cannot produce great art: a great culture cannot produce bad art. England was possibly at her greatest in the Elizabethan period. This was the time of Sir Francis Drake and Hawkins. It was also the time of Bacon, Shakespeare, Donne and Spencer.

France, in the first Empire, produced great writers, painters and architects.

Russia has produced very little artistically since the Revolution that compared with the arts that preceded it. That was the Russia of Tolstoy, Chekhov and Dostoievsky. The arts are therefore related to politics, to an expanding but at the same time secure society in which the artist can work without interruption.

With Louise I met a Russian writer who was ghost writing a

book about a circus. He collected match-boxes and round cheese cartons which he fastened to the wall with drawing pins. He said he had always been a collector, but now with no money he was reduced to this. I thought once a collector, always a collector. He appealed to me because I am a collector myself - of anything I fancy. Prints, pictures, bits of silver, chunks of mineralized stone. Anything cheap, pretty or interesting I can find.

I went to a lot of parties. An unattached man with a couple of good suits was always in demand. At one of them I met Allen Lane (later Sir Allen) and we became friends. He said one day: 'In a few months I shall be rich or broke.' He was starting the Penguin series and had put all his money into it. He had two brothers, one of whom collected pistols, and a sister called Margaret.

I had a curious little book I had written in a rather cheaply-clever way called *The Way of a Gentleman*. Allen Lane nearly took it for The Bodley Head but turned it down in the end.

I got down to writing. I read short stories – Somerset Maugham, de Maupassant, Michael Arlen. I broke them down to see how they got their effects. I read current magazines and wrote for eight hours a day. One thing I discovered quite soon was that though my contemporaries wrote beautifully, most of them had very little to say and took a long time saying it.

I picked up a few of my old friends. I met others. I was at this time leading a Dr Jekyll and Mr Hyde existence. A social life of parties properly dressed in a lounge suit or dinner-jacket, and my real life as a writer in which I wore old flannel trousers and an odd jacket. In this guise I made several friends, one a coal merchant who delivered his own sacks of coal. I helped him with his horse once, a big black shire mare with white stockings and heavily feathered legs. The coal cart was running back with her on a hill. I put a brick under the wheel. 'Too eager, that's what she is,' the merchant said. After that I often went to see him in his little coal yard with a stable and office attached.

At one pseudo-literary party I was introduced to a Negro writer. He came, I think, from Jamaica and turned out to be very nice. Negroes were not so thick on the ground then and it was quite a traumatic experience for me to shake his hand. This is fascinating to look back on and shows the effect of my conditioning. Later I was to have several coloured friends in America, including Katherine Dunham, the dancer, and the actor Canada Lee. I made friends too with some West African Negroes in the Gold Coast (Ghana) and Nigeria. However, I do not believe in enforced integration such as they have in America, or enforced segregation which is at present in force in the South African Republic, both being infringements on human liberty and the right of men to choose their own associates. I disagree with mixed marriages both on genetic and social grounds. Marriage is difficult enough as the divorce figures show without adding the further complications of colour and culture. Moreover, the position of half caste children is difficult since, as a rule, they are accepted by neither black nor white society. I naturally prefer to associate with my own kind as do most other people, including Negroes. I think the English policy of Negro and Indian immigrants will in the end prove to have been a mistake. Colour, unfortunately, is a uniform we cannot take off. Rights and wrongs do not enter into it as anyone who has seen sailors and soldiers fighting in a bar knows very well. No one knows who started the row or its cause, but if one soldier and one sailor start fighting it spreads at once and all the soldiers and sailors are at each other's throats.

I made friends with the fishmonger who taught me to clean and dress a crab. He smoked his own salmon in a little shed with a smudge of oak chips. Another friend was a man who had a radio shop. He had been in Canada and he told me a story about bear hunting which gave me the idea for *The Dancing Bear* that I wrote in London but did not sell for twenty years when Esquire bought it for $600.

My best friend at this time was Cam Lithgo – a retired naval commander. I was introduced to him by Arnot Robertson. He was also writing.

My cousin Mary Cloete, who had married Robin Byng (now Lord Strafford), was very kind to me. The Byngs lived nearby and often gave me a welcome dinner. Robin, who was in the radio business, gave me an old radio, my first since the crystal set I had been given by Billy Pride in South Africa.

And all the time I worked furiously, convinced that one day I should pull it off.

I had to.

CHAPTER 14

BREAKTHROUGH

I JOINED the Studio Club. It was then in a basement in Regent Street. Members were all on the fringes of the arts. Writers, poets, actors and painters of all three sexes. They served good cheap meals. We drank beer – whisky was for the rich – dispensed by Alfred, a Cockney barman of the old school. We played shove-halfpenny on a board. We talked. We said what we hoped to do. I hoped with the others, for none of us had done anything much yet.

I met some nice people there, one of them, Olga Lely, a painter, is still a friend. She had blonde hair with a page-boy cut, and I remember a brown dress with a cowl neck she wore. I was much attracted to her and recently when she wrote to me I discovered she had liked me too. I had been put off when I saw her picked up at the club by a friend in a Rolls. I could not compete with that sort of thing and gave up.

There was a life class at the club one night a week, and those of us who were interested paid five bob and drew nude girls with black and red conté. The girls in those days were paid 7s 6d an hour, so the classes showed a profit to the club. The girls were always quite pretty and of course had shaved their pubic hair. I have always thought women look better this way, like statues. The Greeks must have thought so too because though they indicate pubic hair on male statues they do not do so on the women. Many women in those days still had hair under their arms which some men find an excitant. Quite obviously, girls in bikinis must depilate themselves at least partially and so, of course, do showgirls who appear practically naked. Some Eastern women keep themselves completely hairless. There is a story about the wife of an air marshal who had served in the East being asked why she shaved. She was being prepared for an operation and the sister found the job already done. The reply became a classic. 'Because the Marshal likes it that way.'

I now met another girl and was soon living with her in a desultory sort of way. She was tall and slim, with fine eyes and lovely legs. She was attracted to me because I reminded her of someone else. The way I wore my hat, I think it was. Another woman, whom I loved later, liked me because I reminded her of her first lover. I have loved women because their eyebrows and eyes reminded me of my mother. I have liked women because their name was the same as that of another woman I have loved, and I have disliked women for the same reason. I have usually fallen in love at first sight. Something occurs to me as soon as I see them. A feeling of faintness, of actual sickness low down in the belly, in the genitals, though at first it has little to do with sex. It has to do with fear, with something that psychologists describe as a castration complex. It is the same feeling I get when I look over a high cliff or over the top of a skyscraper. It is the fear that here is someone who, if she chooses to exert her strength, will have power over me, over those parts of me I am afraid to give away. I think men, at least men like me, fear women because of the power they have. Here are the handcuffs, here is the harness, the chains of the galley slave. This lovely stranger holds them in her red-tipped fingers, in her painted mouth, in the long lashes that fall over her cheeks as she drops her eyes. For it is with her eyes that a woman gives her body and demands yours in return. In my life I have only slept with eleven women and have been attracted to perhaps fifty others. I have known men who have slept with hundreds – Casanovas – but for them it is a form of sport. They remained ignorant of the essential things; of love, which is not the act. The act that can be performed by any young man who is personable with any reasonably good-looking young woman, given proximity, time, place and circumstances, mixed in the correct proportions. This is a function which we share, not only with all mammals but with all living things, and beyond the relief from physiological strain it serves no purpose but that of involuntary increase. Love is something quite different. It is an act of confidence, of trust. To be important, the undressing, the nakedness, must be spiritual as well as physical. But I had to learn a lot about love. It still remains a profound mystery, and is the basis of every great story in the world.

And stories were now my concern. I had plenty to say. I had merely to learn to say it. Others could write. But they had not lived. I had lived – a lot, really, for my age – but I could not write. Therefore I must learn. The way to write is to write. Sinclair Lewis described genius as the application of the seat of the pants to the seat of the chair. I wore out some pants.

And everybody laughed at me. I must have been funny.

At one party I remember Marcelle Quenell, a most beautiful fair girl dressed in black, the wife of the critic, who was at that time modelling at a dress shop in Mayfair, and talked the most beautiful French, having been educated at a convent in Brussels, asking me what I did.

'I write,' I said.

'Have you sold anything?' she asked.

I said, 'No.'

'And you expect to make a living by it?' She said, 'My father who is a professor has been writing for years and has never had anything published.'

How mad I must have sounded. I had not been to a university. I could not even spell. I can't spell now. When I was in America my mother used to send my letters back marked with red ink and corrected like a schoolboy's exercise book. She never understood how I could succeed, even after I had, if I could not spell.

To her the two were synonymous, though I told her thousands of girls who take secretarial courses can spell but they cannot write. Words are just symbols. Even Shakespeare couldn't spell.

So I wrote, bad spelling and all, and as I could not afford a secretary, I used a dictionary.

Meanwhile finances were a difficulty. I had my pension of twelve pounds a month and the rent of my farm – which by great good fortune had been rented to two maiden ladies who liked the view and my garden – for a hundred a year. I had the interest on the two thousand pounds I had invested, that brought in another hundred, but I had to send money to Eileen, and to live myself.

I did my own cooking at night. For lunch I always had a roll eaten dry with cheese, and a bottle of milk, that I ate on Parliament Hill or the Heath. The flat was kept clean by a youngish and not bad-looking charwoman whom I had taken over from Una. She came every second day, always arriving, as far as I could see, when I was changing. She wore very short skirts and low blouses, but when I did nothing about it – a woman scorned – she gave notice and I got an older woman.

Unable to live without animals, I bought myself some mice. A white one called Jacobs after WW whom I had met, introduced by his daughter, a red one that I named Arnot, and a black, very intelligent mouse that I named in Michael Arlen's honour. I bought them at Gamages where I had bought mice as a boy, took them home in a carton and turned them loose. They knew meal-times and would turn up whenever I was having something to eat. They were a very loose lot of mice and soon were having affairs with the wild mice who, when they left the safety of their holes in the wainscotting to come and watch the tame mice eat in the kitchen, would go mad with frustration and beat the floor with their tails. People in the apartments below kept bringing me vari-coloured mice, saying had I lost any? Were they my mice? I said yes, they had escaped. I did not dare say I had turned them loose. One mouse, a very small yellow one, came every night to drink out of the glass of milk I took to bed with me. She would stand up and drink from it, and if it was not full enough would wait till I tipped it for her. She was ill one day, and as I could not leave her I took her out to lunch with me. And she died in my palm while I was talking to the very pretty woman whose guest I was at the Lansdowne Club.

In the end people began to complain, saying they could not keep coming upstairs holding a mouse by the tail, and I had to destroy them, which I did by putting them in a big bread bin and gassing them in my London Gas Coal and Light Company's oven. I had taken over this stove and was buying it on the instalment plan. It had the best griller for steaks and chops I have ever come across.

It is one thing to have a lot of stories written and another to sell them. I had the stories and I had a fine collection of rejection slips printed on white or green paper – they were never pink – that I pasted on the wall of my garret-bed-sitting-work-room. It was all very traditional, a theatrical set, a *mise en scene* of a writer's home. Typewriter, paper, paper clips, pens, pencils and stacks of rejected manuscripts.

I realized that to get anywhere I had to have an agent, but until you are established an agent is hard to get, and when you are established you can, if you have that kind of nature, do without one, though personally I feel they earn their ten per cent by getting better prices than one would oneself, and they know where to send the material. Publishers feel that a manuscript sent to them in an agent's jacket must be a commercial possibility. It has at least been read by competent readers who would not send out anything that was really rubbish. It is hard for beginners to realize that publishers want to publish and are always looking for something good. Every manuscript is read or at least looked through to sort the chaff from the wheat.

I feel an agent is essential to a writer. They bear the same relation to him as a trainer to a racehorse. They train him, they enter him, they won't let him run in a race that is beyond his strength.

At last I had some good fortune. At a literary party I met a lady who had two friends who were agents. They had an office in Piccadilly near Hatchards. She gave me an introduction and I went to see them. They said they would take me on and I left some stuff with them. Eventually they sold a story to the *Daily Express* for six guineas, and *Bad Penny* was published on July 19, 1935. A red-letter day. I got eight guineas for it. A breakthrough. If I'd done it once I could do it again, and I worked with renewed ardour.

It was not a good story, all about Lords and Ladies and Berkeley Square, and was written in the style of Michael Arlen after whom I had named one of my mice, the dark, Armenian-looking chap, very handsome with splendid whiskers. Later when I met Michael Arlen I told him about it and expressed my gratitude. His style was not hard to copy and at one time I admired it.

I left my lady agents because they sold nothing else, would not criticize my work or tell me what was wrong with it.

I then fell in with a lady who worked on the *Daily Herald*. I told her I had sold a story called *Bad Penny* under my pen name of Peter Lawrence. She said, 'Send me the stories and I'll see what I can do.' She did a lot. Through her I sold four more stories. *Daily Herald* would not have bought any of my stuff if it had been bad, but it helped having someone on the editorial staff to give it a push. By this time I had written a hundred-odd stories and was beginning to learn. I wrote a novel called *They Said* – a love story set on my African farm. Gollancz saw it and said it had too many commas; he gave me the name of someone who would take them out. This he did for a fee of £30 and it was still no good, so I might as well have left the commas in without the dabs of white paint that now covered them.

I started on a novel about the Great Trek. This had been at Spencer Curtis Brown's suggestion. He said, 'Write about something you know about,' confirming what Morna Stuart had told me previously. Curtis Brown were now my agents. I had been recommended to them by Arthur Calder Marshall, one of their writers. He had a beautiful wife, Ara, who wore her long golden hair loose down her back like Alice in Wonderland. This is the fashion today but that was the first time I had seen it.

All this time I was practically celibate. I had to work and had no time for women. I needed all my energy to write.

I met a Mrs Harmsworth who was married to one of the publisher's sons. A tiny, very beautiful and charming woman, the daughter of a French colonel and an Indo-Chinese woman. I used to meet her sometimes in Green Park and walk with her and her dachshund, Otto, who had a passion for Alsatians. She had a perfection which I was only to find again when, many years later, we went to the Orient. I am sure that had I gone to the Far East as a young bachelor I should never have returned, so much did I admire the looks of the women and the general atmosphere of flowers, temples, pagodas, water buffalo, palms and rice paddies. The wonderful scents of frangipani and jasmine mixed with wood smoke and urine. This was indeed a magic world before it was riven by the impact of war and Western technology.

I have never understood men not being moved by a beautiful girl. No wonder the church was so prejudiced against them, for they would be easy to worship. The fertility and phallic cults were the first religions. They linger on vestigially in Europe but actively in Africa and the East. Women, love, birth and death are the forces, the mysteries that not only concern but make a writer. Feminine beauty is nature's trick, the flower and the bee trick, to draw a man and woman together in the sex act. If this were unpleasant the human race would soon cease to exist. By and large, as women always say, men only want one thing. They are driven to it, and women, even if they deny it, want it too, but their need is less urgent.

This is what I thought about. Couples, couples everywhere – outside, inside houses. This was the life force. Men wanted success, but a by-product of success was the pick of the women. In a way this was a form of Darwinian selection. In theory the most successful men would produce children from the pick of the women. This of course does not work except among the Jews, where for a thousand years the daughter of a rich merchant has married a rabbi, thus producing the most intelligent race in the world. Curiously enough, the Christian world till the late Middle Ages sterilized their élite by insisting on monastic celibacy, as the Catholics still do today.

Thoughts, speculations, people. I was still meeting people, filtering ideas, moving on the periphery of a number of circles. I used to go to the Wheatsheaf, to the Bunch of Grapes for cider, to the Antelope for very heavy Coldstream beer. I ate cheap curry meals at the Delhi restaurant in the Tottenham Court Road, Chinese meals in Soho, French meals at Le Diner Français in Old Compton Street, and at pubs where meat, two veg and pudding used to cost 1s 6d. 1s 6d was about my mark.

One person introduced me to another. I had a letter to Eddie Marsh (Sir Edward later) who had the first collection of modern art I had ever seen. The pictures touched each other so no wall was visible, and very strange I thought them.

I took a correspondence course in writing. People may laugh at correspondence courses, but they can be very valuable and I learnt a lot from mine.

I also took a correspondence course in textile design which interested me. I learnt to do the repeats of patterns such as appear on window curtains and cretonnes. I was interested in design. I designed a white evening dress with black panels on the side for stout women. Many years later I saw a photograph of the Queen Mother in a dress like mine.

For story ideas I listened to people talking and went to the South Kensington Museum of Natural History and looked about till some animal took my fancy. I wrote a story about a white tiger and one about a Spanish fighting bull, both of which I sold to the *Daily Herald*, all under the name of Peter Lawrence. I did not want to use my own name till I wrote better.

Now that I had some published work, even if they were only newspaper stories, I was eligible for the Savage Club. My brother

Ronald got a friend who was a member to put me up and, duly seconded, I was elected a Savage. I bought a Savage tie at once. It was black and pale blue like an old Etonian tie, except every second stripe was pale yellow.

CHAPTER 15

THE LAST PHASE

In these few years while I was living in a state of hope, despair and marital confusion, great events were taking place in the world.

The Italians had taken Abyssinia, Hitler had built his concentration camps and his ovens. The Spanish Civil War was in full swing, with one's friends split into anti- and pro-Franco groups. Tom Garland, who lived in the flat below me, joined the International Brigade, so did George Orwell. I had other friends fighting with Franco. It was difficult to follow what was going on, as according to what newspapers one read the loyalists were called either government forces or reds or rebels, while Franco's Fascists were called loyalists or anti-Communists. It was a horrible war of atrocities and counter atrocities, an arena where the Germans blooded their young officers and tried out weapons and tactics for a more serious conflict. I astonished the local paper shop by taking both *The Times* and *Daily Worker*, feeling that the truth was to be found somewhere between the two.

The King, Edward VIII, involved with the American divorcee Mrs Wally Simpson, abdicated, and his brother King George VI was crowned.

London was ablaze with flags – they hung like heraldic laundry from every window.

But none of this affected me, sunk as I was in my own affairs in a one-man fight for survival, which now turned in my favour. My luck that had carried me through the war had not deserted me.

When Gollancz turned down *They Said* I gave it to Curtis Brown to see what they could do with it. They sent it to Heinemann who called me up and said they would like to see me. I presented myself in a state of great excitement. At last someone was interested.

Charlie Evans greeted me in his office with the news that he would take the book.

This was really something. To have a book accepted by an important publisher.

Mr Evans was, however, a little worried about libel. *They Said* was partly true, based on a love story that had taken place at Constantia where two of my unmarried friends came almost every second weekend and climbed in through each other's windows. They were very annoyed when I fly-netted the spare room because that made it more difficult for them. I assured Mr Evans there was no libel, and then, going downstairs, was called into his son Dwye's office who, in the course of conversation said I would be interested as a South African to know that Francis Brett Young was writing a story of the Great Boer Trek, about which there had never been a novel. Now came the decision. The moment of truth. I, too, had begun a book about the Great Boer Trek which I called *Turning Wheels*. Both Morna Stuart and Spencer Curtis Brown said people liked factual novels. 'You know about Africa, why not write an African romance?' I had done about ten thousand words when Heinemann accepted *They Said*. Fortunately I had not mentioned the other book.

Obviously the same publishing house could not publish two similar stories. So next day I called up Heinemann's and said I wanted an interview. Mr Evans saw me that afternoon and I told him I would withdraw my novel as I had decided that, after all, it was libellous. He seemed quite relieved and I went home.

Now I really had to work. It was a race with time. Sometimes I worked for twelve hours without stopping. This had been a difficult thing to do – to get such a break and throw it away. On the other hand it was perhaps an even greater break to find out that someone else was writing the same book.

A couple of months later Arnot, who was helping me with *Turning Wheels*, showed what I had written to Billy Collins (now Sir William), the publisher. He took me to lunch at the Carlton Grill and told me he would give me a contract on what I had already done – some 50,000 words. This took my breath away. Then Arnot showed the book to Ferris Greenslet of the Houghton Mifflin Company in Boston. He was in England looking for books. He, too, accepted it, told me to hurry with it and when it was done to come to the United States to promote it. Speaking of books, and he was one of the most famous editors in America, he said, 'There is only one test of a book, does it bleed if you prick it?' Evidently *Turning Wheels* bled.

This double success on an unfinished book flabbergasted me. I returned to my desk to work as I had never worked before, knowing that Francis Brett Young was writing the same book in so much as it too was a story of the Great Boer Trek from the Cape of Good Hope into the wilderness of the north, a thousand miles away.

I had one advantage. Brett Young was an established and successful writer whereas I was neither, but I knew the race was on and he did not. A new world had opened to me. I had money – both publishers had given me an advance – and I was going to America. The land of opportunity. A few more months and the book would be finished.

At this moment Eileen came back to me and we tried to iron things out. My mother gave her some bright red material which she had made into a skirt. Joy van der Byl gave her four ermine skins which I had made into a little round cap for her. There were no rows, we were neither of us quarrelsome, but there was no real communication. We each went our own way. Eileen took a course in beauty culture and built up a small practice with friends and friends of friends. I just worked on.

When Eileen had joined me in the flat my current romance ended, as Muriel had scruples about a married man who was living with his wife, so I found another lady, a very attractive married blonde, whom I used to meet in various parts of London and go into the country with her in her car. She had that peculiar softness of flesh that some blondes have. I was ready to run away with her, but she only wanted to go just so far.

Arnot came to my help again. Two or three times a week I went to her apartment at 96 Heath Street, within easy walking distance, and read her what I had written. She made great changes in the book. She cut out one block of twenty-five thousand words. She destroyed a character I had who resembled Ryder Haggard's Umslopogas, the big Zulu. I changed him into Rinkals, a small wizened witch doctor.

I worked day and night. I hardly stopped to eat. *Turning Wheels* had been accepted by two great publishers, but there was still the race. I must win it. I must finish before Brett Young. At the end I had no idea how to finish the book, so I killed the lot. Thank God I left a baby, because I was to need him later on. I won, but it was a neck-and-neck finish and we were reviewed together. It was a coincidence and a great one – that a subject that had never been touched in fiction before should be chosen by two novelists simultaneously.

That is one side of those few months, but there were other more personal facets. Eileen and I were, as they say, leading our own lives, and I actually finished the book at the Guards Club, having left her again, the situation having become impossible. While she was out for the day I got Egan Plesch, my mother's Hungarian doctor who had become a great friend, to come and fetch me in his car. I took a couple of suitcases and my leopard kaross which had become a kind of fetish, my last link with Africa. I left no letter. No explanation. Eileen tried to get in touch with me but I avoided her and did not answer her letters. This was the end. A characteristic running out of a situation on my part.

I was going to America and I was going alone. I was fitted for two new suits by Humphrey & Crook in the Haymarket. I bought three very nice second-hand suit cases from Benjamin in Mayfair, and a most beautiful vicuna overcoat, satin lined, from Moss Bros. I was all set to go.

While I still had my mice, I had one rather amusing incident with a very nice white one that I had in my pocket when I was at George Orwell's bookshop, looking at some second-hand books I wanted but could not afford. It got out of my pocket and started running about on the floor. A woman screamed. Orwell said: 'What's that? Whose mouse is that?'

'Mine,' I said, as I picked her up and put her back in my pocket. That was before Orwell went to Spain and became disillusioned there. Like myself, he was at that time very Left, and had been much upset by the Abyssinian business.

Hampstead was filled with Leftist intellectuals. I knew a lot of them. We used to meet and go to the Everyman Cinema where they showed advanced and foreign films.

A doctor, Tom Garland, lived in the apartment below me. He attended to the Black Cat cigarette factory. He had a charming wife, a sculptress, who had shown in the Salon. I saw quite a lot of them and through them met a German Communist who had escaped from a concentration camp. It was from him that I first heard of the horrors that were being perpetrated in Germany.

In the interval before I left Eileen again, I invented something that could have made my fortune if I had had the sense to patent it. A brassiere. Watching her dress one day I thought her breasts would look better if raised, so getting a piece of material and a saucer I cut two circles. Then I cut a section out of each as if they were pies and sewed them up to form cones. These I joined to a short piece of material. On the outside of the cones I put two more pieces and tapes to fasten at the back. It worked perfectly when Eileen put it on. I had learnt to sew as a child so had no problems.

I now met another woman, one of the most charming I have known, a *jolie laide*, which to me is preferable to a real beauty, with a wonderful figure. I was very happy with her. How few women are both attractive and kind. Pictures – there are plenty that I have left out. I think in pictures. I see the moment when beauty is suddenly crystallized. One such instant was in Richmond Park with my friend where we saw a doe with a small fawn standing beneath a thorn tree white with flowers – a magic moment. Ideas like this are now considered sentimental.

Sometimes we dined at a little place on the embankment with the light of candles, the only illumination, on her fair hair.

I went to the Café Royal quite a lot. I had gone there during the war years, though it was all changed now. The women's orchestra with its red-headed conductress had gone and the building was altered, the upper floor with its private rooms was now a gallery, but there were still interesting people to be met there.

I was not in things but on the edge of them. I met John Grierson who made the first important documentary. I met Bob Everitt, who won the Grand National on Easter Hero and ran an aerial taxi service. I moved on that strange periphery where the arts touch the aristocracy at one point and merge into the demi-monde at the other.

This was the last phase of our old civilization. Decadent it may have been – people said it was – although the Battle of Britain seems to refute the charge, but interesting and varied, brilliant. At parties one met all sorts of people – peers, admirals, generals, actors, actresses, journalists, writers, painters, dress designers, models and mannequins, gentlemen riders, trainers, masters of hounds, chorus girls, kept women, barristers, judges, men who had fought with Franco and men who had fought against him. The world was beginning to fragment, to break into the two halves of left and right. I was caught in the middle with all my social friends pro-Franco and all my intellectual friends against him. There were refugees, White Russians, Germans, Spaniards, the pick and the riff-raff of Europe, all milling round with cocktail glasses in their hands in the drawing-rooms of London.

At one time during this period I almost joined the mounted police as a special constable. I think I was so lost that I wanted to wear uniform again, and of course there were the horses. All I had to do was to buy a uniform and I would get a horse again. The mounted police at that time were very active, as there were many clashes between the Communists and Oswald Mosley's British Fascists. I often listened to both sides speaking on the Heath, which was where, talking to a special constable, I learnt how to join the force. I was turned down on account of my wounds, but it is hard to believe now that I wanted to be employed in mounted baton charges against a crowd. I think it was a combination of the horses and uniform. To someone who has been brought up a soldier there is a kind of security in a uniform. I also wanted an impersonal break in my routine.

Later, when I was in London in the early part of the war, I was very much afraid of what would happen to me as a civilian. I had no experience of crisis alone.

These political scuffles were somewhat brutal, with a lot of kicking and strong arm stuff. One weapon used could never be found, since there was no weapon. A thick pencil was held in the hand and a penny between each finger. This made a most savage knuckle-duster that inflicted frightful wounds on the face, but could be dropped and would resolve itself into its harmless component parts as soon as it was allowed to fall.

When things had been at their worst, before I had sold *Turning Wheels*, my mother stepped into the financial breach and came up with a job that she had obtained through some friend of a friend. I had the offer of travelling for a gin distillery – Gilbeys, I think, or some other well-known brand. Three hundred a year, a car, and commission on sales. It meant going round the public houses and persuading them that this gin was better – stronger, purer, more delectable – than any other sort. She was much upset when I turned it down. She had been to a lot of trouble, she said. But so had I. My foot was all ready on the ladder. I had even scaled a few rungs, the first and the worst, the most fragile which would scarcely bear my weight.

One Christmas I got an interesting job. I was Master of Ceremonies at the Washington Hotel in Curzon Street – a pound a day, all found, and free drinks. I drank a lot. I met a pretty woman there, the grass widow of an admiral. She had persuaded him to take a foreign appointment and to leave her at home. I think it was the China Station – in the East at any rate – she pretended she could not stand the climate. She was a redhead with a pencil face. Her face all came together into a point, like the mask of a fox, a pretty vixen. We had a mild flirtation and danced together. I stood her some of my free drinks – champagne cocktails.

Those few years are blurred in my mind. I do not really remember what I did with Eileen, and what I did alone. I do not remember precisely on which trip home things happened. But I was distraught with love, deranged, at the same time miserable and unbelievably keyed up. My mind was in a turmoil of attempted creation. I can only shake the kaleidoscope of memory and describe the pictures. Some come without sequence, in an odd concatenation. When I was stuck writing, I would go to Lyons Corner House and sit right under the orchestra with a pencil and block. I like to work with loud music provided it has a beat or rhythm. I felt it occupied my mind and allowed my unconscious to function in freedom. I thought about my book all the time, writing it as it was in my head. Sentences, paragraphs. With music they came out unhampered by worries about Eileen or money.

I would go for long rides on the top of a bus. I would go to the Regent Palace Hotel and pick up girls who had gone there for that purpose, or to the Criterion Brasserie and then, after having passed the time of day with them, unpick them. I remember seeing one beautiful Eurasian dancer there, tall, apparently as boneless as a filleted sole.

I became mixed up in the film business. I acted in a film that Arnot was making, a documentary about the Thames which we sailed in a Thames barge. These were interesting boats because instead of a keel which would prevent them going in shallow water they had on each side a kind of big fin which they could lower into the water.

I photographed very well and asked Egon Plesch to introduce me to Korda whom he knew. But he refused because he thought the film business was not for me. I wanted to try it because I suppose, like so many other people, I am an exhibitionist in spite of being extremely shy, and I knew a film career would put me in close contact with a lot of beautiful girls.

Henry Turner, Arnot's husband, was doing the photography of the Thames picture and she had written the script. We worked on weekends, and on one of them stayed at a very nice inn on the water's edge. I was given the daughter's room and she moved in with her mother for the night. She was a pretty girl and her wardrobe was full of very nice day and evening dresses. I was kept awake all night by bed bugs. This surprised me because they seemed such nice clean people. It just showed one could not go by appearances.

At the club I met my friend Luxmore Ball of the Welsh Guards again. He asked me if I'd like to do some film work as an extra at three guineas a day. I jumped at it and he introduced me to the Bolton Agency which had an office in Soho just behind the Regent Palace Hotel. The front part was a large room with chairs, tables and sofas which the clients used as a kind of club. One could buy sandwiches there and I think beer.

I was introduced and asked questions.

What could I do?

I said, 'Ride, shoot, talk French.'

I was asked what clothes I had.

I said, 'Two good lounge suits, a dinner-jacket and tails.'

I was told that everything was in order and all I had to do was to supply them with some stills. Head and shoulders. I did this and soon got some work.

I had to get up at five to get to the studio by seven. London at this early hour was very interesting, empty, undefiled by traffic or people. I travelled by bus and tube to various studios. I met a lovely blonde extra there who said she liked dogs and next time she came she'd bring a picture of her dog to show me. Next day she brought it. It was a 'Diana of the Uplands' job with the sun in her golden hair and the dog, a toy terrier, hardly visible, in her arms. But it was all experience, all interesting.

I also met on several occasions a man whose name I have forgotten but that I got on with, and we would have sandwiches and tea together. Then one day he told me he was shacking up with a lady trick-cyclist. I never saw him again and wondered what she had done to him.

In one film where I was taking the part of a croupier – it was a talking part, I said: '*Faites vos jeux*' and '*Rien ne va plus*' – I had a run in with Tom Walls who was producing his own films. He was being very rude to a charming, rather old lady, who had fluffed her lines. When I could stand it no longer I stood up and said: 'Excuse me, sir, if you will permit me to take Mrs Patten (I think that was her name) to the restaurant and give her a cup of tea, I'm sure she will be all right.' She was. It was no good shouting at her. But I got a black mark at the agency and no more work.

I used to go to the Bunch of Grapes in Knightsbridge, drink draught cider and visit Dolly Barnard, who had a house in Yeoman's Row. It had a brilliant canary yellow front door and was so haunted that she had to get a priest to come and exorcise it. She said he paid particular attention to the corners of the room. I had no idea ghosts liked corners. It is interesting that the Roman Catholic Church still takes haunting seriously and makes provision for dealing with ghosts.

Dolly certainly took it seriously because she said the house before it had been exorcised was impossible to live in. There were bangs and rattles, doors opened all by themselves, objects were moved – all in the classic manner of correct haunting. By a curious coincidence the photographer who took the stills that the Bolton Agency had required turned out to be her brother.

I went to picture exhibitions, to exhibitions of sculpture. I saw Epstein's heroic alabaster, Adam, and was shaken by its power. A nude male with a horizontal penis and the weight of the world on his shoulders. He was always surrounded by suburban housewives who muttered to each other and said: 'Just fancy! How disgusting!'

On Sundays I went to Tattersalls to see the horses in their stalls and boxes – just to smell horses again. On Mondays I went to see them sold and guess the price they would fetch.

I went with my mother to the White Horse Inn at Shepherds Market, where we had splendid English cooking – boiled beef and carrots with dumplings and things like that. I found a shop that specialized in ladies' handmade belts. I have never seen anything more beautiful than some that they made. I remember one – wide, thick white suède, spotted with big imitation jewels.

At one gallery I went to there was a small Picasso about 12 by 14 of a bull fight. The bull had six heads, the matador two or three. The whole effect was one of action and confusion. The price, I think, was three hundred guineas. I often wonder what it is worth today.

I went up to Scotland to stay with George Buchanan at Gask, and worked on *Turning Wheels* there. I went grouse shooting with the house party and never hit a bird. Later, when we were rough shooting, I killed every hare and rabbit that we put up. A colonel in the Black Watch, who was on my right, said, 'You're good with rabbits, Cloete.' 'Yes, sir,' I said, 'rabbits and lions, anything that does not leave the ground.' Of course I had never shot a lion, but I didn't tell him so.

Buck, as the laird, had a gallery with curtains at the back of the kirk. So that although we all had to go to church because it was expected of us, there was no need to pay any attention to what was going on. The gallery even had a fireplace.

Buck had just married a very charming American wife called Margaret and they had continual arguments about the central heating which she had installed against his will. He kept opening the windows and she kept closing them. He said the heat spoilt his books and she said to hell with the books. She was cold. She was the first American I had known since I was a boy, and I was astonished at the freedom of her conversation about sex. I had read Freud but had no idea people talked about oedipus and electra complexes and similar erotic matters. When I told her I was going to America she gave me introductions to some friends there.

George did petit point embroidery in the evenings, and one occasion spent two hours at it only to find he had sewn the long white hairs of his best dress sporran into it. He had made a good job of it too, since every thread was pulled tight. Margaret was always being upset at the careless way he sat with, I suppose, some reason as, like all true Scotsmen, he wore nothing under his kilt. I was amused to compare the way the Highland colonel and civilians wore their kilts. The soldiers swung them as they walked as provocatively as tarts, and made the civilians look like a lot of housewives.

I saw my first capercailzie. They had been re-introduced from Scandinavia, and I was astonished at how silently these great birds flew through the larch and pine woods – as silently as woodcock.

I was having a bit of trouble at that time with abscesses under both arms, which were very painful, but I said nothing about them, so when George asked me to try a new fire escape he had just had installed for the servants, I could not get out of it. This device was a strong thin rope which revolved round a drum. The weight of the man going down acted automatically as a break. The bad part for me was the belt that went under the arms, so I was suspended by my boils as soon as I stepped out into space from the fourth-floor window. It worked very nicely and I only put my foot through one window on the way down.

I had one curious experience with a charming girl who turned out to be a Roman Catholic, and though she was quite ready to go to bed with me refused to have anything to do with a contraceptive, which left me helpless and impotent. I was terrified of the idea of a child. I had previously sheered off from a very attractive girl who said one day that she would like to give me a son – as if it was a wonderful present.

I have always been attracted to the pomp and ceremony of the Roman Catholic religion, to its roots in the pagan past from which it drew so much. But apart from not being religious, the things that put me against it were its attitude to divorce, contraception and its refusal to accept any but the most ordinary method of making love. Apparently fornication was not a serious sin but the use of contraceptives was unforgiveable.

I believe that the Pope could have stopped the First World War by excommunicating those who fought. Almost the whole of the Nazi hierarchy and most of the German army were Roman Catholics, but the Church was too afraid of Communism to intervene; yet by Pope Paul VI's encyclical of July 1968 in which he forbade the use of contraceptive devices, he created the massive overpopulation of Latin-America, opening the doors to Communism there, since hunger is the father of revolution.

I spent a week with Bunny Small at his caravan in Dorsetshire near Corfe Castle. He had often stayed with us in Africa. It was a real gipsy job, beautifully painted with scrolls and flowers, set up in a field near a farm from which we bought our milk, eggs and vegetables. It had two bunks with a table between them and a tiny galley with an oil stove. I was very happy with him. He painted all day and I got on with my book. We went to see friends of his about five miles away. They had a magnificent grey stallion they had bought from a bull fighter in Portugal. I asked if I could come back next day and make a drawing of him, which I did, and was fairly pleased with the result.

Bunny had a young son at Dartington Hall in Devon. I went down there with him and stayed a few days. This was a beautiful property, a stately home that had been brought back from a near ruin to its pristine grandeur. It was one of the first co-educational boarding-schools in England and very liberal in outlook, boys and girls going about together as they pleased.

They pressed a very nice cider and sold it in small barrels with a stand to hold them. When I got back to Hampstead I ordered one and so had draught cider on tap in my kitchen.

I was enchanted with Devonshire. The rich red earth, the voluptuously foliaged trees, the sunken lanes where the banks were a tapestry of wild flowers.

I saw a magnificent sight here. An enormous bay shire stallion being led through a lane by a small wizened groom. He was at stud and visited farmers who had mares to be served. A splendid seventeen-hand beast dressed for a wedding with red ribbon plaited into his mane and tail. This glory has gone from the earth. The tractor has replaced the splendid stallions and the flowery banks have been purified with weed killer.

But seeing him I have never forgotten him in his glory. To see him was to understand the ancient cults of stallion and bull which epitomize masculine power and beauty.

I had met Morna Stuart who was later to influence me a lot in a rather curious manner. One day I was lunching with Dolly Barnard and when we had finished coffee she said she was going to see Harry Jonas, a painter. Did I want to come?

I said, 'Yes.' I liked artists and studios.

Jonas's studio was in Thackeray House, a very old building in Maple Street, off Charlotte Street near Fitzroy Square. It had, I found out later, belonged at various times to such famous men as Whistler, Sickert and Thackeray. It did not appear to have been cleaned since their time and seemed to be held together with cobwebs, but its atmosphere was as thick as the dust that lay like hoar-frost over everything except the working area. The dirty great north window was leaded and filtered a soft light over the scene. Jonas, a handsome dark man, greeted us, his left hand full of brushes. He was painting the portrait of a beautiful dark olive-skinned girl. Her black hair was shoulder length. Behind her was dark blue sky and a white trellis.

We sat as he went on working to catch the last of the light till Dolly decided it was time to go. I said I would wait and let her go alone. She did not take this very kindly but I wanted to meet the girl. I took her home in a taxi to a large basement apartment in Exhibition Road where she lived with her husband, a barrister, and her young son. Her name was Morna Stuart and she worked for the BBC and did freelance writing on the side. She had been at Oxford and was highly educated and sophisticated. She was born in India in the days of the Raj which were so soon to come to an end though we did not know it then. Morna was small, slight, exotic and brilliant. She asked me to her parties which I enjoyed, though her friends – all writers, artists or in the theatre – intimidated me. I often called on her and saw her alone. I liked to talk to her and look at her. I did no more. I was still too shy and diffident, too impressed by her intellectual qualities to approach her. I was afraid of her and now, forty years later, she says she was afraid of me. I wrote to her saying what I could do. Build a house, kill, dress and cook a buck, put up a fence, build a dam. But all this had seemed irrelevant in this intellectual society where people talked of books, pictures and films I had never even heard of. Where everyone had travelled – they talked of Italy and Sweden. Morna said I stood out from them as something real. I did not know this. All I knew was that I stood out.

At one of her parties I did meet a girl who attracted me. Very small with a perfect figure wearing a silk evening dress of Hunting Stuart Tartan which looked as if she had been poured into it. Her name was Bobby and she came out to Hampstead several times for tea or drinks and I would take her to some cheap place for dinner. That affair could have gone the whole way, but she was not interested in my writing and put me off by telling me how she had aborted herself and flushed the foetus down the toilet. I was at this time very highly strung and sex-starved but did not really want to become involved with a woman. I was taking a terrific gamble, one that no one thought I should pull off, and could not afford to get sidetracked.

I had no help, no one except Arnot believed in me. I was offered various not very good jobs, apart from selling gin, which I turned down.

I believed in myself. I knew there was something in me trying to burst out and so I worked on, putting all I had into it.

There are two ways to succeed at a time like this. Friends who believe in you and help you or, as in my case, a kind of furious 'God damn it, I'll show you'. The other ingredient was luck and I had always been lucky.

There were other girls. I took them for walks on the Heath, to the pictures, to cheap lunches in Soho. But that was all. I did not want to sleep with them because I have never been able to make love to a girl without some emotional involvement, though I have always liked the society of attractive women. I like to talk to them, to watch them.

Among the people I met was someone connected with an Oxford group, now Moral Rearmament. They made great efforts to enlist me, sending me books and literature, visiting me and trying to persuade me to join them – even when I told them they were wasting their time.

By some accident I was invited to a wine and food tasting 'do'. The wine was Burgundy and the food ham. There were sixteen varieties of ham, York, Polish, American peach-fed among them. There must have been twenty kinds of Burgundy. Beside each was a small packing case half-filled with sawdust. One was supposed to swill the wine round one's mouth and spit it into the box, which looked like the floor of a butcher's shop – filled with this bloody spit. I was not so stupid; I drank every glass and walked home singing.

About this time it occurred to me suddenly that a man's character, his self-respect, his *amour propre* was, apart from his health, his most valuable possession. This had been why I had changed my name back from Graham to Cloete. Why I intended to succeed. Why I controlled my desire for women. I knew they were my weakness and that if I gave way I would find myself on the skids. It was the emotional involvement with women I enjoyed much more than the actual sex act which was always in a sense anti-climactic. It was the sensuous and sensual that attracted me. The fetishism of pretty clothes, of perfume. The coquetry of courtship, the companionship in which both postponed the logical conclusion. This approach must seem decadent today where instant copulation seems to have replaced the uncertainties and dilemmas of passionate flirtation. I enjoyed watching women dress and undress, do their hair, paint their nails, make up their faces. Clean, dainty women, vastly interested in their personal appearance, knowing that their bodies were their most valuable asset. Nor were such girls necessarily stupid any more than the plain ones were bright. It is easy to say that these girls are useless, but so is a rose or a carnation: after all, one cannot eat them. The sight of a pretty, well-dressed woman always brightened my day, even if she was a prostitute on a street corner. Sex in the sense of beauty has always moved me. A pretty woman being the chef-d'œuvre of evolution. All this must sound like nonsense today when women's lib and unisex are the fashion. But it was not nonsense to the men and poets of the past. It was of beauty that they sang.

But as far as I was concerned, driven as I was to work, without means, without time, pretty women remained abstract. Something to look at but not touch, and I liked touching. They resembled valuable objects behind glass in a museum. For rich men there was no glass, for they too were inside. I envied them.

CHAPTER 16

A QUEEN OF THE SEA

THIS was the last phase of the gamble. I had come to London to do something impossible, and by a combination of lucky breaks had pulled it off. Even today it seems incredible.

Turning Wheels was finished at the Guards Club. I posted the manuscript to the American publishers and took a copy to Collins.

Ferris Greenslet wanted me to come to America at once, so I got my visa and booked a passage tourist-class on the *Normandie*. I always travel tourist. I am such a bad sailor that, since I cannot enjoy the amenities of cabin-class, it seems a waste of money to pay for them. What I like is an inside cabin amidships, very low down, below the waterline, where I cannot hear or see the ocean, and there I remain till I arrive, unless the sea is exceptionally calm. Unfortunately I am never really sick. I merely feel terrible, as if I had the worst possible hangover. I used to be so susceptible to seasickness that I could not even go to a film which showed waves, or watch them from the shore for long. Curiously, later on I changed and I began to enjoy the sea.

I said goodbye to my mother, my brother Ronald, Morna and my other friends, one of whom knew a man, an actor, sailing on the *Normandie*. We met and agreed to share a cabin.

We boarded the *Normandie* by night from a tender. She was floodlit and I do not think there was a more beautiful ship afloat. It was a wonderful sensation staring up at the great scarlet cliff of her flank from the level of the ocean. She was more like a floating hotel than a ship. It was even quite hard to get any sea air, the decks being glassed in. The decoration was superb, sumptuous to the point of vulgarity with black-and-gold mirrors and palms in pots. It swarmed with little page-boys – 'chasseurs' – dressed in scarlet with pillbox caps to match. There were thick carpets, the food was excellent, with carafes of red and white wine on every table. There was a splendid orchestra which never seemed to stop playing. I was to make three more trips on her and finally saw her end – watched her burning in New York harbour. A strange end – death by sabotage – for so beautiful a queen of the sea.

My cabin mate – the actor Alec Sand* – was on his way to Hollywood. We discussed my book and a play he had written, a comedy about a dentist.

The voyage was calm and I spent the first day wandering about the ship with Alec. Then he met a beautiful blonde. She was about thirty, but at the full peak of her voluptuous beauty. She had enormous blue-grey eyes which she used to perfection. She had three looks. One upwards, if she was sitting, a 'Oh, you great big beautiful man' look, a downward demure look with her superb lashes sweeping her cheeks, the modest look – the 'you mustn't say things like that to me' and a sideways look, very welcoming – a 'come up and see me some time' glance – that was very fetching. Alec told me the hours he wanted the cabin. I said, 'That's fine, just leave me the rest' – to which he agreed.

Left to my own devices, I soon found myself a friend, a very small American girl with a beautiful slim figure and a reasonably pretty face. The kind of girl who would cause me no trouble, someone I could not fall in love with, just a companion for the voyage. That was in June, the early summer of '37. We have been together thirty-five years now and this, though I did not guess it then, was the moment of my greatest luck, for I had met my future wife. From that moment until today the time has passed swiftly, the months like days, the days like hours. From now on the story is hers as much as mine. But then it was just a shipboard romance. We went to the pictures together, she joined us at meals, we drank Pernod in the lounge. I knew her name – Mildred Elizabeth West. I knew her profession – she was a fashion artist. I knew her address – 16 El Mora Avenue, Elizabeth, New Jersey. I knew her birthday – the fifteenth of July, within a fortnight of my own. Her age was twenty-two. She had been divorced. And when we reached the docks I kissed her goodbye. Ships that pass in the night. I thought the four-day romance was over. I saw her again at the Customs where she was struggling with a suitcase that she could not close. As she only weighed eighty-seven pounds, sitting on it did no good. I came over and closed it for

*Not his real name

her. I had the feeling then that something so small, so gentle, so fragile, must find it hard to stand alone. I felt little more than that. But after I left her I thought about her. I could not get her out of my mind. I felt someone should look after her.

This was not love at first sight as it had been with Eileen. Mildred, a name she hated that we changed to Tiny later, was very slight – only five feet tall. One had to get close to her to realize her dainty perfection as one does with a miniature painted on ivory. My love came slowly, surely, growing like an organic thing – like a flower from a hidden bulb.

With Eileen it had been a *coup de foudre* – a lightning strike. She had come into my private ward, tall – five feet eight – a slim Irish type, dark, with great grey eyes in which a man could drown. She wore the pale blue uniform of the VADs with a white apron, starched cap and cuffs. She said I stared at her but she had stared right back. I wanted her. I, who had never had a woman, was mad for her at once. It is unfashionable today when people no longer believe in love, much less love at first sight. But it still happens. It is an arrow shot into the heart by the eyes of a stranger. Nothing can come of it or a lot.

Tiny and I sat alone in a corner of the bar drinking Pernod and talking. Not just passing the time but really talking. She spoke of her life, her hopes, her thoughts. Her mind was naked to me. Here was a woman before whom I could take off my armour. I have never put it on again. Next afternoon we made love. It was friendly, safe, like the love of two children, as innocent, with neither seeking an advantage of the other. It was something I had never known. I had tried to possess Eileen and failed, with this small woman there was a beautiful merging. I did not know at the time how deeply she had struck me. I had thought naturally enough it would end on the New York docks.

That first night I said, 'Let's dance,' and we danced. She said, 'Swirl me,' and I swirled her. She was wearing a long dress of green, yellow, purple and red psychedelic colours, the first I had ever seen, on a black ground. When I swirled her her dress spread like an inverted flower about her. As she raised her face, laughing, I kissed her. She had another evening dress, a brown accordion-pleated silk with a paisley design. She loved paisley. She had no fur jacket or fancy wrap to put on when we went on deck to look at the stars from the upper deck, and over the stern at the white churning wake that ripped over the black sea behind us. She wore a heavy lumber jacket with tartan-like squares of two shades of blue. It was rough to the touch like the back of a wire-haired terrier, but warm she said. I found her enchanting. She has continued to enchant and surprise me ever since.

I thought of the talk we had had after that first dinner. It had gone on till nearly three in the morning. We talked about love, about life, about religion. Like me she had none, she had been brought up in a sterile, almost bookless home. She had escaped it by marriage but had found life as the wife of an executive intolerable.

Her parents were religious and had not stood by her in her divorce. It seemed strange to have a home with no atlas, no encyclopaedia, no books but a bible, and no cooking on Sunday. She had been saved at a revivalist meeting when she was six and had had her bellyful of religion by the time I met her. Her husband had been an executive in Standard Oil, but she had not proved a suitable company wife, being neither a social climber nor interested in company affairs. She lived by her work as a commercial artist. She had been to Paris with two other girl artists and was now going back to work again as a freelance.

No one had ever listened to her. No one had ever answered her questions. She doubted the tight little society that life had flung her into - first the hypocrisies of her non-conformist home, then the equally hypocritical world of business men and their wives. No one had in fact told her anything about the world she lived in. She was so innocent that I thought her sophisticated.

She liked Pernod and we drank a lot of it, which freed our tongues. I had never met anyone like her before. I think she thought the same of me. I told her I was going to America to launch my book. I told her how I had worked and the gamble I had taken. I told her of my hopes for the future and the story of my life in the past. The war, my marriage, the farm and ranch in Africa. It was all very curious because neither of us seemed to be holding anything back. I asked her if she had a boy-friend in New York. She said she had had one, a band leader, but had broken with him. It was partly for this reason she had gone to Europe.

I quoted the humanist Ludovic Kennedy to her.

'The humanist does not believe that God created man in his own image, but that men, at all times, have created gods for their own needs. In the beginning man created gods to guard him, and be the explanation for such grave perplexities as thunder, lightning, and the eclipse of the sun. Later in his evolution he developed the idea of a single personal god.

'Later still came the twin discoveries of science – which gave man an account of the physical world – and of psychiatry – which explained man to himself.

'The humanist asks himself the same questions as the Christian. When and where did it all begin? Why are we here? What lies beyond the furthest star? But unlike the Christian, he does not know, or feel a need to know, the answers.'

I said I am not a humanist in the full sense because I associate myself with all living things, both animal and plant life. I believe myself immortal, since as matter, the water, lime, phosphorus and other minerals which compose the body of any living thing, I have existed since time began and will continue to do so after death. I regard all animals as cousins a million times removed.

I have been accused of anthropomorphism, that is, of giving animals human feelings and emotions. But the boot though is on the other foot. Men have the emotions of animals – they are merely more highly developed. Animals know love, hate, fear, doubt, pleasure, sorrow, which they show by the expression on their faces and the movements of their ears and tails, or the erection of their hair. Animals play games. Tug-of-war. Tag, in which they chase each other. Hide-and-seek. King of the castle. They can communicate. They love or hate each other. Some animals or birds if they lose a mate never take another. In many ways animals are more admirable than men whose supremacy is due to their savagery and the brain power that enables them to exploit their environment.

I cannot believe that a loving god could create such an animal as man in his own image. If he was created in the image of god then that god must be terrible, like the Old Testament god of the Jews. What other god could kill men by the million in war, allow disasters, epidemics, earthquakes, floods and storms which decimate whole countries? To believe in God a man must have faith. I have no faith and can find no evidence of his existence. The Bible was written by man. It has been altered by men.

Whole books of it have been discarded by men. God, as I see it, is the whole world. The whole living world. He is the blade of grass, the elephant, the man. He is the red geranium growing in a pot. God is life and not to be defined or interpreted. This is the true blasphemy. I do not deny God for I see him everywhere. What I deny is Man's ability to understand God, or the life force. I believe in good and evil. Good is what goes with life, evil is the destructive force that goes against life, against beauty.

I told Tiny about the ranch and the terrible drought when I was losing thirty head of cattle a day. More than I could skin. Of how, since that time, I had become so careful of water I never even filled a wash-basin full to wash my face and hands. I told her about the first-aid we did with the people in our native villages, bandaging up wounds, dishing out aspirin and Epsom salts. The worst case we had was a little girl, eighteen months old, who had sat down in a fire and burnt her crutch. Her mother held her upside down and every day for a week I poured a mixture of Kerol – a cattle remedy – and salad oil on to her. By that time she was healed. The natives would never go to a doctor if they could help it; he was too far away and had too many patients. I told her about Primrose, a pedigree Friesland heifer, that got bloated on some wilted grass. She was blown up like a football and lying on her side. I sharpened one of Eileen's steel knitting needles and drove it into her left side just behind the last rib. The air came out sounding like a punctured tyre. I was amazed at how hard it was to stab anything. It took a real effort of will. Then I told her about Hartley, our marmalade tom cat, and how the vet had castrated him by putting him head first into one of my top boots. The job took less than a minute and he seemed quite unperturbed when we pulled him out. I told her about de-horning cattle and all the other things we had to do with livestock.

I told her about the silver ash-blonde artist I had been in love with in London. Of how I had left an order with a florist to send her a bunch of dark red carnations every week – and how she gave me a piece of her hair which I cut off with the razor blade she used to sharpen pencils. I had nothing to put it on so I wrapped it in a 10s note. I said, 'That about takes the cake for a bit of sentimentality, doesn't it?'

Tiny was easy to talk to. We talked and made love for three days.

Then we kissed goodbye, and if I had not come to her help in the Customs counter I should not have seen her again. When we had kissed goodbye once more, we wished each other luck and thought everything was over.

This was New York where everyone, as we came in, said, 'What a shame it's not a clear day so that you can see the skyline.' Who wanted to see the skyline? I had seen it a hundred times in pictures, in the illustrated papers, in films. I could almost have sketched the New York skyline. What I saw before me was fairyland. Rising out of the pale mist above the cool, green sea were sunlit golden towers, pinnacles, domes – a mythical heavenly city rooted in the clouds. Never has anyone had a more beautiful approach to New York, the wonder city of the world.

In a few hours I was to see it. To drive down these man-made canyons, made in a few decades, but deeper than a great river could have cut them in ten thousand. And at the bottom, between the high cliffs, ran – not water – but a tide of men and women, no bigger from where I stood looking down on them from the top of my skyscraper than pin-heads, legless spots, that moved this way and that among the chitinous shining cars that crawled insect-like through the thoroughfares.

Accustomed to cities – to London and Paris – I was still enthralled. Never had I dreamed of this immensity, of so many people moving at such speed along the streets, up and down the buildings vertically, swiftly, in silent elevators, and horizontally again – to and fro – at every level. Twenty floors up, thirty, fifty, sixty, and still they moved about their work, calmly, neatly, industriously, like ants. Like swarming ants pressed for time, for here time was a palpable force. I was exposed to such noises as I had never heard before. The scream of sirens, the throbbing of a thousand engines, the inaudible vibrations from hundreds of thousands of others. The people's bodies were pierced by waves of radio music. They were breathing air strong with gasoline, with steam, with sweat. These were supermen. America and Americans, a place and a race apart. The latest thing. The last product of our age. All this came to me, not on the first day, though I felt it then, but over the years, building up a picture of this might, this colossal power.

What are the things that struck me most? Uniformity. That is the basis of America's greatness. There can, after all, be no efficiency without standardization. No mass production of the custom-built. This seems strange at first, but it makes sense. For instance, heaven must be uniform. Can one imagine angels of various colours with different coloured wings? No, angels are white, with white swans' wings. Perhaps for a Negro they are black with sable wings. But each of us sees them as uniform. It seems to me that these manifold vibrations and tensions, combined with the astonishing clearness of the atmosphere and savage climatic variations, produce a particular type of man – active, nervous, of an unparalleled energy. They are the people who get things done, and fast.

Impressions. The immediate impressions were first the slim, svelte beauty of the women, their well-dressed neatness, their perfect figures. They had not the chic of the Parisienne, this was something different, crisp, girdled, silken, rayonned, shod in high heels as neat as the hooves of a deer.

In the great boulevards – the rich avenues – was more uniformity. A uniformity of mink, of women superbly dressed, coiffed, with plucked eyebrows and painted lips. Even their mouths were standardized. The latest mouth from *Vogue*, from Elizabeth Arden, from Helena Rubinstein. Never were there so many women at one time so beautiful, so perfumed, and at the same time so odourless – so alike that they might all have been sisters.

I was surprised at the shabbiness of the police. New York's finest, and certainly one of the most courageous, forces in the world, armed and ready to do battle with the underworld of gangsters and hold-up men who roamed the city like wolves, singly and in packs. Later, this was explained. It appeared that the police had to buy their own uniforms. I was also interested in the quality of the police horses. I saw a squadron ride past. They were not of the same class as those of the London mounted police, which are nearly all thoroughbreds, but they were wonderfully matched, as alike as peas in a pod. Uniformity again, all bays with black points. I was surprised to see that they only had leather reins, no chains. In a riot they would be quickly rendered helpless by a few slashes with a razor, but American crowds are motor-minded and more nervous of horses than the British.

And Grand Central Station – I think you could put Nôtre Dame into it and still have lots of room left over. I saw, on that first day, men carrying bags of money over their shoulders accompanied by armed guards with drawn guns. There were armed guards in the banks, an armed guard outside jewellers' shops. It was just like the films.

This was not the America of the school books, of the atlas. This was the New World. The land of the silver screen, filmland, fairyland.

One of the things that struck me as very typical was the big red second hand on the clocks in the cafeterias. It swept on round and round. It seemed to force me to watch the seconds pass. Each one gone forever. Hurry up with the sandwiches and coffee. Time is money. There is need for haste – this was the land of haste. No one had the time to pass the time of day. Questions were answered with a monosyllable, as if words cost money. Money and time were synonymous.

I spent the night in New York and then went up to Boston to meet my publishers. I saw Ferris Greenslet again and he introduced me to the other members of the firm, Houghton Mifflin, all of whom subsequently became friends – Paul Brooks, Lovell Thompson, Harwick Moseley, Dale Warren and Bob Linscott. They were doing a wonderful publicity job on *Turning Wheels* and spent over fifteen thousand dollars on its promotion. I do not think a bad book can be sold by advertising, but I think some good books have missed the market through lack of it.

Bob Linscott took me out to lunch and we walked over the common. An incident of some interest now occurred. At one point he left the path and cut catty-cornered across the grass. I continued round and met him. He was waiting for me and said, 'Why didn't you follow me?'

I said, 'We aren't in a hurry, are we? And just look at your grass.' There was an ugly track, like a scar, running diagonally across it. 'It's your grass, not mine,' I said, 'but I think if everybody walked round the place would look prettier.'

There was nothing to this, just an approach to public property. The American public is less orderly than the European, less patient of restraint, even if such restraint is to their benefit. Of course, it has its good side – it enables them to cut vital corners and get results which, to slower moving and thinking people, are fantastic. But it was the first example of the difference in attitude and, as I found later, in language, between the English and the

Americans. They are different peoples who speak a similar though different language.

We had an excellent lunch and I was taken to the St Botoph Club where I had been made a temporary member while I worked on the galleys of my book. It was here I first tasted real American seafood. Soft-shelled crabs, steamed clams, cherry-stone clams and blue-point oysters.

I was taken to see the sights by Dale Warren, who did the Houghton Mifflin publicity.

Bob Linscott introduced me to Minna Curtis, a widow who had taught English at Smith. She had a lovely place called Baptists Pool in Massachusetts. At one time the Baptists, who believe in total immersion, had used the pool for baptismal purposes. I bathed in it when I stayed with Minna. It was bitterly cold.

It was here that I met Archie McLeish, the poet, who was a neighbour of Minna's, and her brother Lincoln Kirstein, famous for his interest and patronage of the ballet. I talked to him about the Joos Ballet and Dartington Hall and found we had much in common, including horses. He had a nice black stabled here which I took out one day and it gave me the fright of my life. Overfed and under-exercised, it shot out of the stable yard like a bullet into country I did not know, across roads that were full of cars. By the time I got him quiet we were ten miles from home and I had a lot of trouble finding the way back.

Minna was a wonderful hostess, a beautiful, brilliant dark woman and a fine critic. I spent a couple of weekends in her Guest House. When I said goodbye to her she gave me a big picture of a Zulu girl painted by Neville Lewis, the South African artist. He had given it to her when he was in America but she had no place to hang it. I was delighted.

Another weekend I remember was spent with some friends of Margaret Buchanan's. I had sent them her introductions and went up to their country house, which was beautiful, with a lovely swimming pool. There was only one other guest. I did not meet her till we were having cocktails. Then she came downstairs dressed in a magnificent blue period dress that was almost a costume. She was small, dark-haired with grey eyes, very pretty and had a beautiful figure. She was divorced, immensely rich, and a Catholic. All this came out later. I was allergic to Catholic ladies, but since she had been divorced she could not be too religious. She had obviously been invited to meet me and we got on well. We spent most of Sunday swimming and sitting talking on a raft in the middle of the pool. I arranged to see her in New York where she owned a house in the East Sixties, the most fashionable neighbourhood. I went to her house several times. It was splendidly furnished, the small sitting-room having hand-painted Chinese silk wallpaper.

She was what I had come to America to find – a rich and beautiful woman – but I never so much as kissed her because I knew I had found something better than riches. My being married would have been no great obstacle, I could have gone to Mexico and got a Mexican divorce. I could have done the same with Tiny, but I did not really want to get married. This time I wanted to be really sure, and for that matter so did she. Anyone can make one mistake but the second time there should be no error, though I have a friend in Hollywood who has been married six times.

I stayed in Boston about a month, meeting many interesting people. On the fourteenth of July – for the fifteenth – I sent Mildred a birthday telegram. She replied with a 'thank-you' letter and went on to describe at great length an electrical storm that she had witnessed. I was lonely and decided to go back to New York and to her. I did this and went to the Chatham Hotel where I had been lent an apartment. Mildred came there when she could and we went about a great deal together exploring the city. She had left her parents' house in New Jersey and gone to Allerton House, a place that only took single ladies, secretaries and business women. Men were only allowed in the lobby. As this way of life seemed impractical, Tiny took an apartment where I could visit her. I used to walk home at two or three in the morning through empty streets which were then completely safe.

She drew the map for the endpapers of *Turning Wheels*. We went to parties and on one occasion she took me to visit a palmist, Mrs Baldwin, with whom she and some of her friends had arranged a visit. It was a Dutch treat, and as one of the girls had fallen out I agreed to let her read my hand in her place. Mrs Baldwin was astonishingly accurate, not only about my character, but knew, although at this time I was quite unknown, that I was a writer and that my book would have a great success. I have never understood palmistry but have several times been surprised at the accuracy of palmists in reading both the past and the future. It now appears that some doctors use it in diagnosis, and regard the palm as a visible part of the brain. Tiny, as I now called Mildred, has recently become interested in palmistry, and certainly character, if nothing else, does show in the hand, but many hands are as blank and dull as the lives of the people who show them.

Astrology is even more strange, but here too I have been astonished at some of the forecasts that have been given to us.

I went to the country to stay with Dale Warren. He had a beautiful house and drove me all over, to the Plymouth Rock – a name I had previously only associated with poultry – to Dartmouth University, where I saw the Orosco murals, the first of this kind that I had ever seen. He took me to a lake near his house where a man who lived in a shack was breeding brent and Canada geese. Here I found a bathing-suit half in and half out of the water, rotting. I asked him about it and he said the summer was over now and next year they would buy a new one. I found a canoe lying on its side instead of being hung between two trees, and got the same answer. New bathing-suits, new canoes. This was indeed a rich and prodigal country. I saw motor graveyards with cars that seemed quite good, just thrown away. Later they were sold as junk to the Japanese. It was a great lesson to me. Dale had a very pretty Negro maid called Lerline who had a car of her own. Everyone had cars, every workman went to work in his own automobile.

It is difficult for other nations to understand the richness of America. And even Americans, though they speak of God's own country, seem sometimes not to understand how true this is, and how fortunate they are. In no country in the world is there such opportunity for success. Success on every level, from the highest academic honours to success on the lowest gangster and criminal terms – in his way Al Capone was a great success. There is success through brains, through hard work, through luck, through beauty, through strength, through religion. In no country, because of its vastness, is there so much room at the top. I have thought of America as if it were the keyboard of a piano. There are extra notes at both ends of the scale. Unheard of idealism at the one end and unparalleled crime at the other. The range of these extra notes are the key of American culture, of her greatness, of the paradox of immense variety and incredible uniformity –

again extremes. America is like its climate – a country of violent change – where life is never dull, and the word 'impossible' without meaning.

There were then only two great nations, China had still to be born, two great forces left in the world. The USA and the USSR, both moving by opposite paths in the same direction, towards mechanization and uniformity, the one with freedom of democracy, the other with the cruelty of repression. The one moving forward with hope, the other driven forward by fear. The world's hope is obvious – a stable economy where machines must one day do most of the work of men, releasing them from the curse of hard labour. And this period in which we live is the transition period, the time of change. But within this period, we each in our little lives are the victims of great events.

This was '37, the world was simmering like a pot, but I went on happily enough, concerned only with my own affairs – my book, my love, and my new friends. Everything was going well for me. God was in his heaven.

It was wonderful to be well off. I bought Tiny a silver fox fur and a white evening dress ornamented with gold brocade. On this particular evening we dined at the Ritz in the Japanese room. It was very pretty with water and ferns and little red painted wooden bridges. We were celebrating a cheque I had received from Houghton Mifflin, but at last it was time to take Tiny home, so I ordered a taxi. When we got to her apartment we found it occupied. Her ex-boy-friend Jack Winters was waiting for her. He had not accepted the fact that she was through with him. There was a scene in which he threatened to bash Tiny's teeth in. He was livid at Tiny's new white dress and fur, but at last I persuaded him – or thought I had – that the situation had changed and got rid of him. Tiny was nervous and thought he might break in later, so I went out and at an 'open all night' store bought a gimlet and a punch. I went back to the apartment, bored a hole in the floor against the door, and showed Tiny how to put the steel punch into it thus preventing the door being forced. I then kissed her good night and went off.

Fortunately Tiny still felt insecure and went to spend the rest of the night with a girl-friend, for during the night, after she had gone, Winters did break in and went off with all her clothes. The people in the neighbouring apartments had heard nothing. They never do in New York – not even screams. They do not want to be involved. She called the police, who were very unsympathetic. They had more to do than sort out a triangular situation between a young divorcee and her two lovers. However, they did get the clothes back.

We looked for a new apartment, and finally finding one with two adjoining suites in East 37th Street, we moved in. My sitting-room had one bright canary wall with a fireplace, and the Zulu girl Minna had given me looked very well over the mantelpiece as the background of the picture was a very deep, almost indigo, blue.

While we were there Tiny's mother came to see her on some pretext, but really to have a look at me. Mrs Ellison was a small, partridge plump, dark woman of forty-five who must at one time have been a very pretty girl. She took one look at Mildred's room and realized that it was not used for much except the storage of clothes, and there were quite a few new things, including the fox fur, she had not seen.

She obviously disapproved of me. I was too old for Mildred, I had no regular nine-to-five job, I was married, I was a foreigner – not American, that is. I could see her point of view. Nothing was said because she had no control over Tiny's actions, but a lot was implied.

I disliked her intensely for her treatment of Tiny and her trick of throwing a heart-attack any time she did not get her own way. I was sure next time Tiny went to visit her there would be a scene culminating in an attack of the vapours, which Tiny was too innocent to understand till I explained that this technique was adopted by many mothers. Even when she did realize it, it continued to upset her for some years.

CHAPTER 17

JACKPOT

DALE WARREN introduced me to Catherine Cornell, the famous actress, and her husband, the producer Gutherie Mc Clintic. We stayed the night in her country house in Martha's Vineyard, a charming big cottage right on the water. In the morning I walked out of my room naked on to a pebbly beach and bathed. The sitting-room was panelled in plain wood with inside shutters so that when they were closed it was impossible to see where the windows were as the grain of the shutters matched the wall. I also visited them a few times at their house in Sutton Place.

Dale introduced me to Dorothy Thompson, a well-known columnist, who later married Sinclair (Red) Lewis, the author of *Babbit*. I got to know both Dorothy and Red quite well.

Dorothy showed me a remarkable piece she had written about animal experiments in American high schools and gave me a copy which I kept.

A few months ago the British Advisory Committee of the Universities Federation for Animal Welfare complained to the American ambassador regarding an article describing experiments on live animals being carried out in the biology courses of American public schools. Because of the very close relations that exist between this country and Great Britain, and the Americanizing influence on British cultural life, this committee felt moved to scotch something that might spread outside our borders.

The article that occasioned the protest revealed that the National Science Teachers' Association in Washington is encouraging certain practices. Its author, a biology teacher in a Buffalo, New York high school, wrote of blowing pepper, dusts and smoke into the lungs of mice to provoke 'violent shutting off of the glottis'; toxicity tests to find out what dose of nicotine will kill animals; substitution of external artificial hearts; and routine and periodic transfers of cancer cells to healthy animals. These tests are carried out by teenagers, and the simplest of them are practised even in the lower grades in some schools.

The teacher-author of the article also reported student reactions. 'Surgical procedures are especially *thrilling* to pupils. After the first few weeks there is an *amazing* absence of *squeamishness* and *fear*. In fact, it frequently surprises me to see the *avidity* with which pupils *plunge into* the dissection of rats, mice, rabbits and dog sharks.'

The pupils, we are told, are never allowed to give names to animals. 'I prefer to have the pupils develop an impersonal and objective attitude. It is *too easy to become emotionally attached* and thus *strongly disturbed* at seeing a "friend" handled directly.'

I have italicized certain words in this teacher's account, in which I think he quite unwittingly reveals a good deal. It clearly demonstrates the unintellectual approach of adolescents to experimentation on live animals and records a reversal of normal emotions. Pupils start by being squeamish, but in a few weeks they find the work, not soberly interesting or important but *thrilling*; they *plunge into* dissection of living creatures with *avidity* once their normal ('too easy') emotional attachments to living creatures are suppressed. They are then no longer strongly disturbed, but excited and titillated.

A few years later, while still in elementary school, this same child may be conducting a 'cookbook experiment' on mice, guinea pigs or rabbits, depriving half of them of proteins or carbohydrates and feeding the others a balanced diet, to prove what any child can be taught without such scientifically worthless cruelties; that a diet of nothing but sugar will kill animals and presumably humans. Or he may be, as a Pennsylvania high school reports, conducting research into the effects of high-voltage radiation on mice, deliberately inducing damage to the tissues and organs of the animals, without adding a jot or tittle to knowledge already possessed. Afterward he will cut up his victim for examination.

Or he may have the experience that caused one sensitive high school girl to become sick and rush from the class, when a half-anaesthetized kitten being 'surgically dissected' started to scream – as did the pupil.

One eighteen-year-old high school student was greatly praised for making Siamese twins out of two rats.

As Dorothy said, if children become callous about animals they become callous about people when they grow up.

Curtis Brown, my agents in London, had an office in New York which was run by Allan Collins with Edith Haggard, a very good-looking blonde with beautiful hair, taking care of the story side of the business. I saw her every day, as I went to the office in East 48th Street to collect my mail. She was very helpful to me and said as novels were so uncertain I should try some short stories. To this end she introduced me to Erd Brand, an editor of the *Saturday Evening Post*. He was a big sunburnt man, a very fine type of American and the brother of another literary agent. He told me to try a story, so I bought a *Post* and set about with some coloured pencils analysing the style of the stories they published. I marked the dialogue in red, the scenery and descriptive passages in blue, and the action green. Having worked on this for a couple of days, I wrote a story called *Plenty of Water*, and Edith sold it to the *Post* for $500. A good price in those days, though Sinclair Lewis got $5000 for a story of the same length – five thousand words approximately. But at that time money was money. One could hardly carry home a dollar's worth of groceries, and a good three-course dinner, including steak and a bottle of wine, at a small restaurant cost a dollar a head.

The summer was hotting up so I asked Edith if she knew anywhere we could go for the rest of the summer. She introduced me to Struthers Burt, a writer who had a ranch in Wyoming. He said I could have one of his log cabins if I paid a small rent and a share of the food and the running expenses of the ranch. I said I had a friend, Tiny, whom I could not leave and did he mind us not being married? He was very broadminded and agreed. Things were nothing like as permissive in those days and Tiny showed a lot of courage in, as they say, 'shacking up' with me.

Just before leaving New York I got a wire from Gutherie McClintic asking me if I would like to go to the coast with him.

Here was a real chance for a Hollywood career, Gutherie knew everyone. But I declined because I knew myself. I knew that confronted with all that glamour I should become involved and lose Tiny, something I had no intention of doing. This was another decision that would have changed my life.

We had an amusing incident in the apartment. I had bought a couple of white mice and set them up with a little nest box full of cotton wool on the mantelpiece, where they were very happy peering over the edge and good company for me while Tiny was out at work. I have always found it hard to live without anything alive to look after. Then one day a man appeared to repair something, I forget what, in the apartment, but spotting the mice he refused to come in till I had shut them up in a carton. I was amazed. I knew of course that many women do not like mice, but that a tradesman should be nervous of them really surprised me.

Americans as a whole are not animal lovers or keepers of pets. Very few of my friends even had dogs.

When we were ready to go I took my mice back to the pet shop where I had bought them and gave them to the owner.

We left New York in a monster train – a giant aluminium caterpillar, all set to rush screaming across a continent. It was the last word in luxurious travel. The food was wonderful, the service excellent. The decor could only be described as Victorian Vulgar, opulent. There was even a stuffed canary in a cage hanging in the club car. We had brought books but did not open them. We never left the observation car except to eat and sleep.

When we reached Chicago I was determined to see the stockyards and went between trains without even waiting for breakfast. Since reading Upton Sinclair's *The Jungle*, I had always dreamt of seeing them. They are one of the wonders of the world. So, taking a sight-seeing bus, we left the Stevens Hotel and rode through some of the most terrible slums I have ever seen – waste lots, tumble-down houses, rubbish dumps swarming with dirty children, slatternly women and savage men, all of them black. Over the whole hung a pall of thin, greasy smoke, from the great flesh processing plants. The two arguments against meat eating were here emphasized. The tragedy of the animal itself, withdrawn from the security of its home and subjected to a long journey in crowded trucks, ending in yards that smelled of death, and the inevitable brutalizing of the men concerned with slaughter which we were now to witness on the world's largest scale.

As we approached the meat-packing area the atmosphere changed again, becoming thick and greasy, with a smell of manure and blood. It was palpable.

At the entrance to the packing-plant we were given permit tickets and entered what looked like a large well-appointed shop where all the meat products were shown in glass cases: bacon beautifully packaged in cellophane, even wrapped in ribbon; hams, sausages, steaks and cutlets also wrapped in cellophane;

neat heaps of mince – everything crisp and clean and bearing no relation to the animals on the hoof in the yards outside. The yards covered acres of ground – pens, runs, corrals and fenced passages to the railway where the animals destined for the factory were unloaded on to ramps.

The crowd going over the installation now collected and a guide came to lead us through the various departments. I was astonished to find women with young children among us.

We went down wide passages and looked through plate-glass at headless cattle on an assembly line passing butchers who each performed one act. One man slit the skin, the next stripped one side, the next the other. The timing was perfect.

The guide said, 'Are there any questions?' and I said, 'Yes. I should like to know how you tell the cows' from the steers' carcases when their udders have been cut off. There is a great difference in the quality of the meat between a cow that has had several calves and an ox.'

I got no answer. Presumably because there was none.

The whole operation was hygienic, almost hospital-like, and horrible. The long line of carcases on the assembly line disappeared in the distance of this enormous cathedral-like chamber of death. At the far end they looked no bigger than mice.

In another big chamber we saw Rabbis in rubber boots up to their ankles in blood seeing to the Kosher killing rituals.

One woman held up a child to see the blood better.

But the worst was yet to come. The pigs. The hogs, as they are called, were seized by the ear by one man while another fastened a shackle round their hocks and hoisted them on to a hook on an enormous slowly turning steel wheel from which were suspended some ten hogs at a time, hanging by their hind legs. As they reached shoulder height a man on a platform stuck his knife into their jugular veins. One after another – perhaps two a minute. Reaching the ground the dying pig, for it was not dead yet, was unhooked and passed out to other workers who continued processing it.

The whole operation was one of the most horrible I have ever seen. The great shining disc of the wheel looked about twenty feet in diameter. The pigs hung struggling. When one was in a killing position its head was just over the heels of the one below it. The terrible precision of the killer with his knife and above all the sterile, hygienic atmosphere and the matter of factness of it all appalled me. With its hose pipes scouring blood away, its white tiles, the clean but blood-stained overalls of the workers, all made me think of the Nazi torture chambers of Germany.

The observation-room from which we watched was sound-proofed as the squeals of the pigs would have been intolerable.

Much as I hated it, I was fascinated by the spectacle. I was somewhat more hardened now than when I had been a boy, having slaughtered and dressed a good few animals myself. Tiny, though badly shaken, took it well. It was all so vast, on such a scale, that it lost reality. I think we saw it as a spectacle, but what a picture it would have made, particularly of the Rabbis. It was rather like a ballet in a way, a dance of blood and death.

From here we went to the cooling-rooms where thousands of sides of hot, freshly killed beef hung steaming from hooks, and from there to the vast cold storage-rooms where the naked beasts had grown a new coat. A long fur coat of greenish mould, each hair two inches long. And then it was over. We had seen it. Seen something I shall never forget. Seen everything, from the struggling hog being hung on the terrible wheel, to the bacon wrapped in cellophane, tied with ribbon, and packaged, so that no housewife would ever dream that her rasher had ever been alive – a rootling, grunting pig, happy in its own porcine fashion. For this, too, is a by-product of our great civilization. The processing that comes between the consumer and reality.

Who, seeing them in a shop, would dream that eggs were actually laid by triumphant, cackling hens – this was before the invention of batteries – that milk had come from a cow, quite sterile when it left her udder, and naturally homogenized, or that vegetables, so clean and neatly tied in bundles, had been grown in muck and dung?

We now found ourselves back in the showroom with the finished products of the slaughter we had seen.

Eighty per cent of the meat in the United States comes from Chicago and the hands of such great meat packers as Swift and Armour.

Everything in America is very centralized – meat in Chicago, the Motor Industry in Detroit, rubber in Akron. Some years ago when there was an electrical fault on the Canadian border, the east coast, the USA from Boston to Washington, was blacked out for twenty-four hours. America, because of this specialization and centralization, is very vulnerable, much more so than Russia, or China, and its people so sophisticated that they would be lost without the amenities to which they are accustomed.

Going back to the hogs. I was told years later by a psychiatrist who had lived in Chicago that the slaughterers in the packing sheds often suffer breakdowns and become demented. This does not seem astonishing. To kill stock – cattle, sheep and pigs – for eight hours a day must have some effect on those who do it. Particularly as it is done without ritual. A peasant killing a pig to salt down once in six months is one thing, and a mass slaughter job another.

The ordeal over – and it had been one – we returned to the station to pick up our luggage and have breakfast. This was a silent meal for both of us. This had been a great emotional experience and, I think, Tiny's first vision of reality as I knew it – the stark reality of bush, ranch, land and farm.

And now for the West, the romantic land of cowboy and Indian. We took another super train and were on our way, crossing in minutes the ground that it had taken the pioneers weeks of incredible toil and danger to cover. We saw tame Indians selling fake curios at the stations where we stopped – the descendants of the proud red men who had once ravaged the plains we were crossing. We saw giant Joshua cacti, prickly phalli, standing stark in the burning desert sands. We saw the bad lands, the painted country, we passed land where there were sinister black outcrops of coal. We came to Salt Lake, the stronghold of the Mormons, and here saw another spectacle that I have never seen equalled. It was sunset and the great salt lake was scarlet. Vermilion. A blood-red sea.

We passed through scrub and rocky hills, over the prairies where buffalo had once roamed in millions to the tiny town of Cody near the entrance to the Yellowstone National Park. Cody was named after Colonel William F. Cody and was part of a land grant given to him for his services to the Government.

We visited the Cody Museum and I told Tiny how my father had introduced me to him when I was a child and he had presented his 'Buffalo Bill' Wild West show in Paris. I must have been about five years old, but I remember him clearly. He had long yellowish grey hair and wore a fringed buckskin shirt. He gave me a buckskin cushion cover also frilled, with a picture of Sitting Bull burnt into it. I took it everywhere till I had sat it shiny and my mother, much to my regret, disposed of it.

I still remember the show. The parade with Colonel Cody leading it on a big white horse. He was followed by mounted cowboys and Indians. The main feature was the capture of a stage-coach by Indians. The coach with horses galloped round the arena pursued by yelling braves on their painted ponies.

From Cody, after seeing all the Indian relics such as guns, tomahawks, eagle-feather war bonnets and beadwork in the museum, we took a bus tour of the National Park.

The scenery was magnificent but the animals very thin on the ground compared to those in South Africa. We saw a lot of black bears standing by the roadside like mendicants waiting for a hand-out. They reminded me of prostitutes on their beat waiting at lamp-posts. I did not care for them. There had been accidents with tourists who could not realize that they were wild animals. One man, we heard, even tried to put his baby on a bear's back to take a picture of it. We saw grizzly bears being fed oranges, bread and vegetables standing behind some chicken wire which certainly would have been useless if they had decided to do anything, but did keep the tourists from going too close. I was amazed at how little the tourists saw until it was pointed out, even missing moose the size of a horse. We saw moose, elk that resembled a Scottish red deer, pronghorn antelopes and a herd of buffalo, forty or fifty, that were all that remained of the millions that once roamed the prairies and the west. The buffalo were exterminated by hunters like William Cody – Buffalo Bill – partly to supply meat to the workers laying the railway line to the Pacific, and partly because they were the source of life to the plains Indians who hunted them for food, for their skins to make tepees, and robes to keep them warm in winter. While there were still buffalo it was impossible to destroy these mounted warriors who were doing no more than defend their homeland. The whole story of the treatment of the American Indian is disgraceful. Every treaty the white man ever made with them was broken. They were sent on death marches, women and children were killed, they were given blankets infected with chicken pox which proved fatal to them. These wars ended with a death charge of mounted warriors in 1905. The remnants of the tribes are now living in reserves and do not have full rights as American citizens. They could with ease and without genetic damage have been absorbed into the white population. They had many virtues. They were courageous and kept their word and were in many ways an admirable people worthy of a better fate.

We went to a wayside restaurant for lunch, and here an interesting incident occurred. We were shown to a corner behind some potted palms and a screen put round us. The management evidently didn't think I was suitably dressed. I wore my farm khaki, a shirt and trousers only, whereas the rest of the people were dressed for an Easter Parade or Ascot in their best. This is a rather American characteristic – to dress and talk to impress people they will never see again.

That night we stayed in a log cabin camp. We were disturbed by the noise black bears made fishing in the garbage cans. Having my stock whip with me, I went out, cracked it and scared them off. This brought people out of the cabins thinking it was a shot, so I clapped it again for luck and we went back to bed. The bears did not return.

We were next taken to the geyser area where there were potholes of hot, bubbly mud and geysers that sent sprays into the air. The most famous being Old Faithful that went up very high and repeated itself at regular intervals as it had probably done for hundreds of years before the white man's arrival in the New World. It was like a severed artery, pumping watery mud instead of blood, and one could imagine a pumping heart beating under the skin of the earth.

We saw some Indians dressed in Great Eagle-feather war bonnets for the benefit of the tourists who took snapshots of these noble red men. What a shameful comedown for the descendants of men who had been among the last really free people in the world with a culture that was in many ways democratic and admirable.

The scenery in the Rockies was grand, using the word in its correct sense. It was like Switzerland infinitely exaggerated. There was nothing cosy. The beauty was filled with menace, and it is not surprising the Indians avoided the mountains and considered them evil.

By the time we left the Park we had seen pretty well every

variety of game except for the white Rocky Mountain goat and wild sheep.

It seemed to me it would be possible to naturalize the European ibex, mouflon and chamois without any danger to the local fauna or ecological conditions in general.

Next day we made our way by coach to Struthers Burt's rail-head, and he picked us up and drove us to the Three Rivers ranch where we met the other visitors who owned cabins on a co-operative basis. Meals were in a large central cabin which combined dining- and sitting-room facilities. Struthers had two cowboys and a farm manager. He ran a small herd of white-faced cattle which had to be hand-fed through most of the winter months when the ground was under deep snow. They were fed on Timothy, a grass rather like South African teff, which will give several tons of hay to the acre.

Struthers had half a dozen horses. A rather common lot, strong but without quality. I used a big bay horse with two white stockings and a blaze which showed some Clydesdale blood, called 'Heart'.

Tiny had a buckskin, a yellow horse with a black mane and tail, so fat she could not get her knees on to the saddle flaps, but very tame. I taught her to ride on him and she would have become a good horsewoman if she could have brought herself to pull his head up when he wanted to graze or to turn him. She was afraid of hurting him and thought if he wanted to eat he must be hungry.

Still, these animals, coarse as they were, were good on the mountains, though I think a well-bred horse would have equalled or surpassed their performance.

I had a long argument with Struthers about the horses they used here – cold-blooded, they called them. Common, I called them, more suitable to a van than the saddle. He said they had to be of this type because of the heavy going in the mountains. But I maintained that I could have gone wherever they went on one of our Basuto ponies, also mountain bred, but with a lot of Arab blood. I noticed that all the top horses used in the rodeos had blood in them.

It is rather hard to define what is meant by blood in this case. I do not mean thoroughbred, not race horses, but horses with some of this blood in them, quarter-bred, half-bred, or even three-quarter-bred. The fundamental difference is that a blood horse will go on till he dies under you, whereas a cold blood will lie down when he is tired. This definition may apply to men too. With blood there is no limit except death.

But there were plenty of things to think about. It was strange that all our garden flowers were wild somewhere, were weeds even, like escholtzia, the Californian poppy, that I was to see later in Hollywood, the delphiniums, sunflowers, aconite, columbines of Wyoming.

When riding, the sunflowers, a smallish-flowered branchy kind, came up to my stirrup-irons. The ranchers complained about monkshood and delphiniums because cattle eating them were poisoned. But the flowers were wonderful and I had seen nothing like them since I was a child in Switzerland.

The stockyards were still in my mind. It seemed to me that animals should be killed at home by the man who bred them, so that they made no journey by road or train, so that they were killed with some panoply, some feeling. Their deaths should be discussed. Next week we shall slaughter the black hog. Tomorrow. It should be an event, but above all there should be some measure of regret, some knowledge that life is being taken. I thought of the pigs I had seen killed, as a child, in the village street, of the blood being caught for blood pudding, of the bowels being washed out to make sausage skins – that one could eat, instead of the linoleum now used, a by-product of the cotton seed meal factories.

I kept thinking of reality, of the funerals in Paris, of the woman I had heard when I was about ten, screaming in childbirth. All this was almost over today – the great sailing ship, the horseman riding over the plains, the row boat on the inland lake, but it was all old. It had a thousand years of tradition behind it. Above all, it had reality. It could be understood. Many things could even be made at home. It was here I decided that mechanization, wonderful as it was, did something to man. It made him helpless. Even the best mechanic cannot make a bicycle out of the things he finds on his farm or the tools in his shop. Something has been lost which must be weighed against what has been gained. Perhaps this was because I was not competent in this new world, not mechanical. On the other hand, I could fell a tree, saw planks, build a boat that would not sink, build a house, breed a horse and break it, tan a hide, make – not a saddle but rough saddlery – a bridle anyway. I could breed a cow and milk it, I could kill a steer, dress and cook it, I could grow my own vegetables and fruit.

These are all things that men have done for thousands of years. They have only recently ceased to do them. The vast majority of the people of the world still do them, and perhaps for this reason suffer much less from the neuroses which are the curse of our time, and which may be due, in part at least, to this severance from reality. I, at any rate, have not moved with the times, and remain an anachronism.

Struthers's wife, Katherine Newlin Burt, was also a writer and editor of the *Ladies Home Journal.* They had two children, teenagers, Nathaniel, who later became a writer and by profession a professor of music at Princeton, and a daughter, Julie. Struthers, who was a small man, rode a big 16.2 white horse. Small men often like big horses. I like small ones. Less to go wrong my father used to say. A Shetland pony can carry a man whereas many big horses are weak in one place or another. Few Arabs are over 14.2. We often all went out together on horseback and had some fine rides over the trails.

On one picnic expedition we had a fascinating para-normal experience. We were having a picnic beside a small rippling river. We were right on the path that ran along the bank. On the other side of the river, ten yards or so away, was the forest. Tiny and I were sitting in the middle of the path eating when we heard a horse galloping towards us. The hoofbeats got louder and louder. When they were right up to us we crouched down. The horse passed over us and the hoofbeats became fainter and finally faded away. But there had never been a horse. Margaret Mead, the anthropologist, was with us; she owned one of the lodges. The Burts and a couple of other people – four of us – heard the horse. The others heard nothing. I wish I had taken affidavits from those who did have this experience.

I think almost everyone has in their lives had at least one such inexplicable experience. Dan Walker, a hard-boiled newspaper man who covered the night-club beat, wrote a book which was a collection of such incidents. I wrote this one for him. Burl Ives wrote about a phantom yacht. John Steinbeck wrote a story and so did many others. Dan himself had an old house which was haunted. British red-coats marched through hedges. Pewter, which he collected, was damaged. Snowballs came in through closed windows.

Ghosts. Poltergeists. Who knows? But certainly there are events which cannot be explained logically.

Later we heard a story about the horse incident. A kind of 'dead man's gulch' story of a murder for gold dust and a man escaping along the river on a horse. We also saw a cabin with bullet holes from a .45 in the timber.

We now left the Burts and went to stay on a dude ranch in Jackson Hole, then quite a small village famous for the number of elk that assembled there in winter and had to be fed.

Fred, our host, was a guide and hunter in the shooting season and had many stories of bear, moose and elk hunts.

We had some good rides. Tiny rode a bay horse called Slim that she could get her legs round for a change, and I had a nice grey called Charlie. On one occasion when we were out it began to snow, though it was August. Tiny got so mad with the cold she galloped home and could not sit down for a week. She rode Slim very well but he had a trick of trying to rub her off on the gate of the corral, which annoyed her.

We talked about the ghost horse a lot. We were in no doubt about the reality of the experience. But what did it mean? Were there really ghosts? If so there was an after-life of some kind. Nothing to do with the Church or God, but perhaps the spirit had an existence, perhaps it had electrical waves or elements that continued under certain conditions to exist. There were too many stories of ghosts, poltergeists and other para-normal events for them to be utterly dismissed. Very few people would acknowledge that they believed in ghosts, but very few of these sceptics would spend a night alone in a house that was said to be haunted.

Ghosts, spirits, reincarnation – all seem possible. We recognize places where we think we have been before. We take a dislike to some people on sight because we may have met them in some other existence. We all know if a house has a happy or unhappy atmosphere. Both Tiny and I are convinced we have met before as lovers or as twins.

A dude ranch is really a guest house with horses and cowboys laid on. The cowboys sing western songs at night round a fire and take the dudes on conducted rides by day. A dude in western terminology is a city slicker who buys levis, a bright silk shirt. high-heeled boots, a ten-gallon hat and plays cowboys and Indians without any Indians.

At that time Jackson Hole had one street and two saloons. There was the old cowboys' saloon and a new one, all chrome and stainless steel, for the tourists. That at least was the idea, but what actually happened was that the cowboys went to the new saloon and the tourists to the old one which still had a lot of the 'old West' atmosphere.

There was a church with a remarkable layout. Behind the altar was an enormous picture window having a view of the snow-covered twin peaks of the Tetons. It was most impressive.

In our explorations we found a beaver dam and spent some happy hours watching them at work, felling aspens, cutting them and dragging them through the water to their lodge for winter food.

On one of our walks in the evening Tiny suddenly said, 'Show me a rabbit.' 'There,' I said, pointing, for as she spoke a big jack rabbit had got up in front of us.

We picked up some pretty pebbles, many of them rounded by water, showing they must have been swept here in the valley by some prehistoric storm. We found a dark red one that Tiny said looked like liver, which made me laugh as so many of her similes were culinary.

We went to a rodeo where all the participants were working cowboys, and saw all the usual things. Bulldozing, where a man chases a steer, jumps from his horse on to it, throws it by twisting its horns till it falls, pinning him to the ground between them. The calf tying. Here the calf is roped, the rope kept taut by the horse backing up while the cowboy ties the calf's feet together. We saw bucking horses ridden, bulls ridden, wild cows milked – a few drops into a bottle – and all the rest of the competitions that go to make up the spectacle.

We went to a stock show where the most interesting thing was a competition between cart horses moving a sled laden with rocks.

Then at last we decided to go home to New York once again, contravening the 'Mann Act' – a piece of legislation forbidding a man to cross a State line with a woman with whom he was having intimate relations. It was designed to check pimps and white slavers and rarely worked. It was, however, a godsend to lady hitch-hikers bent on blackmail.

But looking back on this period, what are the outstanding things I remember? The stockyards, the wild flowers of the West, the Rockies that reminded me of Switzerland, infinitely multiplied, the vastness of the continent I had crossed.

This was the last of the West I was to see till I went to Hollywood some years later. We returned to New York to find that the apartment we had rented and had paid for while we were away had been sub-let without our knowledge or permission to a young lady. After some recriminations but no refund, we reinstalled ourselves and resumed our normal lives – Tiny continuing with her work as a fashion artist, and I doing publicity, interviews and promotion, things that my publishers said would assist the sale of the book. I went to Toronto to see Collins' Canadian branch. I was charmed with the Canadians, the women as beautiful as Americans, but more explicable to an Englishman. They seemed to combine the best of both countries.

I went to literary teas and lunches, where I found myself quite out of my depth. I dined out and lunched. I stayed in the country with friends and waited for publication.

I was staying at Minna's country house in Massachusetts when a wire came. I was in the garden, on a close-mown grass path, a smooth green carpet, looking at a lead statue of a nude woman – pale grey against a background of forest trees. There was an herbaceous border on each side of the path, tall delphiniums and white lilies were in flower. It was hot, and humming birds – green and scarlet jewels – hung suspended in the soft evening light – brave little birds that migrated each year from Mexico. I always like to think of them hitching rides on the wild geese when they travelled. This was an ancient superstition, now disproved, like so many other pretty theories.

My hostess came to me with the wire in her hand. There was the usual hesitation before I opened it. I was afraid it might be from Tiny.

Telegrams are strange, strong things. Almost every blow that is struck at us comes by wire – news of death, of illness, that the girl you wanted has married another man. But good news comes too. And this was good. It was from Ferris Greenslet. *Turning Wheels* had been chosen by the Book of the Month Club.

The effect of the wire on me was interesting. I burst into tears. It was the jackpot. The fight was over. I was out. I was free. I had money. I had Tiny. I had a future, the past was dead, wiped out by that telegram. My tears were like the first cry of a newborn child. I had fought my way out of another womb.